THE
EVERYTHING.
PIE
COOKBOOK

Dear Reader,

Baking is one of my very favorite activities. I grew up in a family with a strong tradition of cooking and baking at home. Happily those traditions and recipes have been passed down to me. One of my fondest memories is of my mother teaching me how to make my first apple pie from scratch. Step by step she showed me how to measure out the flour, rub in the butter, and slice the apples just like her mother had taught her. It is a skill I have perfected with time, and I can still hear my mom's instructions every time I make an apple pie today.

I hope in this book you find tips, recipes, and information that will make your own pie baking easy and fun. Pie is unlike anything else out there since it comes in savory varieties as well as sweet. Be it breakfast, lunch, dinner, or dessert, when you learn how to make a pie, you have learned a skill you can use at every meal. Pie is a wonderful treat for special occasions, holidays, potlucks, picnics, or anytime you want something fun and special to give your friends and family. Remember, when it comes to pie, you are limited only by your imagination!

Kelly Jaggers

Welcome to the EVERYTHING® Series!

These handy, accessible books give you all you need to tackle a difficult project, gain a new hobby, comprehend a fascinating topic, prepare for an exam, or even brush up on something you learned back in school but have since forgotten.

You can choose to read an Everything® book from cover to cover or just pick out the information you want from our four useful boxes: e-questions, e-facts, e-alerts, and e-ssentials.

We give you everything you need to know on the subject, but throw in a lot of fun stuff along the way, too.

We now have more than 400 Everything® books in print, spanning such wide-ranging categories as weddings, pregnancy, cooking, music instruction, foreign language, crafts, pets, New Age, and so much more. When you're done reading them all, you can finally say you know Everything®!

QUESTION

Answers to
common questions

FACT

Important snippets
of information

ALERT

Urgent
warnings

ESSENTIAL

Quick
handy tips

PUBLISHER Karen Cooper

DIRECTOR OF ACQUISITIONS AND INNOVATION Paula Munier

MANAGING EDITOR, EVERYTHING® SERIES Lisa Laing

COPY CHIEF Casey Ebert

ASSISTANT PRODUCTION EDITOR Jacob Erickson

ACQUISITIONS EDITOR Lisa Laing

SENIOR DEVELOPMENT EDITOR Brett Palana-Shanahan

EDITORIAL ASSISTANT Ross Weisman

EVERYTHING® SERIES COVER DESIGNER Erin Alexander

LAYOUT DESIGNERS Colleen Cunningham, Elisabeth Lariviere, Ashley Vierra, Denise Wallace

Visit the entire Everything® series at *www.everything.com*

THE
EVERYTHING®
PIE
COOKBOOK

INCLUDES:

Apple Pie with a Spicy Cheddar Crust • Salted Peanut Pie •
Spinach, Mushroom, and Swiss Quiche • Pomegranate Cream
Cheese Pie • Blackberry Cheese Tart . . . and hundreds more!

Kelly Jaggers

3

Aadamsmedia
Avon, Massachusetts

*This book is dedicated to anyone who loves
to bake. Embrace your bliss.*

An Everything® Series Book.
Everything® and everything.com® are registered trademarks of F+W Media, Inc.

Published by Adams Media, a division of F+W Media, Inc.
57 Littlefield Street, Avon, MA 02322 U.S.A.
www.adamsmedia.com

ISBN 10: 1-4405-2726-1
ISBN 13: 978-1-4405-2726-5
eISBN 10: 1-4405-2758-X
eISBN 13: 978-1-4405-2758-6

Printed in the United States of America.

10 9 8 7 6 5 4 3 2 1

Library of Congress Cataloging-in-Publication Data
is available from the publisher.

This publication is designed to provide accurate and authoritative information with regard to the subject matter covered. It is sold with the understanding that the publisher is not engaged in rendering legal, accounting, or other professional advice. If legal advice or other expert assistance is required, the services of a competent professional person should be sought.

—From a *Declaration of Principles* jointly adopted by a Committee of the American Bar Association and a Committee of Publishers and Associations

Many of the designations used by manufacturers and sellers to distinguish their products are claimed as trademarks. Where those designations appear in this book and Adams Media was aware of a trademark claim, the designations have been printed with initial capital letters.

*This book is available at quantity discounts for bulk purchases.
For information, please call 1-800-289-0963.*

Contents

Acknowledgments

First and foremost, I want to thank my mother, Carol, for taking the time to instill in me a love of cooking and baking. Your love and constant support are appreciated more than you know. I want to thank my father, Howard, for always being an honest and appreciative critic. You tell it like it is . . . and yes, I know it needs more cream cheese. To my friends on Twitter and Facebook, and to those who follow my blog, please know you inspire me to be better, to work harder, and to find all that is delicious in life.

Finally, I want to thank my husband, Mark, for all the little things, for all the big things, and for talking me off the ledge more times that I care to discuss. You know how much I love you, how much I appreciate you, and, maybe most important, how invaluable you are to me as a taste tester. I could not do it without you.

Introduction

PIE, IN ITS MOST basic form, is a baked food with a filling that is prepared in a pastry and often topped with a pastry crust or other topping. The tradition of pie spans the globe, with most cultures having some sort of pie that speaks to the food and the people of that region. What gives pie its universal appeal is that it can be made with what is available fresh, such as meat, produce, grains, and dairy, but it can also be made with preserved ingredients. In fact, pies are a great way to perk up preserved, dried, or frozen fruits, meats, and vegetables.

Pies, in one form or another, have been around for centuries. Originally created as a method of food preservation, pies were also used as a way to make food easier to transport. The first recorded information regarding pies goes all the way back to the ancient Egyptians. Their pies more closely resembled modern freeform tarts called galettes and were filled with grains, fruit, and honey. Ancient Greeks made record numbers of pies, both sweet and savory, and with the Romans, pie spread across Europe. Encasing meat or fruit in a pastry crust made pies a preferred food for traveling, so pies were popular with the military and on sea voyages.

The term pie comes from medieval England where pastry cases, or "coffyns" as they were called, were used to house fillings. The crusts were very tough, being used primarily as the cooking vessel. Among the wealthy the filling was the only thing eaten and the crusts were given to the less fortunate or the servants. Pies traveled across the sea to America with the Pilgrims, who created new recipes to use what was locally available. Fruit pies, as they are known today, were most likely perfected by the Pennsylvania Dutch and became popular. As Americans settled the West, pies became a staple of most meals, with pioneer cooks making as many as twenty-one pies in a week!

Pies come in all shapes and sizes and can be served for breakfast, lunch, dinner, and dessert. When it comes to dessert, the most popular flavor in

America is apple. The phrase "as American as apple pie" speaks not only to the pie's popularity, but to what is considered traditional and wholesome. Since pies—and apples for that matter—are not originally from America, the phrase can also be seen as a nod to America's immigrant culture. Aside from apple, other popular flavors include chocolate, pecan, and coconut.

Pie is a comfort food, bringing back memories of home, love, and tradition. Mile-high meringue pies found in roadside diners are the stuff of road trip legend. In the South, deep-fried pies, often served with a tall glass of ice-cold lemonade, can be found in shops dotting the landscape. Pies filed with ice cream and candies are a staple of many ice cream shops and grocery stores. In the days after Thanksgiving, potpies made with leftover turkey and vegetables are often as anticipated as the big meal itself.

Delicious as pie is, it has a reputation for being difficult to prepare. Horror stories of tough, flavorless crusts and runny fillings have some too intimidated to try making a pie from scratch, and that is a shame. It does not take long to develop the skills needed to make good pies, and of course the more pies you make, the better you will become. So roll up your sleeves and get ready for a very tasty journey!

CHAPTER 1

Pie Basics

The first step in creating the perfect pie is to understand the pie-making process. From technique to ingredients, a good pie begins with knowledge. Happily, pie is pretty simple, and you only need to learn some basic fundamentals before getting started. In this chapter you will learn how ingredients function, what tools you need and how to use them, ways you can get ahead, and tips that will help you make better pies.

Ingredients for Success

A pie is only as good as the ingredients used to make it. Understanding the ingredients and how they function in recipes is one of the most important things any baker can learn. When you know how certain ingredients act in a recipe, it is easier to make substitutions or identify and correct problems. Creating new recipes, or making changes to an existing recipe to suit your personal preferences, will be more successful when you understand how ingredients function in the overall formula.

Flour

In most cases all-purpose flour is the best option for pie making. All-purpose flour is usually a blend of flours with high and low gluten content. *Gluten* is a protein that is formed when the wheat proteins glutenin and gliadin are mixed with water. Gluten gives baked goods their structure and helps give pie crusts structure and flakiness. As dough is mixed and kneaded, gluten forms, and the more you mix, the tougher the gluten will become. For some baked goods, like breads, a lot of gluten development is a good thing. In pies, reducing gluten development is preferred for tenderness, so it is important to use a light touch when kneading and rolling out pastry. All-purpose flour can also be used as a thickening agent in some pie fillings. The starch in the flour absorbs liquid, causing the filling to gel; however, flour takes some time to cook out the raw taste, making it less desirable for its thickening ability in cream-pie fillings. For fruit pies, where there is a longer baking time, the raw taste of the flour will be cooked away by the heat of the oven.

FACT

In general, ingredients function in one of two ways in recipes. The first is as a strengthener. Strengtheners are ingredients that help build structure in baked goods and include flour, milk, whole eggs, and egg whites. The second is as a tenderizer. These are ingredients that weaken or help reduce the amount of gluten in baked goods. Some tenderizers include sugar, fat, egg yolks, and leaveners.

Fat

Fat serves many purposes in baked goods. In pie production, perhaps the most important role it plays is in the crust. When fat is rubbed into flour, it acts as a tenderizer, coating some of the flour and preventing the production of gluten. As well as tenderizing the crust, fat acts to make pie crusts flaky. As fat melts in the oven, the water in the fat evaporates, causing steam. As the steam expands, it causes layers to be created, which results in flakiness. In crumb or cookie crusts, fat is used as a binder to help the crumbs keep their shape. It also serves to crisp the crumbs and inhibit moisture absorption from the filling. Butter is the preferred fat for pie fillings since it has a melt-in-your-mouth feel and superior taste. For pastry crusts, there are more fats that can be used. Aside from butter, you can also use vegetable shortening, lard, or even combinations of different fats.

Eggs

Eggs are primarily composed of water, protein, and fat. In baked goods, eggs perform a number of important functions. Beaten whole eggs can be used as a glaze for pastries. The protein in the eggs will brown and become shiny during baking, giving the finished product an appealing look. Beaten eggs can also be used as pastry glue for applying decorative cutouts onto pies and to seal top and bottom crusts. Egg whites can be whipped to provide structure and volume in pie fillings. Beat those same egg whites with sugar and you have a meringue topping for pies. In custard and cream pies, eggs and egg yolks add flavor and function as thickeners. Egg yolks can also be added to pie crusts to add flavor and color, and to assist in reducing the gluten.

ALERT

When working with raw eggs, it is important to avoid cross contamination. Eggs can contain salmonella, a bacteria that can cause the foodborne illness salmonellosis. Cross contamination happens when ready-to-eat food comes into contact with contaminated hands, utensils, and surfaces. Always wash your hands with hot water and soap after handling raw eggs, use a fresh whisk or spatula for cooked fillings, and never pour cooked pie fillings into bowls that contained raw or undercooked eggs.

Thickeners

Starch thickeners are used to keep pie fillings from becoming runny. Common starch thickeners in pie include flour, cornstarch, and tapioca. Thickeners work by absorbing liquid and forming a gel. In fresh fruit pies, simply toss the fruit with a starch thickener, such as flour or cornstarch, before baking. The oven heat will activate the starch and thicken the filling. When adding a starch thickener to a custard or sauce, mix the starch with a cool liquid before cooking. If the starch is added once the liquid is hot, it will form lumps. Once the thickener is added, cook only until the mixture begins to bubble and is just thickened. Overcooking will cause most starches to lose their thickening power, resulting in a runny filling.

Sugar

In baking, sugar helps aid in the browning of pie crusts and helps extend the shelf life of your baked goods. There are two forms of sugar used in baking. The first is granular sugar. *Granular sugars*, such as white, brown, or powdered sugar, are sugars that come in a dry, or crystalline, form. These sugars provide sweetness to pies, help control gluten development, and help egg whites and heavy cream foam when whipped. The second type of sugar comes in liquid form, such as corn syrup, honey, golden syrup, and molasses. These sugars are classified as *invert sugars*, and they are hygroscopic, which means they absorb moisture from the atmosphere. Invert sugars extend the shelf life of baked goods and provide sweetness to recipes.

Salt

As odd as it may seem, salt plays an important role in pie making. Salt contributes to tenderizing the crust, but its biggest contribution is in flavor. When adding salt to a pie crust, it is best to whisk it into the flour to ensure even distribution. Free-flowing, or table, salt offers the best flavor for most pie recipes, but if you prefer kosher, you will need to add 1½ times the amount of salt to the recipe. Salt is also a flavor component to fillings, making sweet fillings taste more sweet and helping flavors like chocolate and spice stand out. Omitting the salt will result in a pie with lackluster flavor.

Dairy

After water, milk is one of the most important liquids used in baking. From whole milk, cream, evaporated milk, and cream cheese, dairy products play a prominent role in many sweet and savory pies. Whole milk is preferred in pie making for its rich flavor and fat content. Low-fat and skim milks have much less fat than whole milk, and it is not recommended that they be used in pies unless specifically called for. Skim milk in particular is tricky to work with because heating it too long or too vigorously can cause splitting in custards. When it comes to cheeses, the same rule regarding fat applies. To achieve the best results, the full-fat versions are preferred since they do not contain additional emulsifiers or other products that can affect overall flavor and texture.

ESSENTIAL

A pie is not the place to use up dairy products that are past their prime. When using dairy products in pie making, it is best to use the freshest products available. If you use old milk, cream, or cheese, the quality of the finished product will be affected. Custards may not thicken properly, and using old dairy products will cause pies to spoil more quickly.

Pie-Making Tools

Ask any professional in any trade and they will tell you that having the right tools makes your job easier, and pie making is no different. The type of pan you bake in, the shape of your rolling pin, and what you use to create your pie will all make a difference in the final product. This does not mean you have to spend a fortune on tools, however. Some of the most valuable tools in the kitchen are the least expensive. Once you have the right tools, the next step is learning how to use them properly.

Pie Plates

Pie plates come in countless shapes, sizes, and materials. Among the most common for home bakers are glass, or Pyrex, pie plates. Glass pans are valuable for pie making because they heat pies evenly and help crusts crisp. Metal, or aluminum, pie pans are also common. These pans can be reusable or disposable, which makes them good for travel. Since metal pans tend to be shiny, it is important to keep an eye on baking times. The shine can actually reflect heat away from the pie, which will increase baking times. If your oven has hot spots or cold spots, you may need to rotate pies baked in metal pans halfway through baking to avoid overbrowning in those areas.

QUESTION

Should I use a pie pan with a nonstick coating?
Nonstick coatings are great on a variety of pans, but they are not usually necessary for pies. The crust, be it pastry or crumb, will have a sufficient amount of fat in it to prevent sticking. Sometimes the filling of a pie may escape under the crust, and in that case the pie may stick slightly, but it is nothing a pie server cannot handle. The biggest drawback to a nonstick coating is scratching. Since most pie is sliced and served from the pan it was baked in, you run a risk of marring the nonstick surface.

Tart pans come in two main varieties. The first are metal pans with removable bottoms for freestanding tarts. These pans are available with nonstick coatings, so releasing the tart is very easy. When buying one of these pans, look for sturdy metal with a surface free from scratches. Ceramic tart pans are also available and are good for tarts with softer crusts made with graham crackers or cookies. These pans allow for even cooking, but they make removing the whole tart almost impossible and are best used when the tart is to be served in the pan.

Rolling Pins

What type of rolling pin you use depends, in large part, on personal preference. For most jobs in the kitchen, a wooden rod-style rolling pin is perfect. These are good all-purpose pins, and when selecting one, it is best to choose one that is heavy for its size and at least 20 inches wide and 2 inches thick. Ball bearing rolling pins are also common, and what most people think of when they think of a rolling pin. These make a good all-purpose rolling pin and are especially helpful when large quantities of dough need rolling out. The heavier the better when it comes to this type of pin since the goal is to have the pin do most of the work. The last style of pin is the tapered, or French, rolling pin. This type of pin does an excellent job of rolling out round dough, such as pie dough. Again, you want a pin that is at least 20 inches wide and 2 to 3 inches thick in the center.

Other Helpful Tools

Good pans and rolling pins are important, but the small tools are important, too. The following is a list of very helpful hand tools for pie making. None of these tools are strictly necessary, but having them can take some of the stress out of baking. Since these tools are fairly common, and can be used for other kitchen tasks, a small investment now will pay off in a variety of ways later.

Pastry Brush

Pastry brushes are very helpful when making pies. It is a good idea to have two types. Natural bristle brushes are good for dusting excess flour off of pie dough and puff pastry. Purchase brushes with natural (not nylon or plastic) bristles that are at least 1 inch wide. Natural brushes should be hand washed only and allowed to air-dry. The second type of pastry brush is silicone. These brushes are good for brushing liquids, like egg washes, onto pies. Since silicone is dishwasher-safe, they are also easy to clean and sanitize.

Pizza Wheel

A pizza wheel or pizza cutter is a good tool to use when cutting pastry strips for lattice tops or trimming pastry before placing it into the pan. The wheel should be sharp and no smaller than 2 inches wide.

Bench Scraper

A bench scraper is a metal scraper with a handle that is good for transporting chopped food from a cutting board to a bowl. Bench scrapers are also helpful for releasing pastry crusts that become stuck to the work surface. Look for a bench scraper that is 5 to 6 inches wide and made of sturdy metal.

Heatproof Spatula

When stirring custards or toasting nuts, a heatproof spatula is invaluable. Silicone spatulas are available in many shapes and sizes. Be sure that the spatula is rated for temperatures over at least 450°F.

Pie Shield or Foil Rings

Pie shields are designed to protect the edges of the pie crust from burning. Commercial pie shields are available in kitchen stores and should be made of shiny metal to reflect the heat away. If you do not wish to buy one, you can easily make one with aluminum foil. Simply wrap the edge of the pie in a 3-inch-wide strip of foil, shiny side out.

Techniques for Perfect Pastry Crusts

For some the thought of making a pie from scratch can be daunting, but it is truly easy with the right technique. Taking the time to make a properly baked crust from scratch can be the difference between a good pie and a pie that will become the star of the meal. Below are tips to help you make delicious, perfectly formed pastry crusts.

Rolling Out Pastry

Rolling out pastry requires a little know-how. For many people, the rolling-out process is the most frustrating. From crusts that stick to crusts that crack or develop holes and tears, it is easy to understand why rolling out pie dough can be intimidating, but it does not have to be. It is important to note that much of the gluten in pie crust is formed during this stage, so working with well-rested, cold pastry is a must. The following tips will make rolling out your pie crusts much easier and prevent many common problems.

- Once the pastry dough is formed, be sure to let it rest in the refrigerator for at least thirty minutes. This will help the gluten formed in the initial mix relax so that when you roll out the dough, it will not spring back.

- Dust your work surface evenly with all-purpose flour, but do not use too much. You can always add more if the pastry begins to stick, but if you add too much it can make your pastry tough.
- When rolling, use light, even pressure to avoid thin spots and never roll the pin off the edge of the dough. Instead stop the pin just at the edge. Do not worry if it looks thick; when you turn the dough, it will flatten out.
- Roll from the middle out, meaning place the pin in the center of the dough and roll once up to the top, then return to the center and roll once back toward you. Do not roll the pin back and forth across the dough as this will cause friction that will warm the dough and make it tough.
- Turn the dough one-quarter turn after each series of strokes with the rolling pin. This will help keep the dough round, even out thick spots, and prevent sticking.
- Dust the bottom and top of the dough lightly throughout the rolling process with flour, especially if things get sticky.
- If the dough starts to spring back, stop rolling and chill it, wrapped in plastic, for thirty minutes. This will relax the gluten and prevent shrinking.

Lining a Pie Pan

Lining your pie pan may sound easy, but this is an area where many bakers run into trouble. The most important thing to remember is that you should never pull the dough; rather you should press it into place. Pulling the dough will stretch it, which can result in cracking and shrinking during baking. Also, remember to roll the dough out at least 3 inches wider than the pan it will go in so that you have enough overhand for a fluted edge. Once the pan is lined, trim the overhanging dough to 1 inch of the pan's edge, then tuck the dough under so that you have a double thickness of dough around the rim. Flute or crimp the dough as desired. To further prevent shrinking and cracking, chill the dough for at least thirty minutes before filling and baking.

Pie crusts can be made up and frozen before baking for as long as two months. To save room in the freezer, you can stack them. Place a piece of parchment or wax paper between each crust to help prevent sticking. When you are ready to bake, you can fill the frozen crust and proceed per the recipe directions, adding an additional five minutes to the cooking time. This is a great get-ahead tip for the holidays!

Using Pie Weights

Pie weights are used for weighing down crusts while *blind baking*, or baking without the intended filling such as with cream pies. When blind baking, be sure your weights fill the pie crust nearly to the top so that the sides get adequate support, which will prevent slipping or collapse. The easiest and least expensive options for pie weights are dry beans. Beans heat evenly and are not too heavy, so the crust will not become compressed.

Can I use my baking beans for soup later?
Sadly, no. Once you use the beans for pie weights, you cannot use them for any other purpose. Happily, if you store them properly, you can reuse them for years. Once the beans are cool, store them in an airtight container and be sure to mark them as baking beans. Making a soup with baking beans is a mistake you do not want to make.

Ceramic pie weights are available in kitchen and gourmet stores. Ceramic weights hold down the crust well, and since they get hot while baking, they help ensure the crust cooks evenly. You will need at least 2 cups of ceramic weights to weight down a pie and to hold the sides of the crust in place. A third option is pie chains. Pie chains are metal beads on a thin chain that are wound around the bottom of a pie crust. Pie chains will hold the bottom of a pie crust down, but they do little to help support the sides of the crust.

Pie Varieties

If you can think of it, you can most likely make it into a pie. Pies come in numerous flavors, textures, and sizes. Knowing, and understanding, the type of pie you are making will help you to be successful. Since the certain types of pies are generally cooked in the same way, knowing the pie type will also help you know where you might run into problems and how to fix them.

- **Quiche** is an egg-based custard filling baked in an unbaked, or par-baked, pastry crust. It can be filled with a variety of meats, vegetables, and cheeses. Quiche is popular for breakfast, brunch, and even dinner, and can be made to suit any theme.
- **Potpies** are pastry-encased savory pies with creamy sauces. Most potpies are filled with a kind of meat, typically chicken, turkey, or beef, along with diced vegetables or rice. Potpies are an economical way to feed a crowd and a good way to use up leftover meat and vegetables.
- **Fruit pies** can be filled with raw, preserved, or cooked fruit. These pies can be topped with a full crust, a lattice, or a crumb topping, or left open-faced. Fresh seasonal fruit makes delicious pies; however, pies are a good place to use preserved or frozen fruit.
- **Cream pies** are pies with a pudding or pastry cream filling that is cooked before being poured into a fully baked crust. Most of the fillings used in cream pies are starch thickened, with either cornstarch or flour. Meringues and whipped cream are traditional toppings for cream pies.
- **Custard pies** are pies with an uncooked custard filling placed in an uncooked or partially cooked crust and then baked. As the pie bakes, the filling cooks until it sets and the crust bakes. Examples of custard pies include pecan pie, pumpkin pie, and chess pie. Beware of overcooking custard pies. Overcooking can cause them to become watery or grainy.
- **Chiffon pies** have a light, fluffy texture thanks to whipped egg whites, and sometimes whipped cream, that are folded into a flavorful base. Gelatin is typically used to help these pies set and retain their cloud-like texture. Chiffon pies may contain raw egg whites, which can be dangerous for people with certain health issues. If raw egg whites are a concern, use pasteurized egg whites.

- **Hand pies**, or pocket pies, are simply large pies that have been scaled down to a more portable size. They can be either sweet or savory and can be either baked or deep-fried.

Tips for Special Diets

More and more people are on special diets. Be it due to an allergy, a medical condition, or a healthy living preference, knowing how to make pies for friends and family members with special dietary considerations is valuable. Modern food science makes it possible to cook delicious pies for any diet without missing a thing!

Sugar Substitutes

Over the last ten years, sugar substitutes have improved in flavor and function. Granulated sucralose is an increasingly popular option in diabetic cooking. Since sucralose can be measured cup for cup like sugar, it also makes conversions easy. When using sucralose in fruit pies, there will be less liquid released by the fruit before baking, but the juices will release during cooking, so do not reduce the amount of thickener. In cream-pie fillings cooked on the stove, reduce the heat used for cooking the custard to medium-low. If the filling becomes lumpy while simmering, blend the filling in a blender for a few seconds to release the lumps, then return to the stove to cook for a minute or two.

Some pies, like custard pies or nut pies, contain corn syrup. Agave syrup is a good substitute for corn syrup. While it contains natural sugars, it is low on the glycemic index and does not cause spikes in blood sugar like regular sugar or corn syrup. To substitute agave syrup for corn syrup, you should use half of the amount because agave syrup is sweeter. You may need to increase the liquid in the recipe. In nut pies, an additional egg should do the trick.

Gluten-Free Substitutes

Gluten intolerance and celiac disease are conditions where the body cannot process gluten, causing pain and other physical symptoms. Gluten-free baking requires mixing different types of gluten-free flours, such as brown or white rice, sorghum, and potato flours. These flours are often available at natural food stores or on the Internet. Baking mixes for those with gluten intolerance are becoming readily available in grocery stores and can be used to make crusts as well. For cookie crusts, gluten-free cookies can be easily used with no significant changes. Cornstarch is naturally gluten-free and can be used for thickening fruit pies and custards in place of flour. Fresh fruits and vegetables, as well as fresh meat, eggs, and most fats, are also gluten-free. Be sure to check processed foods, like sausages, for gluten content since processed foods often contain wheat, gluten, or gluten by-products.

Pies for Vegans

Vegan and vegetarian diets are very popular and the numbers of people following them are on the rise. Knowing how to make pies that can be enjoyed by everyone, regardless of dietary restrictions, may seem difficult but it does not have to be. Happily there are a variety of products available in most grocery stores that can make pie making for vegans a breeze!

- The easiest substitution for vegan baking is fat. Vegetable shortening is a excellent option to replace butter or lard in pastry crusts, however if you want to use something with more flavor look into vegan butter substitutes. Many are suitable for baking, but be sure to check the label. Because vegan butter substitutes are softer than butter it is a good idea to pop it in the freezer for a few minutes before use. Butter in pie fillings can be replaced with vegan butter substitute, or with oils such as coconut oil, olive oil, or canola oil.

- Soy milk and almond milk are good replacements for regular dairy milk in pie fillings, while coconut cream, the thickened part of coconut milk, is a good replacement for dairy cream in pie fillings. Certain products like sour cream and cream cheese can be replaced by silken tofu blended with a little lemon juice for tang.

- Eggs are used in many pie recipes and can be a little tricky to replace depending on their function in the recipe. In quiche and custard pies where the eggs act as thickeners silken tofu can replace eggs in a ratio of ¼ cup blended tofu mixed with 2 teaspoons of cornstarch per egg. Another option is to use fruit or vegetable puree in place of eggs where the function is flavor and texture. Applesauce, pureed banana, and pureed squash can replace eggs but can also change the flavor of the pie. They are used in a ratio of ¼ cup of puree per egg.

- For savory pies, such as potpies and quiche, meat and cheese are easily replaced by soy products. Soy cheese, for example, is available in most grocery stores and provides the flavor and melting qualities of regular cheese. Soy cheese is frequently located in the produce department in grocery stores. Chicken, beef, and pork products, such as sausage and bacon, can be replaced with soy- or vegetable-based products. Commonly these products are found in the freezer section with other vegan meat replacements.

Reduced-Fat and Calorie Substitutes

Whether you are trying to lose weight or maintain a healthy lifestyle, you do not have to sacrifice things like pie. Taking simple steps will help make your pie lighter in calories and fat. Here are a few easy ways to cut the fat:

- When reducing fats, remember that you cannot omit them entirely, especially in pastry crusts. Simply cutting the amount of fat in half will still provide some flavor and richness but less fat. Some additional liquid may be needed to help the dough come together, so add it a few drops at a time.
- Low-fat or 2% milk can be used in most custard and cream pie recipes with no appreciable effect. If evaporated milk is called for, again 2% milk works fine. The cooking time may need to be reduced, so start checking for doneness five minutes early. Avoid skim or nonfat milks for pies as they tend to break when heated.
- In quiche, cream, or custard pies that call for more than one egg yolk, whole eggs can be substituted. One whole egg can stand in for two egg yolks. Do not use only the whites as they will leave your pie grainy.
- In quiches and potpies, you can substitute heavy cream and half-and-half with low-fat evaporated milk. It provides richness and flavor just like cream but will not make the filling watery.
- Other low-fat dairy products, like reduced-fat cream cheese and low-fat cheese, can be substituted for the full-fat versions. Due to some

additives in reduced-fat cheeses, the texture of the finished pie may be slightly different than the full-fat version. Again, avoid fat-free dairy products as they contain additives that do not bake or cook well.

Storage and Safety

Once you have successfully created your masterpiece, the next steps are among the most vital, but they are often overlooked: cooling and storage. Taking the proper precautions while cooking and cooling the pie will prevent the growth of harmful bacteria. Proper storage will extend the life of your pie and prevent premature spoiling. All pies are different, so it is important to know how each type of pie should be handled.

Cooking and Cooling

Cooking does more than soften fruits, thicken custards, and cook meats. The cooking process, when done properly, kills the bacteria that can cause illness. For any fruit pie that is cooked only in the oven, you want to make sure that the filling is bubbling throughout, including the center, but an exact temperature is not required. For potpies, particularly those that contain poultry products, it is wise to test the internal temperature of the filling with a digital cooking thermometer. You are looking for the center of the filling to reach a minimum temperature of 160°F. Quiche is also ready when your thermometer reaches 160°F. Remember, once the pie is out of the oven, the temperature will rise an additional five degrees. This is called *carryover cooking*.

ALERT

You may think that the hotter the better when it comes to the internal temperature of pies and quiche, but you would be wrong. As long as the pie reaches 160°F, and eventually reaches 165°F during the carryover period, your food is safe to eat. Overcooking will lead to dry, split, and burned food. The same goes for reheating. Do not heat over 160°F or your delicious leftovers will become dry and tough.

Properly cooling your pie may seem easy, and sometimes it is, but there are a few things you should keep in mind.

- Cream pies should always be chilled in the refrigerator, unless the recipe specifies differently. Cooling at room temperature can be unsafe and may not properly set the filling.
- Never cover a warm pie completely with plastic or store in a covered container. The heat from the pie will lead to a soggy, mushy crust. The only exception is a cream pie where you cover the hot filling with plastic. The crust should be loosely covered, but not tightly.
- Potpies and quiche should never sit out at room temperature for longer than four hours before being refrigerated, and any potpie or quiche that has sat out longer than six hours should be discarded.
- Cool pies on a wire rack. The rack will encourage air circulation around the whole pie, which will ensure speedy and even cooling.

Storing Fruit Pies

Fruit pies that do not contain a dairy element, like a custard, cheese, or cream, can be safely stored at room temperature for up to two days. To keep the pie fresh, keep it in an airtight container or wrap the pie in aluminum foil. Fruit pies can be kept in the refrigerator for storage longer than a day or two, but the crusts can soften.

Storing Cream Pies

Cream pies should be kept refrigerated to keep them fresh. Since the fillings are typically egg- and milk-based, they are not safe for counter storage. Properly stored cream pies will keep for two or three days. Cover cream pies tightly in plastic wrap to prevent the absorption of off-flavors from the refrigerator.

Storing Custard Pies and Nut Pies

Most nut pies can be safely stored at room temperature for a day. For example, if you bake a pecan pie the night before you plan to serve it, just wrap it in a clean dishtowel and keep it on the counter. If the pie will be kept beyond that time, wrap it in plastic and store it in the refrigerator. Custard pies should be stored in the refrigerator since they contain egg and milk products. Both types of pies will last for up to three days.

Storing Potpies and Quiches

Potpies and quiches should be refrigerated within four hours of baking to ensure they are safe to eat. Cool the pie on the counter until just warm, then place it in the refrigerator. Once cooled, they should be covered with plastic or foil and kept chilled. Refrigerated, they will keep for up to two days.

Reheating and Refreshing

Cold pie can be disappointing, and a little soggy. Happily you can reheat and refresh most pies in the oven. Reheat potpies in a 350°F oven for 20 to 30 minutes, or until the filling is bubbly and reaches an internal temperature of 160°F. Fruit pies and quiches can be reheated the same way, but reduce the warming time to 10 to 12 minutes, or until warmed through. Discard any reheated pie and never reheat any type of pie more than once. Doing so will increase the chance of foodborne illness and bacteria.

Crusts

Flaky Pie Crust

This recipe is best for pies where the crust is blind-baked, such as with cream pies, or used as the top crust for fruit pies. This also works beautifully for a lattice top.

INGREDIENTS | YIELDS 1 (9-INCH) CRUST

1¼ cups all-purpose flour

2 tablespoons sugar

½ teaspoon salt

6 tablespoons butter, cubed and chilled

2 tablespoons lard or vegetable shortening, chilled

2–4 tablespoons ice water

What about the Scraps?

Ever wonder what to do with your pie dough scraps? Reroll them and use decorative cookie cutters to make festive decorations for your pie. Brush them with a little egg wash for a shiny finish.

1. In a large bowl, sift together the flour, sugar, and salt.

2. Add the chilled fats and rub them into the flour mixture with your fingers until 30 percent of the fat is between pea- and hazelnut-sized, while the rest is blended in well.

3. Add 2 tablespoons of water and mix until the dough forms a rough ball. Add more water, 1 tablespoon at a time, if needed.

4. Turn the dough out onto a lightly floured surface and form a disk. Wrap in plastic and chill for at least 30 minutes or up to 3 days.

5. Remove the dough from the refrigerator about 10 minutes before rolling out. Roll out on a lightly floured surface to a ⅛-inch-thick, 12-inch circle, turning the dough often to make sure it does not stick. Dust the surface with additional flour if needed.

6. Place the crust on a baking sheet and chill for 30 minutes before use.

Mealy Pie Crust

Mealy pie crusts are best used as the bottom crust for fruit pies and custard pies.

INGREDIENTS | YIELDS 1 (9-INCH) CRUST

1¼ cups all-purpose flour

2 tablespoons sugar

½ teaspoon salt

4 tablespoons butter, cubed and chilled

¼ cup lard or vegetable shortening, chilled

2–4 tablespoons ice water

What's the Difference?

Flaky pie crusts use large pieces of fat to create flaky layers, but those layers can absorb liquid in the pie filling, making them soggy. In a mealy crust, the fat is better incorporated, resulting in a denser crust that resists moisture absorption. It is still tender and crisp, just less flaky.

1. In a large bowl, sift together the flour, sugar, and salt.

2. Add the butter and shortening to the bowl and with your fingers rub the fat into the flour until the mixture looks like coarse sand with no large pieces of fat remaining.

3. Add 2 tablespoons of water and mix until the dough forms a rough ball. Add more water, 1 tablespoon at a time, if needed.

4. Turn the dough out onto a lightly floured surface and form a disk. Wrap in plastic and chill for at least 30 minutes or up to 3 days.

5. Remove the dough from the refrigerator about 10 minutes before rolling out. Roll out on a lightly floured surface to a ⅛-inch-thick, 12-inch circle, turning the dough often to make sure it does not stick. Dust the surface with additional flour if needed.

6. Fold the dough in half and place it into a 9-inch pie plate. Unfold and carefully push the dough into the pan. Use kitchen scissors or a paring knife to trim the dough to 1 inch of the pan's edge.

7. Cover with plastic and chill until ready to bake.

Cream Cheese Pastry Crust

This is very rich, tender dough that is lovely for fruit and nut pies.

INGREDIENTS | YIELDS 1 (9-INCH) CRUST

½ cup cream cheese, room temperature
½ cup butter, room temperature
1 teaspoon lemon zest
1½ cups all-purpose flour
¼ cup sugar
½ teaspoon salt
¼ teaspoon baking powder

1. In a large bowl, cream together the cream cheese, butter, and lemon zest until smooth.

2. In a separate bowl, sift together the flour, sugar, salt, and baking powder. Add the sifted dry ingredients into the cream cheese mixture and stir until it forms a soft dough. If the mixture feels sticky, add more flour, 1 tablespoon at a time, until it is smooth and no longer sticky.

3. Turn the dough out onto a lightly floured surface and form a disk. Wrap in plastic and chill for at least 1 hour or up to 3 days.

4. Remove the dough from the refrigerator for 10 minutes to warm up. Roll out on a lightly floured surface to a ⅛-inch-thick, 12-inch circle, turning the dough often to make sure it does not stick. Dust the surface with additional flour if needed.

5. Fold the dough in half and place it into a 9-inch pie plate. Unfold and carefully press the dough into the pan. Use kitchen scissors or a paring knife to trim the dough to 1 inch of the pan's edge.

6. Cover with plastic and chill until ready to bake.

All-Butter Pie Crust

All-butter crusts have a lovely melt-in-the-mouth feel, making them perfect for both sweet and savory pies and tarts.

INGREDIENTS | YIELDS 1 (9-INCH) CRUST

1¼ cups all-purpose flour

1 tablespoon sugar

½ teaspoon salt

8 tablespoons unsalted butter, cubed and chilled

3–4 tablespoons ice water

Working with Butter

Butter can be tricky to work with since it melts at around 90°F. When making a pie crust with butter, it is best to use very cold butter that is cut into ½-inch cubes. Chilling the butter in the freezer for 10 minutes will help make cutting it easier.

1. In a large bowl, sift together the flour, sugar, and salt.

2. Add the butter to the bowl and with your fingers rub it into the flour until the mixture looks like coarse sand studded with pea-sized pieces of butter.

3. Add 2 tablespoons of water and mix until the dough forms a rough ball. Add more water, 1 tablespoon at a time, if needed.

4. Turn the dough out onto a lightly floured surface and form a disk. Wrap in plastic and chill for at least 30 minutes or up to 3 days.

5. Remove the dough from the refrigerator for 10 minutes before rolling out. Roll out on a lightly floured surface to a ⅛-inch-thick, 12-inch circle, turning the dough often to make sure it does not stick. Dust the surface with additional flour if needed.

6. Fold the dough in half and place it into a 9-inch pie plate. Unfold and carefully press the dough into the pan. Use kitchen scissors or a paring knife to trim the dough to 1 inch of the pan's edge.

7. Cover with plastic and chill until ready to bake.

Food Processor Pie Crust

The food processor is a great tool in pastry making because it saves time and makes homemade pie crusts a snap to prepare.

INGREDIENTS | YIELDS 1 (9-INCH) CRUST

1¼ cups all-purpose flour

1 tablespoon sugar

½ teaspoon salt

4 tablespoons vegetable shortening, chilled

4 tablespoons unsalted butter, cubed and chilled

3–4 tablespoons ice water

Butter and Vegetable Shortening

Vegetable shortening has a higher melting point than butter, making it easier to work with, but it does not have a lot of flavor. Using a mixture of butter and shortening means a flavorful crust that is easy to work with.

1. In the work bowl of a food processor, add the flour, sugar, and salt. Pulse 5 times to combine.

2. Add the shortening and pulse until the mixture looks like coarse sand. Add the butter and pulse until the butter is the size of hazelnuts, about 5 pulses.

3. Add 2 tablespoons of water and pulse until the dough begins to clump around the blade. Add more water, 1 tablespoon at a time, if needed. The dough should hold together when pinched and should not feel wet or sticky.

4. Turn the dough out onto a lightly floured surface and form a disk. Wrap in plastic and chill for at least 30 minutes or up to 3 days.

5. Remove the dough from the refrigerator for 10 minutes to warm up. Roll out on a lightly floured surface to a ⅛-inch-thick, 12-inch circle, turning the dough often to make sure it does not stick. Dust the surface with additional flour if needed.

6. Fold the dough in half and place it into a 9-inch pie plate. Unfold and carefully press the dough into the pan. Use kitchen scissors or a paring knife to trim the dough to 1 inch of the pan's edge.

7. Cover with plastic and chill until ready to bake.

Almond Pastry Crust

Ground almonds give this crust a nutty flavor that is perfect for fruit pies . . . particularly cherry!

INGREDIENTS | YIELDS 1 (9-INCH) CRUST

1 cup plus 2 tablespoons all-purpose flour

¼ cup ground almonds

2 tablespoons sugar

½ teaspoon salt

4 tablespoons butter, cubed and chilled

4 tablespoons vegetable shortening, chilled

¼ teaspoon almond extract

2–4 tablespoons ice water

Ground Almonds

Ground almonds can be purchased at most natural food stores, but it is easy to make at home. Grind whole, blanched almonds in a food processor until they are the texture of coarse sand. Be careful not to overgrind or you will end up with almond butter.

1. In a large bowl, whisk together the flour, almonds, sugar, and salt.

2. Add the butter and shortening, and with your fingers rub it into the flour until the mixture looks like coarse sand studded with pea-sized pieces of butter.

3. Add the almond extract and 2 tablespoons of water and mix until the dough forms a rough ball. Add more water, 1 tablespoon at a time, if needed.

4. Turn the dough out onto a lightly floured surface and form a disk. Wrap in plastic and chill for at least 30 minutes or up to 3 days.

5. Remove the dough from the refrigerator for 10 minutes to warm up. Roll out on a lightly floured surface to a ⅛-inch-thick, 12-inch circle, turning the dough often to make sure it does not stick. Dust the surface with additional flour if needed.

6. Fold the dough in half and place it into a 9-inch pie plate. Unfold and carefully press the dough into the pan. Use kitchen scissors or a paring knife to trim the dough to 1 inch of the pan's edge.

7. Cover with plastic and chill until ready to bake.

Lard Crust

Pie crusts made with lard have a refined, flaky texture that vegetable shortening and butter cannot match. They also have a neutral flavor, making them a good crust for any type of pie.

INGREDIENTS | YIELDS 1 (9-INCH) CRUST

1¼ cups all-purpose flour
½ teaspoon salt
½ cup lard, chilled
1 egg yolk
1 teaspoon white distilled vinegar
2 tablespoons ice water

Why Lard?

Lard was widely used in baking and cooking until the 1900s, when vegetable shortening came to the market. Lard is low in saturated fat, high in unsaturated fat, and trans-fat-free. Lard offers the higher melting point of vegetable shortening with the flavor and crisping qualities of butter.

1. In a large bowl, sift together the flour and salt.

2. Add the lard and with your fingers rub it into the flour until the mixture looks like coarse sand studded with pea-sized pieces of fat.

3. In a bowl, whisk together the egg yolk, vinegar, and water. Add 2 tablespoons of the liquid and mix until the dough forms a rough ball. Add more liquid, 1 tablespoon at a time, if needed.

4. Turn the dough out onto a lightly floured surface and form a disk. Wrap in plastic and chill for at least 30 minutes or up to 3 days.

5. Remove the dough from the refrigerator for 10 minutes to warm up. Roll out on a lightly floured surface to a ⅛-inch-thick, 12-inch circle, turning the dough often to make sure it does not stick. Dust the surface with additional flour if needed.

6. Fold the dough in half and place it into a 9-inch pie plate. Unfold and carefully press the dough into the pan. Use kitchen scissors or a paring knife to trim the dough to 1 inch of the pan's edge.

7. Cover with plastic and chill until ready to bake.

Traditional Graham Cracker Crust

For simplicity and versatility, you can't beat a graham cracker crust. Consider this crust for fruit pies, too!

INGREDIENTS | YIELDS 1 (9-INCH) CRUST

1⅓ cups graham cracker crumbs

3 tablespoons sugar

6 tablespoons unsalted butter, melted

Flavoring Cookie Crusts

Cookie crusts are a good place to add a little extra flavor. Try adding ¼ teaspoon of cinnamon or pumpkin pie spice to give the crust a spicy kick. If you want to add some chocolate flavor, add 1 tablespoon of cocoa powder.

1. Heat the oven to 350°F.

2. Combine the graham cracker crumbs, sugar, and butter in a medium bowl until well combined. Press the mixture evenly into a 9-inch pie pan.

3. Bake for 10 to 12 minutes, or until the crust is golden brown and the center is firm when pressed lightly. Cool completely before filling.

Pretzel Crust

Pretzel crusts are especially good with peanut butter and chocolate fillings, or used with tangy citrus pies.

INGREDIENTS | YIELDS 1 (9-INCH) CRUST

1¼ cups finely crushed pretzels

¼ cup sugar

¼ cup unsalted butter, melted

Getting the Right Crumbs

The best way to get fine crumbs for cookie-style pie crusts is to use a food processor. Process until the mixture looks like sand. Large pieces of cookies or pretzels will make the crust too fragile and the slices will fall apart when sliced.

1. Heat the oven to 350°F.

2. Combine the pretzel crumbs, sugar, and butter in a medium bowl until well combined. Press the mixture evenly into a 9-inch pie pan.

3. Bake for 10 to 12 minutes, or until the crust is golden brown and the center is firm when pressed lightly. Cool completely before filling.

Short Crust for Tarts

This buttery crust is similar to a shortbread cookie and is perfect for dessert tarts.

INGREDIENTS | YIELDS 1 (10-INCH) TART CRUST

¼ cup sugar
1 stick unsalted butter, slightly softened
1 egg yolk
½ teaspoon vanilla
1⅓ cups all-purpose flour

1. Cream together the sugar and butter until just combined. Add in the egg yolk and vanilla and mix well.

2. Add in the flour and mix until the dough is smooth. Wrap in plastic and chill for 1 hour or up to 3 days.

3. Remove dough from the refrigerator for 10 minutes to warm up. Roll out on a lightly floured surface to a ⅛-inch-thick, 12-inch circle, turning the dough often. Dust the surface with additional flour if needed.

4. Roll the dough around the rolling pin and unroll it into a 10-inch tart pan. pressing the dough into the pan. Press your fingers against the rim of the pan to trim the dough. Cover with plastic and chill until ready to bake.

Chocolate Cookie Crust

This crust is a crowd pleaser, and when filled with mocha ice cream, it is absolute heaven!

INGREDIENTS | YIELDS 1 (9-INCH) CRUST

1⅓ cups chocolate wafer cookie crumbs
2 tablespoons sugar
6 tablespoons unsalted butter, melted

Chocolate Wafer Cookie Substitutes

If chocolate wafer cookies are not available, then a good substitute is chocolate graham crackers. To punch up the chocolate flavor, add a tablespoon of Dutch-processed cocoa powder to the crumbs.

1. Heat the oven to 350°F.

2. Combine the cookie crumbs, sugar, and butter in a medium bowl until well combined. Press the mixture evenly into a 9-inch pie pan.

3. Bake for 10 to 12 minutes, or until the crust is firm in the center when pressed lightly. Cool completely before filling.

Graham Pecan Crust

As the pecans bake in this crust, they become aromatic and toasty!

INGREDIENTS | YIELDS 1 (9-INCH) CRUST

1 cup plus 2 tablespoons graham cracker crumbs

⅓ cup ground pecans

¼ teaspoon cinnamon

¼ cup sugar

6 tablespoons unsalted butter, melted

1. Heat the oven to 350°F.

2. Combine the graham cracker crumbs, ground pecans, cinnamon, sugar, and butter in a medium bowl until well combined. Press the mixture evenly into a 9-inch pie pan.

3. Bake for 10 to 12 minutes, or until the crust is golden brown and the center is firm when pressed lightly. Cool completely before filling.

Gingersnap Crust

Gingersnaps give this crust a spicy edge that is perfect with rich fillings.

INGREDIENTS | YIELDS 1 (9-INCH) CRUST

⅔ cups graham cracker crumbs

⅔ cups gingersnap crumbs

2 tablespoons sugar

6 tablespoons unsalted butter, melted

1. Heat the oven to 350°F.

2. Combine the graham cracker crumbs, gingersnap crumbs, sugar, and butter in a medium bowl until well combined. Press the mixture evenly into a 9-inch pie pan.

3. Bake for 10 to 12 minutes, or until the crust is golden brown and the center is firm when pressed lightly. Cool completely before filling.

Blitz Puff Pastry

This recipe produces a flaky pastry dough that can be used in place of puff pastry in most recipes.

What Makes Blitz Puff Pastry So Quick?

Traditional puff pastry incorporates a block of cold butter into dough, which is then rolled out, folded, and chilled repeatedly to get all those flaky layers. It can take all day. This recipe incorporates large pieces of butter directly into the dough, and from start to finish this takes less than an hour. It is essentially a very flaky pie crust.

1. In a large bowl, combine the flour, sugar, and salt. Mix well. Add the chilled butter and blend it into the flour mixture with your fingers until 10 percent of the fat is blended in well, leaving the rest as very large chunks, between hazelnut and pecan size.

2. Add the water a little at a time and mix the dough with a spatula until it just hangs together. It will look very shaggy.

3. Turn the dough out onto a well-floured surface. Shape the dough into a rectangle and roll it out to ½-inch thick. Dust the top with additional flour if the butter is too soft, but do not add too much. Use a bench scraper or a large spatula to fold the dough into itself in thirds, similar to folding a letter. It will be crumbly.

4. Turn the dough 90 degrees and square off the edges of the dough. Roll the dough into a rectangle that's ½-inch thick. Brush off any excess flour from the dough and fold the dough in thirds. Repeat this process two more times, then wrap in plastic and chill for 30 minutes.

5. Remove from the refrigerator and allow to stand for 10 minutes. Roll the dough out into a ½-inch thick rectangle, dust off any excess flour, then fold the 2 shorter sides into the center and then in half at the seam, like a book. Roll out the dough to ½-inch thick, wrap in plastic, and chill for 1 hour before use.

Cornmeal Tart Crust

Cornmeal adds a rustic flavor and an unusual texture that goes well with berry tarts.

INGREDIENTS | YIELDS 1 (10-INCH) TART CRUST

¾ cup all-purpose flour

⅓ cup yellow cornmeal

¼ teaspoon salt

⅓ cup unsalted butter, room temperature

¼ cup sugar

1 large egg yolk

1. In a medium bowl, combine the flour, cornmeal, and salt until thoroughly blended.

2. Whisk together the butter and sugar in a separate bowl until lightened in color. Whisk in the egg yolk.

3. Add dry ingredients to the butter mixture and stir until just combined. Flatten the dough into a disk, wrap in plastic, and refrigerate for 30 minutes.

4. Remove the dough from the refrigerator for 10 minutes to warm up. Roll out on a lightly floured surface to a ⅛-inch-thick, 12-inch circle, turning the dough often to make sure it does not stick. Dust the surface with additional flour if needed.

5. Fold the dough in half and place it into a 10-inch tart pan with 1-inch sides. Unfold and carefully press the dough into the pan. Press the dough against the edge of the pan to trim.

6. Cover with plastic and chill until ready to bake.

Parmesan Pastry Crust

This savory crust is lovely for tarts and quiches.

Add Some Herbs

Adding a tablespoon of finely minced herbs to savory pastry crusts adds a lot of extra flavor. Be sure the herbs are very finely minced, then add them to the flour before you add the butter so that the herbs can be evenly distributed. Use herbs that complement the filling for the most impact.

1. In a large bowl, whisk together the flour, baking powder, salt, and cheese.

2. Add the chilled butter and rub it into the flour mixture with your fingers until 30 percent of the fat is pea-sized, while the rest is blended in well.

3. Add the water and vinegar and mix until the dough forms a rough ball. Add more water, a few drops at a time, if needed.

4. Turn the dough out onto a lightly floured surface and form a disk. Wrap in plastic and chill for at least 30 minutes or up to 3 days.

5. Remove the dough from the refrigerator for 10 minutes to warm up. Roll out on a lightly floured surface to a ⅛-inch-thick, 11-inch circle, turning the dough often to make sure it does not stick. Dust the surface with additional flour if needed.

6. Fold the dough in half and place it into a 9-inch tart pan with 1-inch sides. Unfold and carefully press the dough into the pan. Press the dough against the edge of the pan to trim.

7. Cover with plastic and chill until ready to bake.

CHAPTER 3

Toppings

Butter Crumble

Buttery crumble toppings can take a simple fruit pie over the top!

INGREDIENTS | YIELDS ENOUGH CRUMBLE FOR 1 (9-INCH) PIE

½ cup all-purpose flour
½ cup sugar
¼ teaspoon salt
⅓ cup unsalted butter, cubed and chilled

1. In a medium bowl, blend the flour, sugar, and salt. Using your fingers, rub in the butter until the mixture resembles coarse sand.

2. Chill the crumble for 30 minutes before use.

Crumble It Up!

Crumbles are delicious as ice cream toppings. Just spread the chilled crumble on a parchment-lined pan and bake for 12 to 15 minutes, or until golden and crisp. Any extra crumble can be stored in an airtight container for up to three days.

Pecan Streusel

You can use walnuts or almonds in place of the pecans for some variety.

INGREDIENTS | YIELDS ENOUGH CRUMBLE FOR 1 (9-INCH) PIE

¼ cup packed light brown sugar
¼ cup sugar
½ cup all-purpose flour
¼ cup unsalted butter, cubed and chilled
⅓ cup chopped pecans

1. In a large bowl, blend the light brown sugar, sugar, and flour. Using your fingers, rub in the butter until the mixture resembles coarse sand. Add the pecans and mix well.

2. Chill for 30 minutes before use.

Cinnamon Streusel Topping

This recipe is good on pies and can also be used for topping coffee cakes and muffins.

INGREDIENTS | YIELDS ENOUGH CRUMBLE FOR 1 (9-INCH) PIE

½ cup all-purpose flour

½ cup packed light brown sugar

½ teaspoon cinnamon

¼ teaspoon salt

⅓ cup unsalted butter, cubed and chilled

1. In a large bowl, blend the flour, light brown sugar, cinnamon, and salt. Using your fingers, rub in the butter until the mixture resembles coarse sand.

2. Chill the crumble for 30 minutes before use.

Using Whole Wheat Flour

Whole wheat flour offers a nutty flavor and more fiber than all-purpose flour. In crusts and toppings, substitute whole wheat for no more than half of the flour. Using all whole wheat will make crusts tough and crumbles gummy.

Sour Cream Topping

Tangy and lightly sweet, this topping is great with peach pie or stone fruit tarts.

INGREDIENTS | SERVES 8

1 cup sour cream

2 tablespoons sugar, or more to taste

1 teaspoon vanilla

In a large bowl, mix the sour cream, sugar, and vanilla together until smooth. Chill 1 hour before serving.

Oat Crumble

Oats add a lovely texture and toasty flavor to this crumble.

¼ cup all-purpose flour

¼ cup rolled oats

¼ teaspoon cinnamon

½ cup sugar

¼ teaspoon salt

⅓ cup unsalted butter, cubed and chilled

1. In a large bowl, blend the flour, oats, cinnamon, sugar, and salt. Using your fingers, rub in the butter until the mixture resembles coarse sand.

2. Chill the crumble for 30 minutes before use.

Keeping a Crumble Crisp

Crumbles are popular because of their crispness. The best way to keep leftover crumble-topped pies and tarts crisp is to allow them to cool completely to room temperature before storing. Avoid plastic wrap, which does not allow for air flow. Instead cover the pie loosely with aluminum foil or store in a plastic container.

Foolproof Meringue

The cornstarch in this recipe helps prevent the meringue from shrinking, beading, or weeping.

INGREDIENTS | SERVES 8

1 tablespoon cornstarch
⅓ cup cold water
4 egg whites, room temperature
1 pinch cream of tartar
6 tablespoons superfine sugar
1 teaspoon vanilla

The Trick to Fluffy Meringues

Start with room-temperature egg whites, which will whip up faster and hold more air than cold egg whites. Beat on a low speed for the first few minutes, allowing them to get foamy and frothy before increasing the speed. Finally, add a little acid such as cream of tartar, which will help the protein set up and stay fluffy.

1. Whisk the cornstarch into the water until smooth. Pour the mixture into a small pot and cook over medium heat, stirring constantly, until the starch thickens, about 5 minutes. Set aside to cool.

2. In a large bowl, add the egg whites and cream of tartar. Beat the egg whites on low speed until they become foamy. Increase the speed to medium and begin adding the sugar, 1 tablespoon at a time. Beat until the mixture forms soft peaks.

3. Continue beating the egg whites and add cornstarch mixture, 1 tablespoon at a time. Beat until the mixture forms firm peaks.

4. Immediately spread over pie filling and bake as desired.

Stabilized Whipped Cream

This whipped cream has a delicate, fluffy texture and holds its shape for up to three days.

INGREDIENTS | SERVES 8

½ teaspoon unflavored powdered gelatin

1½ teaspoons cold water

1 cup heavy whipping cream, cold

3 tablespoons powdered sugar

1 teaspoon vanilla

Blooming Gelatin

Powdered gelatin must be bloomed before it can be used. Blooming ensures that the final product will have a smooth texture and that the gelatin will set up properly. Most liquid is fine for blooming gelatin, but avoid using fresh tropical fruit juices. The enzymes in the juice will inhibit the gelatin from blooming properly.

1. In a small bowl, mix the powdered gelatin with the cold water. Let stand 10 minutes, then melt in the microwave for 10 seconds. Allow to cool for 5 minutes, or until cool to the touch.

2. In a medium bowl, add the cream, powdered sugar, and vanilla. Whip with a stand mixer or with hand mixer on medium-high speed until it starts to thicken. Slowly pour in the cooled gelatin and whip until the cream forms medium peaks.

3. Use immediately, or cover with plastic and store in the refrigerator for up to 3 days.

Spiked Whipped Cream

This whipped cream has a boozy kick, but if you want to skip the alcohol just replace it with Stabilized Whipped Cream.

INGREDIENTS | SERVES 8

1 cup heavy whipping cream, cold
3 tablespoons powdered sugar
2 tablespoons bourbon, rum, or brandy

Chocolate and Spices

Whipped cream can easily be flavored with cocoa powder or other spices. Adding a tablespoon of cocoa powder or a pinch of spice to the cream before whipping will ensure the flavors are evenly distributed.

1. In a medium bowl, add the cream, powdered sugar, and alcohol. Whip on medium-high speed with a stand mixer or with hand mixer until it starts to thicken. Increase the speed to high and beat until soft peaks form.

2. Reduce the speed to medium and slowly add the liquor. Continue to whip until medium peaks form.

3. Use immediately.

Biscuit Topping

If you want a unique topping for a potpie, try this recipe!

INGREDIENTS | YIELDS ENOUGH TO TOP 1 (9-INCH) PIE

1 cup all-purpose flour
1 tablespoon sugar
1 teaspoon baking powder
½ teaspoon salt
1 stick unsalted butter, cubed and chilled
¼ cup buttermilk

1. In a medium bowl, combine the flour, sugar, baking powder, and salt. Add the cold butter and with your fingers rub it in until it is the size of peas.

2. Add the buttermilk and, using a spatula, stir until it is just combined. Do not overmix.

3. Using a disher, or 2 spoons, scoop the dough by rounded tablespoons onto the pie.

Salted Caramel Sauce

Serve this sauce drizzled over a slice of warm pie adorned with a scoop of vanilla ice cream. It is so good!

INGREDIENTS | YIELDS 1½ CUPS

1 cup sugar
2 tablespoons water
2 tablespoons light corn syrup
¾ cup heavy cream
4 tablespoons unsalted butter
1½ teaspoons sea salt, crushed

1. In a medium saucepan with deep sides over medium-high heat, combine the sugar, water, and corn syrup. Brush down the sides of the pan with a wet pastry brush until it begins to bubble.

2. Bring the mixture to a full boil and cook until the mixture becomes dark amber in color and smells like caramel, about 6 minutes. Remove the saucepan from the heat and carefully whisk in the cream, butter, and salt.

3. Allow the caramel to cool to room temperature before serving.

Peanut Butter Fudge Sauce

If you want a sauce with some texture, use chunky peanut butter.

INGREDIENTS | YIELDS 1½ CUPS

¾ cup heavy cream
½ cup semisweet chocolate, chopped
½ cup creamy peanut butter
2 tablespoons honey

In a medium saucepan, combine the cream, chocolate, peanut butter, and honey. Cook over medium-low heat until the chocolate is completely melted and the mixture is smooth. Serve warm.

CHAPTER 4

Traditional Favorites

Home-Style Apple Pie

Simplicity makes this pie so good. Serve it warm with vanilla ice cream for a special touch.

INGREDIENTS | SERVES 8

1 cup sugar

¼ cup cornstarch

1 teaspoon cinnamon

½ teaspoon fresh grated nutmeg

8 medium Granny Smith apples, peeled, cored, and sliced ¼-inch thick

1 (9-inch) Mealy Pie Crust, unbaked (See Chapter 2)

1 egg, beaten

1 (9-inch) Flaky Pie Crust, unbaked (See Chapter 2)

Baking Apples

When it comes to baking, Granny Smith apples are a good choice. Aside from being flavorful, they have a crisp texture that holds up well after cooking. If you prefer a less tart apple, try Gala, Honey Crisp, or Golden Delicious.

1. Heat the oven to 400°F.

2. In a large bowl, mix the sugar, cornstarch, cinnamon, and nutmeg until well blended. Add the apples and toss to coat. Allow to stand 10 minutes.

3. Fill the mealy crust with the apple mixture. Brush the edge of the bottom pie crust with the beaten egg so that the top crust will adhere.

4. Top with the flaky crust and trim the dough to 1 inch of the pan's edge. Tuck the edge of the top crust under the edge of the bottom crust. Crimp the dough using your fingers or a fork.

5. Brush the entire top crust with the beaten egg and cut 4 or 5 slits in the top to vent steam.

6. Place the pie on a baking sheet and bake for 30 minutes, then reduce the heat to 350°F for an additional 30 to 40 minutes, or until the pie is bubbling and the juices are thick. Cool for 2 hours before slicing.

Lattice-Top Cherry Pie

If fresh cherries are available, feel free to use them here.
A few toasted flaked almonds make an excellent garnish.

INGREDIENTS | SERVES 8

20 ounces frozen pitted cherries

1 cup sugar

½ cup cornstarch

1 tablespoon butter

¼ teaspoon salt

1 teaspoon lemon juice

¼ teaspoon almond extract

1 (9-inch) Mealy Pie Crust, unbaked (See Chapter 2)

1 Flaky Pie Crust (See Chapter 2), cut into 10 (1-inch) strips

1 egg, beaten

1. Heat the oven to 375°F.

2. Thaw the cherries and drain the juices into a measuring cup. Add enough water to the juice to equal ½ cup.

3. Combine the juice, sugar, and cornstarch until smooth in a small saucepan. Cook over medium heat until the mixture begins to boil and thickens.

4. Add the butter, salt, lemon juice, and almond extract. Mix well and then fold in the cherries. Cool to room temperature.

5. Pour into the Mealy Pie Crust and top with the pastry strips. Lay out 5 strips of pie dough on top of the filling about ½ inch apart. Starting ½ inch from the edge of the pie, fold back every other strip and lay down 1 strip of pastry. Fold the pastry back down and fold back the other pieces. Lay down a second strip about ½ inch from the first strip. Repeat this process until all the strips are used. Trim the dough to 1 inch of the pan's edge. Tuck the edge of the top crust under the edge of the bottom crust. Crimp the dough using your fingers or a fork. Brush the lattice with beaten egg.

6. Bake for 40 to 45 minutes, or until the filling is bubbly in the center and the lattice is golden brown. Cool for 30 minutes before serving.

Blueberry Pie

In the summer, when blueberries are in season, there is no better way to enjoy them than in a pie! Pour a little cold heavy cream over each slice. It is delicious.

INGREDIENTS | SERVES 8

6 cups of fresh blueberries, rinsed and stemmed

1 teaspoon lemon zest

2 teaspoons lemon juice

¼ cup cornstarch

½ cup sugar

¼ teaspoon cinnamon

Pinch fresh grated nutmeg

1 (9-inch) Mealy Pie Crust, unbaked (See Chapter 2)

3 tablespoons butter (unsalted), cut into small pieces

1 egg, beaten

1 (9-inch) Flaky Pie Crust (See Chapter 2)

Frozen Blueberries

If fresh berries are not in season or are looking less than desirable, frozen blueberries are a fine substitute. Allow the berries to thaw completely and drain off any excess liquid before preparing the filling. Skipping that step will result in a watery pie.

1. Heat the oven to 400°F.

2. In a large bowl, gently toss together the blueberries, lemon zest, lemon juice, cornstarch, sugar, cinnamon, and nutmeg. Pour into the prepared pastry crust. Dot the top with the butter.

3. Brush the edge of the Mealy Pie Crust with the beaten egg so that the top crust will adhere. Top with the flaky crust and trim the dough to 1 inch of the pan's edge. Tuck the edge of the top crust under the edge of the bottom crust. Crimp the dough using your fingers or a fork. Brush the entire top crust with the beaten egg and cut 4 or 5 slits in the top to vent steam.

4. Place the pie on a baking sheet and bake for 30 minutes, then reduce the heat to 350°F for an additional 30 to 40 minutes, or until the pie is bubbling and the juices are thick. Cool completely before slicing.

Peach Pie

Fresh peaches are always best, but frozen can be used if peaches are not in season. Be sure to thaw and drain frozen peaches before use to keep the pie from becoming watery.

INGREDIENTS | SERVES 8

1 cup sugar

¼ cup cornstarch

¼ teaspoon cinnamon

½ teaspoon vanilla

10 medium peaches, peeled, pitted, and sliced ¼-inch thick

1 (9-inch) Mealy Pie Crust, unbaked (See Chapter 2)

2 tablespoons unsalted butter

1 egg, beaten

1 (9-inch) Flaky Pie Crust (See Chapter 2)

Best Peaches for Baking

When selecting peaches for baking consider two things: first, freestone peaches are easier to pit than clingstone, meaning there will be less loss of flesh. Second, yellow peaches tend to have a more robust flavor, making them best for pies. White peaches are better in open-faced tarts where they can be the star.

1. Heat the oven to 425°F.

2. In a large bowl, combine the sugar, cornstarch, cinnamon, vanilla, and peaches. Turn gently to coat and allow to stand for 10 minutes.

3. Fill the Mealy Pie Crust with the peach mixture and dot the top with butter. Brush the edge of the bottom pie crust with the beaten egg so that the top crust will adhere.

4. Top with the flaky crust and trim the dough to 1 inch of the pan's edge. Tuck the edge of the top crust under the edge of the bottom crust. Crimp the dough using your fingers or a fork. Brush the entire top crust with the beaten egg and cut 4 or 5 slits in the top to vent steam.

5. Place the pie on a baking sheet and bake for 30 minutes, then reduce the heat to 350°F for an additional 30 to 40 minutes, or until the pie is bubbling and the juices are thick. Cool for 1 hour before slicing.

Rhubarb Pie

Fresh rhubarb is available in the spring, but frozen rhubarb will also work in this pie.

INGREDIENTS | SERVES 8

½ cup all-purpose flour

1½ cups sugar

¼ teaspoon salt

4 cups rhubarb, cut into 1-inch pieces

1 (9-inch) pastry crust, unbaked

3 tablespoons butter

1 egg, beaten

1 (9-inch) Flaky Pie Crust (See Chapter 2)

The Pie Plant

Rhubarb originated in western China and was used primarily as a medicine. Today rhubarb is nicknamed "the pie plant" in the United States because of its extensive use in pies. Since it is very tart, rhubarb pies use more sugar or are combined with sweeter fruits like strawberries to balance the flavor.

1. Heat the oven to 350°F.

2. In a large bowl, combine the flour, sugar, and salt. Add the rhubarb and toss to coat.

3. Pour the mixture into the pastry crust. Dot the top with the butter. Brush the edge of the bottom pie crust with the beaten egg so that the top crust will adhere.

4. Top with the second crust and trim the dough to 1 inch of the pan's edge. Tuck the edge of the top crust under the edge of the bottom crust. Crimp the dough using your fingers or a fork. Brush the entire top crust with the beaten egg and cut 4 or 5 slits in the top to vent steam.

5. Place the pie on a baking sheet and bake, in the lower third of the oven, for 45 minutes to 1 hour, or until the fruit is tender and the crust is golden brown all over. Cool on a rack before serving.

Key Lime Pie

Key limes are not always available fresh, and they can be time-consuming to juice, so look for bottled key lime juice if fresh is unavailable.

INGREDIENTS | SERVES 8

4 egg yolks
14 ounces sweetened condensed milk
½ cup key lime juice
1 (9-inch) Traditional Graham Cracker Crust, baked and cooled (See Chapter 2)

1. Heat the oven to 350°F.

2. In a large bowl, lightly whisk the egg yolks until they are broken. Add the sweetened condensed milk and stir to combine. Add the lime juice and stir until smooth.

3. Pour the filling into the prepared crust. Bake for 10 minutes, then chill overnight before serving.

Chess Pie

Originally from England, chess pie is now a staple in the southern part of the United States. The filling is very rich, and this pie could easily serve 10.

INGREDIENTS | SERVES 8

4 eggs
1 stick butter, melted
1 cup sugar
1 tablespoon yellow cornmeal
1 teaspoon vanilla
½ cup milk
1 tablespoon fresh lemon juice
1 (9-inch) pastry crust, unbaked

1. Heat the oven to 350°F.

2. In a large bowl, whisk together the eggs, butter, and sugar until smooth. Add the cornmeal, vanilla, milk, and lemon juice. Whisk until well combined.

3. Pour the mixture into the pastry crust and place on a baking sheet. Bake for 50 to 55 minutes, or until the filling is set and the top is golden brown. Allow to cool to room temperature before serving.

Vanilla Cream Pie

Fresh vanilla beans offer the best flavor for this pie and produces a pretty, speckled custard.

Vanilla Bean Paste

Vanilla bean paste, made from vanilla beans and a thick sugar syrup, is available in specialty stores and online. It can be used in the same measure as vanilla extract and is perfect in recipes where the visual impact of the beans matters. One tablespoon of vanilla bean paste is equal to 1 vanilla bean.

1. Heat the oven to 375°F.

2. Line the unbaked pie crust with parchment paper or a double layer of aluminum foil and add pie weights or dry beans. Bake for 15 minutes, then remove the paper and weights and bake for an additional 10 minutes, or until the crust is golden brown all over. Remove from the oven and set aside to cool.

3. In a medium saucepan, combine the milk, sugar, vanilla bean and seeds, cornstarch, egg yolks, and salt. Whisk until smooth, then cook over medium heat, stirring constantly, until it begins to simmer and thicken, about 8 minutes.

4. Remove from the heat and add the butter. Stir until melted. Pour through a strainer into a separate bowl, then pour directly into the prepared crust.

5. Place a layer of cling film directly on the custard and chill for at least 6 hours or overnight.

6. Once the pie has chilled, prepare the Stabilized Whipped Cream and top the pie. Chill for 30 minutes before serving.

Coconut Cream Pie

A chocolate cookie crust or graham cracker crust also work well with this pie. If you have it, fresh shredded coconut can be used here.

INGREDIENTS | SERVES 8

1 (9-inch) pastry crust, unbaked

1½ cups whole milk

½ cup sugar

3 tablespoons cornstarch

1 egg yolk

2 eggs

1¾ cups shredded sweetened coconut, divided

¼ teaspoon salt

2 tablespoons butter

1 teaspoon vanilla

⅛ teaspoon coconut extract

1 recipe Stabilized Whipped Cream (See Chapter 3)

1. Heat the oven to 375°F.

2. Line the pie crust with parchment paper or a double layer of aluminum foil and add pie weights or dry beans. Bake for 15 minutes, then remove the paper and weights and bake for an additional 10 to 12 minutes, or until the crust is golden brown all over. Remove from the oven and set aside to cool.

3. In a medium saucepan, combine the milk, sugar, cornstarch, egg yolk, eggs, 1½ cups of shredded coconut, and salt. Whisk until smooth, then cook over medium heat, stirring constantly, until it begins to simmer and thicken.

4. Remove from the heat and add the butter, vanilla, and coconut extract. Stir until melted. Pour directly into the prepared crust.

5. Place a layer of cling film on the custard and chill for at least 6 hours or overnight.

6. Once the pie has chilled, prepare the Stabilized Whipped Cream and top the pie. Chill for 30 minutes before serving. Garnish with the reserved coconut.

Chocolate Cream Pie

*Nothing beats a simple, rich chocolate cream pie. Make this pie
with a chocolate cookie crust to drive chocoholics wild.*

INGREDIENTS | SERVES 8

2 cups whole milk or half-and-half

⅔ cup sugar

¼ cup Dutch-processed cocoa powder

¼ cup cornstarch

2 egg yolks

¼ teaspoon salt

2 tablespoons butter

2 ounces semisweet chocolate, chopped

1 teaspoon vanilla

1 (9-inch) Traditional Graham Cracker
Crust, baked and cooled (See Chapter 2)

1 recipe Stabilized Whipped Cream
(See Chapter 3)

1. In a medium saucepan, combine the milk, sugar, cocoa powder, cornstarch, egg yolks, and salt. Whisk until smooth, then cook over medium heat, stirring constantly, until it begins to simmer and thicken.

2. Remove from the heat and add the butter, chopped chocolate, and vanilla. Stir until melted. Pour through a strainer into a separate bowl, then pour directly into the prepared crust.

3. Place a layer of cling film directly on the custard and chill for at least 6 hours or overnight.

4. Once the pie has chilled, prepare the Stabilized Whipped Cream and spread it on the pie. Chill for 30 minutes before serving.

The Chocolate Matters

Consumers have become more sophisticated and demand higher-quality ingredients in their grocery stores. Where once only generic baking chocolate was available, now there are chocolate bars to suit all tastes. Consider splurging on a bar with a higher cacao percentage, anything over 65 percent. The end result will be a richer, more robust chocolate flavor.

Banana Cream Pie

Using ripe bananas is the key to a flavorful pie. If your bananas are a little green,
put them in a paper bag overnight to accelerate the ripening.

INGREDIENTS | SERVES 8

1 (9-inch) pastry crust, unbaked

3 ripe bananas, peeled and sliced ¼-inch thick

1½ cups whole milk

½ cup sugar

3 tablespoons cornstarch

1 egg

¼ teaspoon salt

2 tablespoons butter

1 teaspoon vanilla

1 recipe Stabilized Whipped Cream (See Chapter 3)

1. Heat the oven to 375°F.

2. Line the pie crust with parchment paper or a double layer of aluminum foil and add pie weights or dry beans. Bake for 15 minutes, then remove the paper and weights and bake for an additional 10 minutes, or until the crust is golden brown all over. Remove from the oven and set aside to cool.

3. Evenly layer the banana slices in the prepared crust. Set aside.

4. In a medium saucepan, combine the milk, sugar, cornstarch, egg, and salt. Whisk until smooth, then cook over medium heat, stirring constantly, until it begins to simmer and thicken.

5. Remove from the heat and add the butter and vanilla. Stir until melted. Pour through a strainer into a separate bowl, then pour directly into the prepared crust.

6. Place a layer of cling film directly on the custard and chill overnight.

7. Once the pie has chilled, prepare the Stabilized Whipped Cream and top the pie. Chill for 30 minutes before serving.

Butterscotch Meringue Pie

Butterscotch is simply brown sugar custard, but there is nothing simple about the delicious, complex flavor.

INGREDIENTS | SERVES 8

1 (9-inch) pastry crust, unbaked
1 cup milk
1 cup heavy cream
⅔ cup packed light brown sugar
¼ cup cornstarch
2 egg yolks
¼ teaspoon salt
2 tablespoons butter
1 teaspoon vanilla
1 recipe Foolproof Meringue (See Chapter 3)

1. Heat the oven to 375°F.

2. Line the pie crust with parchment paper or a double layer of aluminum foil and add pie weights or dry beans. Bake for 15 minutes, then remove the paper and weights and bake for an additional 10 minutes, or until the crust is golden brown all over. Remove from the oven and set aside to cool.

3. In a medium saucepan, combine the milk, cream, light brown sugar, cornstarch, egg yolks, and salt. Whisk until smooth, then cook over medium heat, stirring constantly, until it begins to simmer and thicken.

4. Remove from the heat and add the butter and vanilla. Stir until melted. Pour through a strainer into a separate bowl, then pour directly into the prepared crust.

5. Prepare the Foolproof Meringue and spread onto the filling while it is still hot, making sure the meringue completely covers the filling and the inside edge of the crust. Bake for 10 to 12 minutes, or until the meringue is golden brown. Remove from the oven and chill in the refrigerator for 2 hours, uncovered, before slicing.

Southern Pecan Pie

No gathering in the South is complete without a fresh pecan pie.
In the summer, try it with vanilla or chocolate ice cream.

INGREDIENTS | SERVES 8

2 tablespoons all-purpose flour

½ cup sugar

2 eggs

1 cup corn syrup

¼ teaspoon salt

2 tablespoons butter, melted

1 teaspoon vanilla

1½ cups coarsely chopped pecans

1 (9-inch) Mealy Pie Crust, unbaked
(See Chapter 2)

1. Heat the oven to 350°F.

2. Whisk together the flour and sugar. Add the eggs, corn syrup, salt, butter, and vanilla. Whisk until smooth.

3. Spread the pecans into the crust in an even layer. Pour the filling over the pecans and tap the pie gently on the counter to release any air bubbles.

4. Place the pie on a baking sheet and bake for 50 to 60 minutes, or until the filling is puffed all over and set. Cool to room temperature before serving.

Pumpkin Pie

Filled with warm spices and creamy pumpkin, this traditional
pie is a perfect ending to a Thanksgiving or holiday meal.

INGREDIENTS | SERVES 8

¾ cup sugar

1 teaspoon cinnamon

½ teaspoon salt

¼ teaspoon allspice

¼ teaspoon ground cloves

⅛ teaspoon fresh grated nutmeg

2 eggs

15 ounces pumpkin purée

12 ounces evaporated milk

1 (9-inch) pastry crust, unbaked

1. Heat the oven to 425°F.

2. In a large bowl, whisk together the sugar, cinnamon, salt, allspice, cloves, and nutmeg until well combined.

3. Add the eggs, pumpkin, and evaporated milk and whisk until smooth.

4. Pour the mixture into the prepared pastry crust and place on a baking sheet. Bake in the lower third of the oven for 15 minutes, then reduce the heat to 350°F and bake for an additional 40 to 45 minutes, or until the filling is set at the edges and just slightly wobbly in the center. Cool for 3 hours on a wire rack before slicing.

Lemon Meringue Pie

Tart and sweet, lemon meringue pie is popular all year round.

Meyer Lemons

Next time you make a lemon pie, why not try Meyer lemons? A cross between a lemon and an orange, this fruit has a sweet, mildly tangy citrus flavor. Originally from China where they are grown in pots, Meyer lemons have gained in popularity in American cooking and can be found in produce markets from November to March.

1. Heat the oven to 375°F.

2. Line the pie crust with parchment paper or a double layer of aluminum foil and add pie weights or dry beans. Bake for 12 minutes, then remove the paper and weights and bake for an additional 10 minutes, or until the crust is golden brown all over. Remove from the oven and set aside to cool. Leave the oven on.

3. In a medium saucepan, whisk together the egg yolks, cornstarch, water, sugar, and salt. Cook the mixture over medium heat, whisking constantly, until it comes to a boil. Boil for 1 minute, then remove from the heat and whisk in the butter and lemon juice. Pour through a strainer into a separate bowl, then pour directly into the prepared crust.

4. Spread the meringue onto the filling while it is still hot, making sure the meringue completely covers the filling and the inside edge of the crust. Bake for 10 to 12 minutes, or until the meringue is golden brown. Remove from the oven and cool to room temperature, uncovered, before slicing.

CHAPTER 5

Fruit Pies

Apple Pie with a Spicy Cheddar Crust

*Cheddar cheese and apples are a traditional combination. This pie
takes that old favorite and gives it a spicy twist!*

INGREDIENTS | SERVES 8

2½ cups all-purpose flour

1 teaspoon salt

¼ teaspoon cayenne pepper

1 cup (2 sticks) unsalted butter, cubed
and chilled

2 cups shredded sharp Cheddar cheese

6–8 tablespoons ice water

3 medium Granny Smith apples, peeled,
cored, and sliced ¼-inch thick

3 medium Golden Delicious apples,
peeled, cored, and sliced ¼-inch thick

2 tablespoons lemon juice

½ cup packed light brown sugar

¼ cup all-purpose flour

¼ teaspoon salt

1 teaspoon cinnamon

¼ teaspoon fresh grated nutmeg

½ teaspoon vanilla

1 egg, beaten

Cheese, Please!

Adding cheese to pie crust is an easy way
to add extra flavor. Quiche and potpies are
good candidates for a cheesy crust, as are
savory tarts. Aside from Cheddar, Gruyére,
Parmesan, and jack cheeses work well in
pastry crusts.

1. In a large bowl, sift together the flour, salt, and cayenne pepper.

2. Add the chilled butter and rub into the flour mixture with your fingers until 30 percent of the fat is between pea- and hazelnut-sized, while the rest is blended in well. Add the Cheddar cheese and mix until evenly incorporated.

3. Add 3 tablespoons of water and mix until the dough forms a rough ball. Add more water, 1 tablespoon at a time, as needed.

4. Turn the dough out onto a lightly floured surface. Divide the dough in half. Form each half into a disk. Wrap in plastic and chill for at least 1 hour or up to 3 days.

5. Remove one of the disks from the refrigerator for 10 minutes to warm up. Once warm, knead the dough 10 times on a well-floured surface. Roll out to a ⅛-inch-thick, 12-inch circle, turning the dough often to make sure it does not stick. Dust the surface with additional flour if needed.

6. Fold the dough in half and place it into a 9-inch pie plate. Unfold and carefully push the dough into the pan. Use kitchen scissors or a paring knife to trim the dough to ½ inch of the pan's edge. Cover with plastic and place in the refrigerator to chill.

Apple Pie with a Spicy Cheddar Crust

(CONTINUED)

7. Remove the second disk of dough from the refrigerator for 10 minutes to warm up. Roll out on a lightly floured surface to a ⅛-inch-thick, 12-inch circle, turning the dough often to make sure it does not stick. Dust the surface with additional flour if needed.

8. Place the crust on a baking sheet and chill for 30 minutes before use.

9. Heat the oven to 400°F.

10. Put the apple slices in a large bowl and toss with the lemon juice.

11. Add the light brown sugar, flour, salt, cinnamon, nutmeg, and vanilla to the apples. Toss to coat and set aside for 10 minutes.

12. Fill the pie with the apple mixture. Brush the edge of the bottom pie crust with the beaten egg so that the top crust will adhere. Top with the second crust and trim to 1 inch of the pan's edge. Tuck the edge of the top crust under the edge of the bottom crust. Crimp the dough using your fingers or a fork. Brush top crust with the beaten egg and cut 4 or 5 slits in the top to vent steam.

13. Place the pie on a baking sheet and bake, in the lower third of the oven, for 1 hour to 1 hour and 15 minutes, or until the filling is bubbling in the center of the pie and the crust is golden brown all over. Enjoy warm.

Raspberry-Peach Crumble Pie

This pie is a perfect Labor Day treat since fresh peaches and raspberries are available at the market.

INGREDIENTS | SERVES 8

4 medium peaches, peeled, pitted, and cut ¼-inch thick

2 cups fresh raspberries

¾ cup sugar

¼ cup packed light brown sugar

¼ cup cornstarch

¼ teaspoon salt

½ teaspoon cinnamon

¼ teaspoon nutmeg

½ teaspoon vanilla

4 tablespoons butter, melted and cooled

1 (9-inch) pastry crust, unbaked

1 recipe Butter Crumble (See Chapter 3)

1. Heat the oven to 375°F.

2. In a large bowl, combine the peaches, raspberries, sugar, light brown sugar, cornstarch, salt, cinnamon, nutmeg, vanilla, and butter. Gently toss until the fruit is evenly coated.

3. Pour the mixture into the prepared crust and spread the butter crumble mixture evenly over the top. Place the pie on a baking sheet and bake, in the lower third of the oven, for 45 to 55 minutes, or until the crumble is golden brown and the pie is bubbling. Cool at room temperature for 2 hours before serving.

Peach Streusel Pie

The spices and nutty topping add a lot of flavor, so this pie is a good place to help frozen or less-than-stellar peaches shine.

INGREDIENTS | SERVES 8

1 cup packed light brown sugar

¼ cup cornstarch

¼ teaspoon cinnamon

¼ teaspoon nutmeg

½ teaspoon vanilla

4 cups frozen peaches, thawed and drained

1 (9-inch) pastry crust, unbaked

1 recipe Pecan Streusel (See Chapter 3)

1. Heat the oven to 375°F.

2. In a large bowl, combine the light brown sugar, cornstarch, cinnamon, nutmeg, vanilla, and peaches. Turn gently to coat.

3. Fill the bottom crust with the peach mixture. Top with the streusel mixture.

4. Place the pie on a baking sheet and bake for 45 to 55 minutes, or until the pie is bubbling and the topping is golden brown. Cool to room temperature before serving.

Apple-Blueberry Crumble Pie

This pie is lovely warm with a scoop of vanilla ice cream or a drizzle of Sour Cream Topping (See Chapter 3).

INGREDIENTS | SERVES 8

6 cups Granny Smith apples, peeled, cored and cut into ¼-inch slices

1 cup fresh blueberries

1 cup sugar

¼ cup cornstarch

1 teaspoon cinnamon

2 teaspoons lemon zest

1 tablespoon lemon juice

2 tablespoons butter, melted and cooled

1 (9-inch) Mealy Pie Crust, unbaked (See Chapter 2)

1 recipe Oat Crumble (See Chapter 3)

1. Heat the oven to 375°F.

2. In a large bowl, combine the apples, blueberries, sugar, cornstarch, cinnamon, lemon zest, lemon juice, and butter. Gently toss until the fruit is evenly coated.

3. Pour the mixture into the prepared crust and spread the oat crumble mixture evenly over the top. Place the pie on a baking sheet and bake, in the lower third of the oven, for 45 to 55 minutes, or until the crumble is golden brown and the pie is bubbling. Cool at room temperature for 2 hours before serving.

Peach Sour Cream Pie

Sweet peaches are surrounded by tangy sour cream custard in this unique pie. It is hard to resist.

INGREDIENTS | SERVES 8

1 (9-inch) pastry crust, unbaked

1 cup sour cream

½ cup sugar

1 tablespoon cornstarch

2 eggs, lightly beaten

1 teaspoon vanilla

¼ teaspoon mace

8 medium peaches, peeled and cut into ¼-inch-thick slices

1 recipe Butter Crumble (See Chapter 3)

1. Heat the oven to 425°F.

2. Line the pie crust with foil or parchment paper and fill with pie weights or dry beans. Bake for 10 minutes, then remove the lining and weights and bake for an additional 10 minutes. Set aside to cool.

3. In a large bowl, whisk together the sour cream, sugar, and cornstarch until smooth. Add the eggs, vanilla, and mace and whisk until well combined.

4. Fold in the sliced peaches, pour them into crust, and top with the crumble. Bake for 30 to 35 minutes. Cool to room temperature before serving.

Apple and Candied-Walnut Pie

Topped with sweet glazed walnuts, this pie is a delicious combination of flavors and textures.

INGREDIENTS | SERVES 8

3 medium Granny Smith apples, peeled, cored, and sliced ¼-inch thick

3 medium Golden Delicious apples, peeled, cored, and sliced ¼-inch thick

1½ cups chopped walnuts, divided

1 cup packed light brown sugar, divided

2 tablespoons lemon juice

¼ cup all-purpose flour

¼ teaspoon salt

1 teaspoon cinnamon

¼ teaspoon fresh grated nutmeg

1 (9-inch) pastry crust, unbaked

4 tablespoons butter, melted

1. Heat the oven to 375°F.

2. In a large bowl, combine the apples, ¾ cup chopped walnuts, ½ cup light brown sugar, lemon juice, flour, salt, cinnamon, and nutmeg. Toss to coat and allow to stand for 10 minutes.

3. Pour the apple mixture into the pastry crust and place on a baking sheet. Bake for 50 to 55 minutes, or until the filling is bubbling and the crust is brown. Remove from the oven and set aside.

4. Heat the broiler. Combine the remaining walnuts with the remaining light brown sugar and the melted butter. Mix well, then spread over the baked pie. Wrap the edge of the crust with aluminum foil to protect it. Broil about 5 inches from the heating element for 2 to 3 minutes, or until bubbly. Cool completely before serving.

Brandied-Pear Pie

Brandy and pears are a common combination, but whiskey or rum also work well.

INGREDIENTS | SERVES 8

1 (9-inch) pastry crust, unbaked

2 tablespoons unsalted butter

8 medium Bosc pears, peeled, cored and sliced ¼-inch thick

1 vanilla bean, split and seeds scraped out

½ cup brandy, divided

½ cup sugar

¼ cup cornstarch

½ teaspoon cinnamon

¼ teaspoon salt

1 recipe Spiked Whipped Cream made with brandy (See Chapter 3)

1. Heat the oven to 375°F.

2. Line the pie crust with parchment paper or a double layer of aluminum foil and add pie weights or dry beans. Bake for 10 minutes, then remove the paper and weights and bake for an additional 8 to 10 minutes, or until the crust is lightly golden brown all over. Remove from the oven and set aside to cool.

3. In a large skillet over medium heat, melt the butter until it foams. Add the sliced pears, vanilla bean, and vanilla bean seeds. Remove the pan from the heat and add ¼ cup of the brandy and the sugar. Return the pan to the heat and cook until the pears are just starting to soften, about 3 minutes.

4. In a small bowl, whisk together the remaining brandy and the cornstarch until smooth. Add to the simmering fruit and stir until thickened. Remove from the heat and add the cinnamon and salt. Carefully remove the vanilla bean.

5. Fill the pie crust with the pear mixture. Place the pie on a baking sheet and bake, in the lower third of the oven, for 25 to 30 minutes, or until the filling is bubbling in the center of the pie and the crust is golden brown all over.

6. Cool the pie completely to room temperature, then top with the Spiked Whipped Cream. Serve immediately.

Apple Rum Raisin Pie

Spiced rum and plump raisins make this pie fancy enough for the holidays or a special occasion.

INGREDIENTS | SERVES 8

¼ cup spiced rum

½ cup raisins

6 medium Gala apples, peeled, cored, and sliced ¼-inch thick

½ cup sugar

⅓ cup flour

¼ teaspoon salt

1 teaspoon cinnamon

¼ teaspoon cardamom

1 (9-inch) pastry crust, unbaked

1 egg, beaten

1 (9-inch) Flaky Pie Crust (See Chapter 2)

Substitute for Raisins

Raisins are either loved or hated; there are few who fall in between. If you or your family dislike raisins, try substituting dried cherries or cranberries. Both of these fruits pair well with apple and rum, and they have plenty of flavor.

1. Heat the oven to 400°F.

2. Heat the rum in a small saucepan until it simmers. Remove from the heat and add the raisins. Allow to steep for 10 minutes.

3. In a large bowl, combine the apples, sugar, flour, salt, cinnamon, cardamom, and raisins with the rum. Toss to coat and allow to stand for 10 minutes.

4. Fill the pie crust with the apple mixture. Brush the edge of the bottom pie crust with the beaten egg so that the top crust will adhere. Top with the second crust and trim the dough to 1 inch of the pan's edge. Tuck the edge of the top crust under the edge of the bottom crust. Crimp the dough using your fingers or a fork. Brush the entire top crust with the beaten egg and cut 4 or 5 slits in the top to vent steam.

5. Place the pie on a baking sheet and bake, in the lower third of the oven, for 1 hour to 1 hour and 15 minutes, or until the filling is bubbling in the center of the pie and the crust is golden brown all over. Enjoy warm.

Almond Cherry Pie

Almonds in the crust, filling, and topping add a lot of real almond flavor as well as lovely texture to this cherry pie.

INGREDIENTS | SERVES 8

20 ounces frozen cherries
1 cup sugar
½ cup cornstarch
1 tablespoon butter
¼ teaspoon salt
1 teaspoon lemon juice
¼ teaspoon vanilla
½ cup toasted flaked almonds
1 (9-inch) Almond Pastry Crust, unbaked (See Chapter 2)
¼ cup packed light brown sugar
¼ cup sugar
½ cup all-purpose flour
¼ cup unsalted butter, cubed and chilled
⅓ cup chopped almonds

1. Heat the oven to 375°F.

2. Thaw the cherries and drain the juices into a measuring cup. Add enough water to the juice to equal ½ cup, if needed.

3. Combine the juice, sugar, and cornstarch until smooth in a small saucepan. Cook over medium heat until the mixture begins to boil and thickens.

4. Add the butter, salt, lemon juice, and vanilla. Mix well and then fold in the flaked almonds and cherries. Remove from the heat and cool to room temperature.

5. In a bowl, blend the light brown sugar, sugar, and flour. Using your fingers, rub in the butter until the mixture resembles coarse sand. Add the almonds and mix well. Chill for 30 minutes before use.

6. Pour the cooled cherry mixture into the prepared crust and top with the almond crumble. Place the pie on a baking sheet and bake for 40 to 45 minutes, or until the filling is bubbly in the center and the topping is golden brown. Cool for 1 hour before serving.

Fresh Apricot Pie

Apricots are in season from late spring to mid-summer and make unexpected filling for a pie.

INGREDIENTS | SERVES 8

20 fresh apricots, pitted and sliced
¼-inch thick
1 cup sugar
⅓ cup all-purpose flour
¼ teaspoon cinnamon
¼ teaspoon nutmeg
1 tablespoon lemon juice
1 (9-inch) pastry crust, unbaked
1 Flaky Pie Crust (See Chapter 2), cut
into 10 (1-inch) strips
1 egg, beaten

When Is That Apricot Ripe?

Here are the best ways to tell if an apricot is ready for eating. First, look for plump, bright orange fruit. Discard any that are pale yellow or white. Second, test for softness. The fruit should just give under slight pressure. Finally, smell them. A strong apricot smell is an indication that they are ripe and ready.

1. Heat the oven to 375°F.

2. In a large bowl, combine the apricots, sugar, flour, cinnamon, nutmeg, and lemon juice. Toss gently until all the fruit is evenly coated. Allow to stand for 10 minutes.

3. Pour the apricot mixture into the pie shell and top with the pastry strips. Lay out 5 strips of pie dough on top of the filling about ½ inch apart. Starting ½ inch from the edge of the pie, fold back every other strip and lay down 1 strip of pastry. Fold the pastry back down and fold back the other pieces. Lay down a second strip about ½ inch from the first strip. Repeat this process until all the strips are used. Trim the dough to 1 inch of the pan's edge. Tuck the edge of the top crust under the edge of the bottom crust. Crimp the dough using your fingers or a fork. Brush the lattice with beaten egg.

4. Bake for 40 to 45 minutes, or until the filling is bubbly in the center and the lattice is golden brown. Cool for 30 minutes before serving.

Strawberry Pie

Fresh strawberries will retain some of their texture after cooking. Frozen berries are too mushy.

INGREDIENTS | SERVES 8

1 quart fresh strawberries, hulled and quartered

¾ cup sugar

3 tablespoons cornstarch

¾ cup cranberry juice

1 (9-inch) Traditional Graham Cracker Crust, baked and cooled (See Chapter 2)

1 recipe Stabilized Whipped Cream (See Chapter 3)

1. In a medium bowl, combine half of the strawberries with the sugar. With a potato masher or a fork, mash the berries until mostly smooth. Stir in the remaining berries and let stand for 10 minutes.

2. In a large saucepan, combine the berry mixture, cornstarch, and cranberry juice. Cook over medium heat until the mixture thickens and bubbles.

3. Pour the mixture into the prepared crust and chill for 4 hours. Once chilled, prepare the Stabilized Whipped Cream and spread over the top. Chill for 30 minutes before serving.

Cherry-Pear Crumble Pie

Dried cherries, plumped up in some orange juice, give this pie a sweet and tangy flavor perfect for the fall.

INGREDIENTS | SERVES 8

1 cup orange juice

1 cup dried cherries

6 Bosc pears, peeled, cored and sliced ¼-inch thick

½ cup packed light brown sugar

¼ cup cornstarch

½ teaspoon cinnamon

½ teaspoon vanilla

1 (9-inch) pastry crust, unbaked

1 recipe Oat Crumble (See Chapter 3)

1. In a small saucepan, bring the orange juice to a boil. Remove from the heat and add the cherries. Allow to stand for 10 minutes, then drain well.

2. Heat the oven to 375°F.

3. In a large bowl, combine the cherries, pears, light brown sugar, cornstarch, cinnamon, and vanilla. Toss to coat and allow to stand for 10 minutes.

4. Pour pear mixture into pastry crust. Evenly top with Oat Crumble. Bake for 45 to 55 minutes, or until the topping is golden brown. Cool to room temperature before serving.

Apple Crumble Pie

Cinnamon and apples star in this crunchy-topped pie.

1. Heat the oven to 375°F.

2. In a large bowl, combine the apples, sugar, lemon juice, cornstarch, salt, cinnamon, and nutmeg. Toss to coat and allow to stand for 10 minutes.

3. Pour the apple mixture into the pastry crust and top with the Cinnamon Streusel Topping. Place on a baking sheet and bake for 50 to 55 minutes, or until the filling is bubbling and the crust is brown.

Other Baking Apples

Granny Smith is a wonderful baking apple, but other varieties can be used with great success. Next time you bake apple pie, try Crispin, Courtland, or Jonathan apples. Avoid Red Delicious, Pink Lady, or Ida Red apples as they become mushy after baking.

Strawberry-Rhubarb Pie

Sweet strawberries are a natural partner to the tangy rhubarb in this pie.

INGREDIENTS | SERVES 8

¼ cup cornstarch

1¼ cups sugar

¼ teaspoon salt

¼ teaspoon cinnamon

2 cups rhubarb, cut into 1-inch pieces

2 cups strawberries, hulled and sliced in half

1 (9-inch) pastry crust, unbaked

3 tablespoons butter

1 egg, beaten

1 (9-inch) Flaky Pie Crust (See Chapter 2)

Strawberry Rhubarb Pie Day

Looking for an excuse to make a strawberry rhubarb pie? Well, if it is June 9, you don't need one since it is National Strawberry Rhubarb Pie Day. While an unofficial holiday, it is a good reason to bake, and eat, this delicious pie!

1. Heat the oven to 350°F.

2. In a large bowl, combine the cornstarch, sugar, salt, and cinnamon. Add the rhubarb and strawberries. Gently toss to coat.

3. Pour the mixture into the pastry crust. Dot the top with the butter. Brush the edge of the bottom pie crust with the beaten egg so that the top crust will adhere. Top with the second crust and trim the dough to 1 inch of the pan's edge. Tuck the edge of the top crust under the edge of the bottom crust. Crimp the dough using your fingers or a fork. Brush the entire top crust with the beaten egg and cut 4 or 5 slits in the top to vent steam.

4. Place the pie on a baking sheet and bake, in the lower third of the oven, for 45 minutes to 1 hour, or until the fruit is tender and the crust is golden brown all over. Cool on a rack before serving.

Pineapple Chiffon Pie

Light and fluffy, this is a unique way to enjoy pineapple.

Fresh or Canned?

For ease of use, canned pineapple is always a good choice. If you prefer to use fresh in a recipe where canned crushed pineapple is called for, simply crush the fresh fruit with a potato masher or pulse it a few times in a food processor.

1. In a small bowl, combine the gelatin and the water. Allow to stand until completely bloomed, about 10 minutes.

2. In a double boiler, combine the egg yolks, sugar, pineapple, and lemon juice. Cook the mixture, whisking constantly, until thickened. Remove from the heat and add the bloomed gelatin. Whisk until dissolved. Allow to cool until it thickens.

3. In a large, clean bowl, whip the egg whites with the salt until they are very frothy. Gradually add in the sugar, beating constantly, until the whites form medium peaks.

4. Working in thirds, fold the egg whites into the pineapple mixture, making sure no large streaks of egg white remain. Pour the mixture into the prepared crust and chill until firm, about 4 hours.

5. Once chilled, prepare the Stabilized Whipped Cream. Top the pie and chill for 30 minutes before serving.

Strawberry Chiffon Pie

This pie tastes like a fluffy strawberry cloud. A little drizzle of chocolate syrup would not hurt either.

INGREDIENTS | SERVES 8

1 tablespoon unflavored powdered gelatin

¼ cup cold water

1 cup crushed strawberries

1 cup sugar

½ cup hot water

¼ teaspoon salt

1 tablespoon lemon juice

2 egg whites

2 tablespoons sugar

1 (9-inch) Traditional Graham Cracker Crust, baked and cooled (See Chapter 2)

1 recipe Stabilized Whipped Cream (See Chapter 3)

Punching Up the Color

Fresh strawberry pies do not always retain their bright pink color. If color is a concern, add a drop or two of red food coloring to the egg whites to help give the color a little boost.

1. In a small bowl, combine the gelatin and the water. Allow to stand until completely bloomed, about 10 minutes.

2. Combine the crushed strawberries and sugar and allow to stand for 10 minutes. Mix the bloomed gelatin with the hot water until dissolved, then whisk it into the strawberries along with the salt and lemon juice. Let the mixture stand until it begins to thicken.

3. In a large, clean bowl, whip the egg whites until they are very frothy. Gradually add in the sugar, beating constantly, until the whites form medium peaks.

4. Working in thirds, fold the egg whites into the strawberry mixture, making sure no large streaks of egg white remain. Pour the mixture into the prepared crust and chill until firm, about 4 hours.

5. Once chilled, prepare the Stabilized Whipped Cream. Top the pie and chill for 30 minutes before serving.

Cranberry-Apple Pie

Apples and cranberries are in season in the fall, making this a great seasonal fruit pie for cooler weather.

INGREDIENTS | SERVES 8

2 cups sugar

¼ cup cornstarch

½ teaspoon cinnamon

½ teaspoon allspice

1 tablespoon orange zest

1 tablespoon orange juice

4 Gala apples, peeled, cored, and cut into 1-inch slices

2 cups fresh cranberries

1 (9-inch) Mealy Pie Crust, unbaked (See Chapter 2)

2 tablespoons butter

1 egg, beaten

1 (9-inch) Flaky Pie Crust (See Chapter 2)

Phytochemicals

Scientists are currently researching whether fruits and vegetables rich in phytochemicals may have medicinal properties. Cranberries, for example, contain the phytochemical quercetin, which is an antioxidant that may help reduce inflammation and defend against cancer.

1. Heat the oven to 425°F.

2. In a large bowl, combine the sugar, cornstarch, cinnamon, allspice, orange zest, orange juice, apples, and cranberries. Toss to coat, then let stand for 10 minutes.

3. Pour the mixture into the Mealy Pie Crust. Dot the top with the butter. Brush the edge of the Mealy Pie Crust with the beaten egg so that the top crust will adhere. Top with the Flaky Pie Crust and trim the dough to 1 inch of the pan's edge. Tuck the edge of the top crust under the edge of the bottom crust. Crimp the dough using your fingers or a fork. Brush the entire top crust with the beaten egg and cut 4 or 5 slits in the top to vent steam.

4. Place the pie on a baking sheet and bake in the lower third of the oven for 10 minutes, then reduce the heat to 350°F and bake for an additional 45 to 50 minutes, or until the filling is bubbling and the crust is golden brown all over. Cool to room temperature before serving.

Mixed-Berry Pie

This pie is the perfect place to use slightly overripened berries.
Their natural sweetness will only make the pie better.

INGREDIENTS | SERVES 8

1 cup fresh blueberries

1 cup fresh raspberries

1 cup fresh blackberries

1 cup fresh strawberries, hulled and chopped

1 cup sugar

¼ cup all-purpose flour

¼ teaspoon salt

1 teaspoon lemon zest

1 tablespoon lemon juice

1 (9-inch) pastry crust, unbaked

2 tablespoons butter

1 Flaky Pie Crust (See Chapter 2), cut into 10 (1-inch) strips

1 egg, beaten

Fruity Variations

If a specific kind of fresh berry is not available at the market, then substitute that amount with fresh chopped peaches or apricots. Peaches, apricots, and berries come into season around the same time, and their flavors complement each other well.

1. Heat the oven to 375°F.

2. In a large bowl, combine the blueberries, raspberries, blackberries, strawberries, sugar, flour, salt, lemon zest, and lemon juice. Toss well and allow to stand 10 minutes, then pour into the pie shell and dot the filling with butter.

3. Top with the pastry strips. Lay out 5 strips of pie dough on top of the filling about ½ inch apart. Starting ½ inch from the edge of the pie, fold back every other strip and lay down 1 strip of pastry. Fold the pastry back down and fold back the other pieces. Lay down a second strip about ½ inch from the first strip. Repeat this process until all the strips are used. Trim the dough to 1 inch of the pan's edge. Tuck the edge of the top crust under the edge of the bottom crust. Crimp the dough using your fingers or a fork. Brush the lattice with beaten egg.

4. Bake for 45 to 55 minutes, or until the filling is bubbly in the center and the lattice is golden brown. Cool completely before serving.

Strawberry Cream Cheese Pie

Rich cream cheese filling is topped with a fresh strawberry topping.

INGREDIENTS | SERVES 8

1 (9-inch) Almond Pastry Crust, unbaked (See Chapter 2)

8 ounces cream cheese, room temperature

1 egg

½ cup sugar

1 teaspoon vanilla

6 cups strawberries, hulled and crushed

¾ cup sugar

3 tablespoons cornstarch

1 cup heavy cream

2 tablespoons powdered sugar

¼ cup toasted flaked almonds

Making It Easy

Want to make fruit-topped pie even easier? Rather than make your own fruity topping, substitute a canned pie filling or marmalade, or combine 1 cup of fresh berries with ½ cup of strawberry glaze from the produce department.

1. Heat the oven to 375°F.

2. Line the pie crust with parchment paper or a double layer of aluminum foil and add pie weights or dry beans. Bake for 10 minutes, then remove the paper and weights and bake for an additional 10 minutes, or until the crust is lightly golden brown all over. Remove from the oven and set aside to cool. Leave the oven on.

3. In a medium bowl, beat the cream cheese until it is smooth. Add the egg, sugar, and vanilla and beat until light and fluffy. Spread into the pie crust and bake for 15 minutes, or until the filling is set at the edges but still slightly wobbly in the center. Set aside to cool.

4. In a medium saucepan, combine the crushed strawberries, sugar, and cornstarch. Cook over medium heat, stirring frequently, until thick. Pour over the cream cheese filling and chill for 4 hours or overnight.

5. Once the pie has chilled, whip together the cream and powdered sugar until it forms medium peaks. Spread over the cooled pie and garnish with the toasted almonds. Serve immediately.

Vanilla Pear Pie

This pie was inspired by vanilla poached pears and is lovely slightly warm.

INGREDIENTS | SERVES 8

1 cup sugar

⅓ cup cornstarch

¼ teaspoon cinnamon

Seeds of 1 vanilla bean pod, or 2 teaspoons vanilla bean paste

8 Bosc pears, peeled, cored, and sliced ¼-inch thick

2 tablespoons brandy

1 (9-inch) Mealy Pie Crust, unbaked (See Chapter 2)

1 egg, beaten

1 (9-inch) Flaky Pie Crust (See Chapter 2)

Picking Pears

When shopping for pears, keep a few things in mind. Pears are harvested before they are ripe, so do not be afraid to buy unripe fruit. They ripen at room temperature and are ready when the flesh at the stem end gives slightly under soft pressure. Avoid bruised or blemished skins, or pears that are ripe at the store.

1. Heat the oven to 425°F.

2. In a large bowl, mix the sugar, cornstarch, and cinnamon until well blended.

3. Add vanilla bean, pears, and brandy. Toss to coat and allow to stand 10 minutes.

4. Fill the Mealy Pie Crust with the pear mixture. Brush the edge of the Mealy Pie Crust with the beaten egg so that the top crust will adhere. Top with the Flaky Pie Crust and trim the dough to 1 inch of the pan's edge. Tuck the edge of the top crust under the edge of the bottom crust. Crimp the dough using your fingers or a fork. Brush the entire top crust with the beaten egg and cut 4 or 5 slits in the top to vent steam.

5. Place the pie on a baking sheet and bake for 20 minutes, then reduce the heat to 350°F for an additional 40 to 50 minutes, or until the pie is bubbling and the juices are thick. Cool for 2 hours before slicing.

CHAPTER 6

Cream Pies

Peanut Butter Cream Pie

If you love peanut butter, then this pie is for you! Peanut butter is featured in the crust and filling, and it is topped with cocoa whipped cream.

INGREDIENTS | SERVES 8

8 graham crackers

4 tablespoons butter, melted

2 tablespoons peanut butter

3 tablespoons sugar

2½ cups milk

⅔ cup sugar

¼ cup cornstarch

1 egg

½ cup peanut butter

2 teaspoons vanilla

2 tablespoons butter

1 teaspoon dry gelatin

2 tablespoons cold water

1 pint heavy whipping cream, cold

¼ cup powdered sugar

2 tablespoons Dutch-processed cocoa powder, plus extra for garnish

Like It Crunchy?

Looking for a little extra crunch? This recipe can be made with either creamy or smooth peanut butter. For extra crunch, top the pie with some crushed, toasted peanuts!

1. Heat the oven to 350°F and spray a 9-inch pie dish with nonstick spray.

2. In a food processor, add the graham crackers and pulse until they form rough crumbs. Pour in melted butter, 2 tablespoons peanut butter, and sugar. Process until crumbs are all coated. Press the crumbs evenly into the dish. Bake for 10 minutes, then cool completely.

3. In a medium saucepan, whisk together the milk, sugar, cornstarch, and egg. Place the pan over medium heat and whisk until the mixture starts to get warm. Add ½ cup peanut butter and whisk the mixture until it thickens and starts to simmer, about 8 minutes.

4. Remove the pan from the heat and add the vanilla and butter. Whisk until completely incorporated. Pour the mixture through a strainer, then into the prepared crust.

5. Place a layer of cling film directly on the custard and chill for at least 6 hours or overnight.

6. Once the pie is chilled, prepare the whipped cream. Combine the gelatin and the cold water. Allow to stand for 5 minutes, or until completely bloomed. Heat for 5 seconds in the microwave, making sure it is completely melted, then cool to room temperature. Pour the cold cream into a large bowl. Add the powdered sugar and cocoa powder. Whip in a stand mixer, or with a hand mixer, on medium-low speed until the sugar and cocoa are blended in, then increase the speed to medium-high. When the cream is softly whipped, pour in the cooled gelatin. Whip until the cream forms medium peaks. Spread on top of the chilled pie. Chill for 30 minutes before serving.

Apple Cream Pie

This unique pie is baked twice, once to set the filling and a second time to crisp the topping.

INGREDIENTS | SERVES 8

¾ cup sugar

2 tablespoons flour

1 cup sour cream

1 egg

½ teaspoon vanilla

¼ teaspoon salt

1 cup Golden Delicious apples, peeled, cored, and finely chopped

1 (9-inch) pastry crust, unbaked

⅓ cup sugar

1 teaspoon cinnamon

⅓ cup flour

¼ cup butter

1. Heat the oven to 450°F.

2. In a large bowl, whisk together the sugar, flour, sour cream, egg, vanilla, and salt. Fold in the apples.

3. Pour into the pastry crust and bake for 15 minutes, then lower the oven temperature to 325°F and bake for 30 minutes more, or until the filling is set.

4. In a medium bowl, combine the sugar, cinnamon, flour, and butter. Mix until the mixture is crumbly. Spread over the pie and return to the oven for 20 minutes, or until golden brown. Cool completely before serving.

Spiced Cream Pie

Warm spices make this cream pie a lovely treat for the fall.

INGREDIENTS | SERVES 8

2½ cups milk

½ cup sugar

¼ cup cornstarch

¼ teaspoon cinnamon

¼ teaspoon allspice

⅛ teaspoon salt

1 teaspoon vanilla bean paste

2 eggs

1 egg yolk

2 tablespoons unsalted butter

1 (9-inch) Gingersnap Crust, baked and cooled (See Chapter 2)

1 recipe Spiked Whipped Cream (See Chapter 3)

1. In a medium saucepan, combine the milk, sugar, cornstarch, cinnamon, allspice, salt, vanilla bean paste, eggs, and egg yolk. Whisk until smooth, then cook over medium heat, stirring constantly, until it begins to simmer and thicken, about 8 minutes.

2. Remove from the heat and add the butter. Stir until melted. Pour through a strainer into a separate bowl, then pour directly into the prepared crust.

3. Place a layer of cling film directly on the custard and chill for at least 6 hours or overnight.

4. Once the pie had chilled, top with Spiked Whipped Cream. Serve immediately.

Pomegranate Cream Cheese Pie

Pomegranate syrup, made by reducing pomegranate juice, gives the pie a burst of tangy flavor.

INGREDIENTS | SERVES 8

2 cups pomegranate juice

6 ounces cream cheese, softened

1 cup powdered sugar

1 cup heavy cream

½ teaspoon vanilla

1 (9-inch) Traditional Graham Cracker Crust, baked and cooled (See Chapter 2)

½ cup fresh pomegranate seeds, for garnish

Reduced Fruit Juices

Reducing fruit juice is an easy and tasty way to make a fruit glaze or marinade. If the juice is too tangy, add a little sugar, but remember that as the water evaporates and the natural sugars caramelize, the sauce will become sweeter. These reductions make good plate sauces or drizzles over ice cream.

1. In a medium saucepan over medium heat, add the pomegranate juice and bring to a simmer. Cook, stirring occasionally, until reduced to ¼ cup, about 20 minutes. Cool to room temperature.

2. In a large bowl, cream together the pomegranate syrup, cream cheese, and powdered sugar. Mix until smooth, then set aside.

3. In a separate bowl, whip the cream with the vanilla until it forms medium peaks. Fold the cream into the pomegranate mixture until no streaks of cream remain.

4. Pour the mixture into the prepared crust and garnish with the pomegranate seeds. Chill for 4 hours before serving.

Vanilla Rum Meringue Pie

A little spiced rum adds a lot of flavor to this pie.

INGREDIENTS | SERVES 8

1 (9-inch) pastry crust, unbaked

2 cups half-and-half

⅔ cup sugar

1 vanilla bean, split and the seeds scraped out

¼ cup cornstarch

2 eggs

¼ teaspoon salt

2 tablespoons butter

1 tablespoon spiced rum

1 recipe Foolproof Meringue (See Chapter 3)

1. Heat the oven to 375°F.

2. Line the pie crust with parchment paper or a double layer of aluminum foil and add pie weights or dry beans. Bake for 15 minutes, then remove the paper and weights and bake for an additional 10 to 12 minutes, or until the crust is golden brown all over. Remove from the oven and set aside to cool.

3. In a medium saucepan, combine the half-and-half, sugar, vanilla bean and seeds, cornstarch, eggs, and salt. Whisk until smooth, then cook over medium heat, stirring constantly, until it begins to simmer and thicken.

4. Remove from the heat and add the butter and rum. Stir until the butter is melted. Pour through a strainer into a separate bowl, then pour directly into the prepared crust.

5. Place a layer of cling film directly on the custard and chill for 2 hours.

6. Heat the oven to 450°F. Prepare the meringue and spread over the pie. Bake for 6 to 8 minutes, or until golden brown. Cool completely to room temperature before serving.

Café Mocha Cream Pie

The popular coffee shop staple has nothing on this luscious pie.

2½ cups milk

½ cup sugar

3 tablespoons Dutch-processed cocoa powder, plus more for garnish

1 tablespoon instant espresso powder

¼ cup cornstarch

2 egg yolks

¼ teaspoon salt

2 tablespoons butter

2 ounces semisweet chocolate, chopped

1 teaspoon vanilla

1 tablespoon coffee liqueur, optional

1 (9-inch) Traditional Graham Cracker Crust, baked and cooled (See Chapter 2)

1 recipe Stabilized Whipped Cream (See Chapter 3)

Instant Espresso

Instant espresso powder has become widely available in most grocery stores, but if it is unavailable, instant coffee can be substituted. For every tablespoon of instant espresso, use 1 tablespoon plus 2 teaspoons instant coffee.

1. In a medium saucepan, combine the milk, sugar, cocoa powder, espresso powder, cornstarch, egg yolks, and salt. Whisk until smooth, then cook over medium heat, stirring constantly, until it begins to simmer and thicken.

2. Remove from the heat and add the butter, chopped chocolate, vanilla, and coffee liquer if using. Stir until melted. Pour through a strainer into a separate bowl, then pour into the prepared crust.

3. Place a layer of cling film directly on the custard and chill for at least 6 hours or overnight.

4. Once the pie has chilled, prepare the whipped cream and spread it over the pie. Garnish with cocoa powder, then chill for 30 minutes before serving.

Cantaloupe Cream Pie

Most people do not think of melon for a pie, but if you love cantaloupe, you need to try this pie.

INGREDIENTS | SERVES 8

1 cup cantaloupe, peeled, seeded, and cubed

2 cups sugar

⅓ cup cornstarch

3 egg yolks

2 cups milk

1 teaspoon vanilla

2 tablespoons butter

1 (9-inch) Traditional Graham Cracker Crust, baked and cooled (See Chapter 2)

1 recipe Stabilized Whipped Cream (See Chapter 3)

1. Purée the cantaloupe in a blender until smooth, about 2 minutes.

2. In a medium saucepan, combine the purée, sugar, cornstarch, egg yolks, and milk. Cook over medium heat, whisking constantly, until it simmers and thickens. Remove from heat, add vanilla and butter. Stir until melted.

3. Pour the custard directly into the prepared crust. Cover the custard with a layer of cling film and chill overnight.

4. Once chilled, prepare the whipped cream and spread over the pie. Chill for 30 minutes before serving.

Cream Cheese Peanut Butter Pie

Serve this pie with strong coffee since it is very rich.

INGREDIENTS | SERVES 8

¾ cup creamy peanut butter

4 ounces cream cheese, softened

1¼ cups powdered sugar, divided

1 cup heavy cream

½ teaspoon vanilla

1 (9-inch) Chocolate Cookie Crust or Pretzel Crust, baked and cooled (See Chapter 2)

1 recipe Peanut Butter Fudge Sauce, for garnish (See Chapter 3)

1. In a large bowl, cream peanut butter, cream cheese, and 1 cup of the powdered sugar. Set aside.

2. In a separate bowl, whip the heavy cream with the remaining powdered sugar and vanilla until it forms medium peaks.

3. Beat half of the whipped cream into the peanut butter mixture until almost combined, then add the remaining whipped cream and beat until no streaks of cream remain.

4. Pour into the prepared crust and chill overnight. Serve with a drizzle of Peanut Butter Fudge Sauce.

Black-Bottom Pie

Three layers of chocolate and rich whipped cream make this a decadent experience.

INGREDIENTS | SERVES 8

2 cups milk

⅔ cup sugar

¼ cup cornstarch

2 egg yolks

¼ teaspoon salt

2 tablespoons butter

1 teaspoon vanilla

1 tablespoon rum

2 ounces semisweet chocolate, chopped

½ cup chopped pecans, toasted, optional

1 (9-inch) Chocolate Cookie Crust, baked and cooled (See Chapter 2)

1 recipe Stabilized Whipped Cream (See Chapter 3)

Melting Chocolate in the Microwave

Melting chocolate in the microwave is a great time-saver if done properly. Start with a microwave-safe bowl and add the chopped chocolate. Heat on high for 30 seconds, then stir well. Continue heating for 15 second intervals, stirring well in between, until melted. Every microwave is different, so watch the chocolate carefully.

1. In a medium saucepan, combine the milk, sugar, cornstarch, egg yolks, and salt. Whisk until smooth, then cook over medium heat, stirring constantly, until it begins to simmer and thicken, about 8 minutes.

2. Remove from the heat and add the butter, vanilla, and rum. Divide the mixture evenly between 2 bowls. Into one add the chocolate and stir until melted. Pour the chocolate mixture through a strainer into the prepared crust. Top with the pecans, if desired.

3. Pour the vanilla mixture through a strainer into a separate bowl, then carefully spread over the chocolate layer. Place a layer of cling film directly on the custard and cool until the custard is just warm, about 10 minutes.

4. Once the pie has chilled, prepare the Stabilized Whipped Cream. Spread over the top and chill for 30 minutes before serving.

White Chocolate Chiffon Pie

In this ultralight pie, white chocolate is transformed into a fluffy treat perfect for any occasion.

INGREDIENTS | SERVES 8

1 tablespoon unflavored powdered gelatin

¼ cup cold water

4 egg yolks

1 cup sugar, divided

2 ounces white chocolate, melted

4 egg whites

¼ teaspoon salt

1 teaspoon vanilla

1 (9-inch) Traditional Graham Cracker Crust, baked and cooled (See Chapter 2)

1 recipe Stabilized Whipped Cream (See Chapter 3)

Separating Eggs

The easiest way to separate eggs is to use your hands. Crack the egg into a cupped hand and let the egg white slip between your fingers into a bowl. This method prevents the yolk from breaking into the whites, which will keep them from whipping up if they are being used for meringues.

1. In a small bowl, combine the gelatin and the water. Allow to stand until completely bloomed, about 10 minutes.

2. In a double boiler, combine the egg yolks with ½ cup of the sugar. Whisk until thickened, about 10 minutes. Remove from the heat and add the bloomed gelatin and melted chocolate. Whisk until completely dissolved. Allow to cool until the mixture begins to thicken.

3. In a large, clean bowl, whip the egg whites with the salt until they are very frothy. Gradually add in the vanilla and the remaining sugar, beating constantly, until the whites form medium peaks.

4. Working in thirds, fold the egg whites into the white chocolate mixture, making sure no large streaks of egg white remain. Pour the mixture into the prepared crust and chill until firm, about 4 hours.

5. Once chilled, prepare the Stabilized Whipped Cream. Top the pie and chill for 30 minutes before serving.

Peanut Butter Cup Pie

Hidden inside this chocolate pie is a creamy peanut butter layer.

INGREDIENTS | SERVES 8

⅓ cup creamy peanut butter

2 ounces cream cheese, softened

⅓ cup powdered sugar, divided

3 tablespoons milk

½ teaspoon vanilla

1 (9-inch) Chocolate Cookie Crust or Pretzel Crust, baked and cooled (See Chapter 2)

1 cup milk

⅓ cup sugar

2 tablespoons Dutch-processed cocoa powder

4 teaspoons cornstarch

1 egg yolk

1 tablespoon butter

1 ounce chopped bittersweet chocolate

½ teaspoon vanilla

1 recipe Stabilized Whipped Cream (See Chapter 3)

1. In a large bowl, cream together the peanut butter, cream cheese, powdered sugar, milk, and vanilla until smooth and creamy. Carefully spread into the bottom of the prepared crust and set aside.

2. In a medium saucepan, combine the milk, sugar, cocoa powder, cornstarch, and egg yolk. Whisk until smooth, then cook over medium heat, stirring constantly, until it begins to simmer and thicken.

3. Remove from the heat and add the butter, chopped chocolate, and vanilla. Stir until melted. Pour through a strainer into a separate bowl, then carefully spread over the peanut butter mixture.

4. Place a layer of cling film directly on the custard and chill for 4 hours, or overnight.

5. Once the pie is chilled, prepare the Stabilized Whipped Cream and spread over the pie. Chill for 30 minutes before serving.

Chocolate Butterscotch Pie

The caramel notes from the butterscotch custard are enhanced by the earthy chocolate.

INGREDIENTS | SERVES 8

1 (9-inch) pastry crust, unbaked

2 cups milk

2 tablespoons Dutch-processed cocoa powder

⅔ cup packed light brown sugar

¼ cup cornstarch

2 egg yolks

¼ teaspoon salt

2 ounces bittersweet chocolate, chopped

2 tablespoons butter

1 teaspoon vanilla

1 recipe Spiked Whipped Cream (See Chapter 3)

1. Heat the oven to 375°F.

2. Line the pie crust with parchment paper or a double layer of aluminum foil and add pie weights or dry beans. Bake for 15 minutes, then remove the paper and weights and bake for an additional 10 to 12 minutes, or until the crust is golden brown all over. Remove from the oven and set aside to cool.

3. In a medium saucepan, combine the milk, cocoa powder, light brown sugar, cornstarch, egg yolks, and salt. Whisk until smooth, then cook over medium heat, stirring constantly, until it begins to simmer and thicken.

4. Remove from the heat and add the chopped chocolate, butter, and vanilla. Stir until melted. Pour through a strainer into a separate bowl, then pour directly into the prepared crust.

5. Cover the custard with a layer of cling film and chill for 4 hours or overnight.

6. When ready to serve, prepare the Spiked Whipped Cream and spread over the top of the pie. Serve immediately.

Peach Cream Pie

This pie combines silky vanilla custard with fresh peaches to make a delightfully refreshing pie.

Berry Good Toppings

Give your pie a special touch with a fresh fruit topping. Purée fresh berries with a little powdered sugar and lemon juice, strain, and you have a delicious sauce for dressing a plate or drizzling over whipped cream. Fresh fruit sauces will stay fresh for up to 3 days in the refrigerator.

1. Heat the oven to 375°F.

2. Line the pie crust with parchment paper and add pie weights or dry beans. Bake for 15 minutes, then remove the paper and weights and bake for an additional 10 to 12 minutes, or until the crust is golden brown all over. Remove from the oven and set aside to cool.

3. In a saucepan, whisk together the milk, sugar, cornstarch, and egg until well mixed. Cook this mixture over medium heat, whisking constantly, until it comes to a boil and thickens.

4. Remove from the heat and add the vanilla and butter. Pour the custard through a strainer, then pour the custard into the cooled pie crust.

5. Press a layer of plastic wrap directly onto the custard. Chill for at least 4 hours or overnight.

6. In a large bowl, mix the peaches with the sugar and cinnamon. Let stand for 10 minutes.

7. In a large skillet over medium heat, melt the butter. Pour the peaches into the melted butter and cook, stirring constantly, until the peaches are soft.

8. In a small bowl, combine the cornstarch and water.

9. Bring the peach mixture to a boil and add the cornstarch. Cook until thickened. Turn off the heat and allow to cool for 10 minutes.

10. Use a slotted spoon to drain off excess juices, top the custard layer with the peaches. Chill the pie covered in plastic for 1 hour. Prepare the whipped cream and spread it over the pie. Chill for 30 minutes before serving.

Chocolate-Covered Cherry Pie

This pie is perfect for Valentine's Day, or anytime you want to treat your sweetie.

INGREDIENTS | SERVES 8

2 cups whole milk

⅔ cup sugar

¼ cup cocoa powder

¼ cup cornstarch

1 egg

2 tablespoons butter

2 ounces semisweet chocolate, chopped

1 teaspoon vanilla

3 ounces unsweetened chocolate, chopped

½ cup sweetened condensed milk

1 (9-inch) Traditional Graham Cracker Crust, baked and cooled (See Chapter 2)

1¼ cups maraschino cherries, drained and patted dry

1 recipe Stabilized Whipped Cream (See Chapter 3)

Fixing a Lumpy Custard

If, after thickening, your custard has lumps, just pour the mixture into a blender or food processor and blend for a few seconds to work out the lumps. Pour the custard through a strainer to remove any remaining lumps the blender missed.

1. In a medium saucepan, combine the milk, sugar, cocoa powder, cornstarch, and egg. Whisk until smooth, then cook over medium heat, stirring constantly, until it begins to simmer and thicken.

2. Remove from the heat and add the butter, chopped chocolate, and vanilla. Stir until melted. Pour through a strainer into a separate bowl. Place a layer of cling film directly on the custard and cool slightly.

3. In a microwave-safe bowl, melt the chocolate with the condensed milk until smooth. Pour the mixture into the bottom of the prepared crust. Top with 1 cup of the drained cherries.

4. Carefully spread the custard over the cherries. Cover the filling with cling film and chill for 4 hours.

5. Once chilled, prepare the whipped cream and spread it over the pie. Garnish with the remaining cherries. Chill for 30 minutes before serving.

Chocolate Mousse Pie

Whipped cream makes this mousse pie extra creamy and decadent.

INGREDIENTS | SERVES 8

1 (9-inch) pastry crust, unbaked

1½ cups milk

½ cup sugar

2 tablespoons Dutch-processed cocoa powder

2 tablespoons cornstarch

2 egg yolks

¼ teaspoon salt

1 tablespoon butter

1 ounce bittersweet chocolate, chopped

1 teaspoon vanilla

½ teaspoon powdered gelatin

1 tablespoon cold water

1 cup heavy whipping cream

3 tablespoons powdered sugar

1 teaspoon vanilla

Shaved chocolate, for garnish

1. Heat the oven to 375°F.

2. Line the pie crust with parchment paper or a double layer of aluminum foil and add pie weights or dry beans. Bake for 15 minutes, then remove the paper and weights and bake for an additional 10 to 12 minutes, or until the crust is golden brown all over. Remove from the oven and set aside to cool.

3. In a medium saucepan, combine the milk, sugar, cocoa powder, cornstarch, egg yolks, and salt. Whisk until smooth, then cook over medium heat, stirring constantly, until it begins to simmer and thicken.

4. Remove from the heat and add the butter, chopped chocolate, and vanilla. Stir until melted. Pour through a strainer into a separate bowl. Place a layer of cling film directly on the custard and chill for 1 hour.

5. In a small bowl, mix the powdered gelatin with the cold water. Let stand 10 minutes, then melt in the microwave for 10 seconds. Allow to cool for 10 minutes or until cool to the touch.

6. In a medium bowl, add the cream, powdered sugar, and vanilla. Whip on medium-high speed until it starts to thicken. Slowly pour in the cooled gelatin and whip until the cream forms medium peaks. Cover and chill for 30 minutes.

7. Add half of the whipped cream to the chocolate mixture and gently fold to incorporate. Pour into the prepared crust and chill for 4 hours before serving. Garnish with the remaining whipped cream and shaved chocolate.

Butterscotch Coconut Pie

*Combining butterscotch pie and coconut cream pie produces
a pie filled with nutty, complex flavors and textures.*

INGREDIENTS | SERVES 8

1 cup packed light brown sugar

¼ teaspoon salt

½ cup sugar

1¾ cups milk

2 egg yolks

¼ cup cornstarch

3 tablespoons all-purpose flour

1 teaspoon vanilla

2 tablespoons unsalted butter

1 cup shredded sweetened coconut, toasted

1 (9-inch) Traditional Graham Cracker Crust, baked and cooled (See Chapter 2)

1 recipe Stabilized Whipped Cream (See Chapter 3)

1. In a large pot, whisk together the light brown sugar, salt, sugar, milk, egg yolks, cornstarch, and flour. Bring to a boil and cook until it thickens and simmers.

2. Remove from the heat and add the vanilla and butter. Stir until the butter is melted. Pour the mixture through a strainer into a bowl and fold in the coconut.

3. Pour into the prepared crust and press a layer of plastic wrap directly onto the custard. Chill for at least 4 hours or overnight.

4. Once chilled, top with the Stabilized Whipped Cream. Chill for 30 minutes before serving.

Toasting Coconut

Toasted coconut is versatile, and kept in a zip-top bag in the freezer, it keeps for up to 3 months. To make it, simply spread shredded, sweetened coconut on a baking sheet and bake at 350°F for 8 to 10 minutes, or until all the coconut is golden brown. Watch it carefully; it burns easily.

Chocolate and Toasted Coconut Meringue Pie

Milk chocolate, toasted coconut, and a fluffy meringue give this pie a lovely delicate flavor.

INGREDIENTS | SERVES 8

1 cup half-and-half

1 cup coconut milk

⅔ cup sugar

2 tablespoons cocoa powder

¼ cup cornstarch

2 egg yolks

¼ teaspoon salt

2 tablespoons butter

2 ounces milk chocolate, chopped

1 teaspoon vanilla

1 cup shredded sweetened coconut, toasted

1 (9-inch) Chocolate Cookie Crust, baked and cooled (See Chapter 2)

1 recipe Foolproof Meringue (See Chapter 3)

Don't Care for Meringue?

Just because a recipe calls for meringue does not mean you have to use it. Whipped cream can be used in place of meringue in almost any cream pie recipe without damaging the overall flavor. Other options include fruit glaze, chocolate sauce, chopped candy, and fresh fruit.

1. In a medium saucepan, combine the half-and-half, coconut milk, sugar, cocoa powder, cornstarch, egg yolks, and salt. Whisk until smooth, then cook over medium heat, stirring constantly, until it begins to simmer and thicken.

2. Remove from the heat and add the butter, chopped chocolate, and vanilla. Stir until melted. Pour through a strainer into a separate bowl, then fold in the coconut. Pour directly into the prepared crust.

3. Heat the oven to 375°F.

4. Prepare the Foolproof Meringue and spread onto the filling while it is still hot, making sure the meringue completely covers filling and the inside edge of the crust.

5. Bake for 10 to 12 minutes, or until the meringue is golden brown. Remove from the oven and chill, uncovered, until set.

CHAPTER 7

Custard Pies

Coconut Custard Pie

For extra flavor, try toasting the coconut before mixing it into the filling.

1⅓ cups milk

2 tablespoons all-purpose flour

1 cup sugar

6 tablespoons butter, softened

2 eggs

¼ teaspoon salt

1 teaspoon vanilla

¼ teaspoon coconut extract

1 cup sweetened shredded coconut

1 (9-inch) pastry crust, unbaked

Little Bakers

Cooking with your kids is a great way to build memories and develop confidence in the kitchen. Rubbing in butter, mixing cold fillings, and even peeling fruit are good jobs for young children. Older children can help whip egg whites, stir custards, and chop fruit. Encourage your children to get involved in baking. Nothing tastes better than a treat they made themselves!

1. Heat the oven to 425°F.

2. In a medium saucepan, bring the milk to a simmer over medium heat. Remove from the heat and cool slightly.

3. In a large bowl, whisk together the flour, sugar, and butter until completely combined. Add the eggs, salt, vanilla, and coconut extract and mix well. Slowly whisk in the warm milk until smooth. Fold in the coconut.

4. Pour the mixture into the prepared pastry crust and place on a baking sheet. Bake in the lower third of the oven for 10 minutes, then reduce the heat to 325°F and bake for an additional 30 to 40 minutes, or until the filling is set at the edges and just slightly wobbly in the center. Do not overbake or the custard will become watery. Cool completely before slicing.

Chocolate Fudge Pie

Serve this pie with some whipped cream if you find it too rich. Want to take it over the top? Drizzle some hot fudge over each slice.

INGREDIENTS | SERVES 8

2 ounces unsweetened chocolate, chopped

2 tablespoons butter

2 eggs

2 egg yolks

½ cup packed light brown sugar

¾ cup corn syrup

1 teaspoon vanilla

1 tablespoon cocoa powder

1 (9-inch) pastry crust, unbaked

1. Heat the oven to 375°F.

2. In a double boiler, melt the chocolate and butter until smooth. Remove from the heat.

3. In a large bowl, combine the eggs, egg yolks, light brown sugar, and corn syrup. Add in the melted chocolate, vanilla, and cocoa powder and whisk until well combined.

4. Pour the mixture into the pastry crust and place on a baking sheet. Bake for 35 to 45 minutes, or until the filling is just set. Serve slightly warm.

Peanut Butter Custard Pie

Any nut or seed butter would work well in this pie, but peanut butter has universal appeal.

INGREDIENTS | SERVES 8

4 eggs

1 stick butter, melted

⅓ cup peanut butter

¾ cup sugar

1 teaspoon vanilla

¼ cup heavy cream

1 tablespoon white vinegar

1 (9-inch) pastry crust, unbaked

1. Heat the oven to 350°F.

2. In a large bowl, whisk together the eggs, butter, peanut butter, and sugar until smooth. Add the vanilla, cream, and vinegar. Whisk until well combined.

3. Pour the mixture into the pastry crust and place on a baking sheet. Bake for 50 to 55 minutes, or until the filling is set and the top is golden brown. Allow to cool to room temperature before serving.

Caramel Custard Pie

The caramel flavor in this the pie comes from browning the butter as the sugar caramelizes.

INGREDIENTS | SERVES 8

1 stick butter
1 cup packed light brown sugar
3 eggs
1¾ cups evaporated milk
2 tablespoons all-purpose flour
1 teaspoon of vanilla
1 (9-inch) pastry crust, unbaked

Browning Butter

Brown butter has a nutty flavor and aroma and can be used in cookie crusts for extra flavor. Browning butter is simple. In a shiny bottom pot, add the butter and cook over medium heat until the butter is nut brown. Be sure to stir the butter often to prevent burning.

1. Heat the oven to 425°F.

2. In a medium saucepan over medium heat, combine the butter and light brown sugar. Bring the mixture to a boil and cook, stirring frequently, for 5 minutes, or until the butter smells nutty. Cool for 2 minutes.

3. In a large bowl, whisk together the eggs, milk, flour, and vanilla. Slowly whisk in the cooled brown sugar mixture. Pour into a blender and process until smooth.

4. Pour the mixture into the pastry crust and place on a baking sheet. Bake for 5 minutes, then reduce the heat to 325°F and bake for an additional 30 to 40 minutes, or until the filling is set and the top is golden brown. Allow to cool to room temperature before serving.

Pumpkin Cream Cheese Pie

This pie has a slightly tangy flavor and a creamy texture. It takes traditional pumpkin pie to the next level.

INGREDIENTS | SERVES 8

8 ounces cream cheese, room temperature

¾ cup packed light brown sugar

1 teaspoon cinnamon

½ teaspoon salt

½ teaspoon ground ginger

¼ teaspoon ground cloves

3 eggs

1 cup pumpkin purée

1 cup evaporated milk

1 teaspoon vanilla

1 (9-inch) Traditional Graham Cracker Crust, baked and cooled

1. Heat the oven to 375°F.

2. In a large bowl, cream together the cream cheese, light brown sugar, cinnamon, salt, ginger, and cloves.

3. Add the eggs, one at a time, and beat until thoroughly incorporated. Add the pumpkin, evaporated milk, and vanilla and mix until smooth.

4. Pour the mixture into the pastry crust and place on a baking sheet. Bake for 45 to 55 minutes, or until the pumpkin filling is set at the edges but still slightly wobbly in the center. Cool for 1 hour at room temperature, then chill overnight before serving.

Apple Butter Pumpkin Pie

Apple butter adds a tart, refreshing edge to the traditionally sweet pumpkin pie. Reduce some apple cider to use as a drizzle for special occasions.

INGREDIENTS | SERVES 8

¾ cup sugar

1 teaspoon cinnamon

½ teaspoon salt

¼ teaspoon ginger

¼ teaspoon ground cloves

2 eggs

1 egg yolk

1 cup pumpkin purée

¾ cup apple butter

1 cup evaporated milk

1 (9-inch) pastry crust, unbaked

1. Heat the oven to 425°F.

2. In a large bowl, whisk together the sugar, cinnamon, salt, ginger, and cloves until well combined.

3. Add the eggs, egg yolk, pumpkin, apple butter, and evaporated milk and whisk until smooth.

4. Pour the mixture into the prepared pastry crust and place on a baking sheet. Bake in the lower third of the oven for 15 minutes, then reduce the heat to 350°F and bake for an additional 40 to 45 minutes, or until the filling is set at the edges and just slightly wobbly in the center. Cool for 3 hours on a wire rack before slicing.

Cheesecake Pie

Chopped fresh fruit drizzled with melted chocolate makes a great accompaniment to this pie.

INGREDIENTS | SERVES 8

8 ounces cream cheese, room temperature
⅓ cup sour cream
⅓ cup heavy cream
½ cup sugar
1 egg
1 egg yolk
1 teaspoon vanilla
1 (9-inch) Traditional Graham Cracker Crust, baked and cooled (See Chapter 2)

1. Heat the oven to 350°F.

2. Cream together the cream cheese, sour cream, heavy cream, and sugar until well blended and smooth.

3. Add in the egg, egg yolk, and vanilla and mix well.

4. Pour the mixture into the pastry crust and place on a baking sheet. Bake for 40 to 45 minutes, or until the center is just set. Turn off the oven and crack the door. Leave the pie to cool for 30 minutes, then remove from the oven and cool to room temperature. Chill for 2 hours before serving.

French Coconut Pie

Rich and sweet, this pie is for coconut lovers. Garnish the finished pie with some toasted coconut for a special touch.

INGREDIENTS | SERVES 8

1½ cups sugar
3 eggs
1 stick butter, melted
1 tablespoon white vinegar
1 teaspoon vanilla
1 cup shredded, sweetened coconut
1 (9-inch) pastry crust, unbaked

1. Heat the oven to 400°F.

2. In a large bowl, whisk together the sugar, eggs, butter, vinegar, and vanilla. Stir in the coconut.

3. Pour the mixture into the pastry crust and place on a baking sheet. Bake for 10 minutes. Reduce the heat to 375°F and bake for 15 minutes, then reduce the heat to 350°F for 20 to 30 minutes, or until the pie is golden brown and the filling is set. Cool to room temperature before serving.

The Gift of Pie

Pie makes a delicious gift, and if you give it in a beautiful pie dish, wrapped in a pretty tea towel, you have a perfect hostess gift or bridal shower present.

Egg Custard Pie

Egg custard, with a hint of fresh nutmeg, is a classic dessert. Bake it in a pie crust and you have a pie that is a standout!

INGREDIENTS | SERVES 8

3 cups whole milk
4 eggs
¾ cup sugar
½ teaspoon salt
1 teaspoon vanilla
¼ teaspoon fresh grated nutmeg
1 (9-inch) pastry crust, unbaked

1. Heat the oven to 425°F.

2. In a medium saucepan, bring the milk to a simmer over medium heat. Remove from the heat and cool slightly.

3. In a large bowl, combine eggs, sugar, and salt. Whisk until smooth, then gradually whisk in milk and vanilla.

4. Pour the mixture into pastry crust and dust with nutmeg. Place pie on a baking sheet and bake in the lower third of the oven for 8 minutes, reduce heat to 325°F and bake for an additional 40 to 50 minutes, or until the filling is set at the edges and just slightly wobbly in the center. Cool to room temperature before slicing.

Maple Chess Pie

Real maple syrup is required to give this pie its delicious flavor.

INGREDIENTS | SERVES 8

4 eggs
1 stick butter, melted
¼ cup maple syrup
¾ cup sugar
1 tablespoon yellow cornmeal
1 teaspoon vanilla
¼ cup milk
1 tablespoon white vinegar
1 (9-inch) pastry crust, unbaked

1. Heat the oven to 350°F.

2. In a large bowl, whisk together the eggs, butter, maple syrup, and sugar until smooth.

3. Add the cornmeal, vanilla, milk, and vinegar. Whisk until well combined.

4. Pour the mixture into the pastry crust and place on a baking sheet. Bake for 50 to 55 minutes, or until the filling is set and the top is golden brown. Allow to cool to room temperature before serving.

Irish Coffee Pie

Top this pie with a little Irish cream–laced whipped cream for the adults or some cocoa whipped cream for the kids.

INGREDIENTS | SERVES 8

2¼ cups milk

2 eggs

2 egg yolks

¾ cup sugar

½ teaspoon salt

¼ cup Irish cream liqueur

1 teaspoon vanilla

¼ teaspoon instant espresso powder

1 (9-inch) pastry crust, unbaked

1. Heat the oven to 425°F.

2. In a medium saucepan over medium heat, bring the milk to a simmer. Remove from the heat to cool slightly.

3. In a large bowl, whisk together the milk, eggs, egg yolks, sugar, salt, Irish cream, vanilla, and espresso powder until well blended.

4. Pour the mixture into the prepared pastry crust and place on a baking sheet. Bake in the lower third of the oven for 10 minutes, then reduce the heat to 325°F and bake for an additional 35 to 45 minutes. Cool completely before slicing.

Peach Custard Pie

The custard in this pie is sour cream based. The tang of the sour cream complements the sweet peaches.

INGREDIENTS | SERVES 8

1 cup sour cream

4 egg yolks

1 cup sugar

2 tablespoons cornstarch

⅛ teaspoon cardamom

1 teaspoon vanilla

4 peaches, peeled, pitted, and cut into ½-inch slices

1 (9-inch) pastry crust, unbaked

1 recipe Butter Crumble (See Chapter 3)

1. Heat the oven to 425°F.

2. In a large bowl, whisk together sour cream, egg yolks, sugar, cornstarch, cardamom, and vanilla. Set aside.

3. Arrange the peach slices on the bottom of the pastry crust. Carefully pour the custard over the top. Bake for 25 to 30 minutes, or until the custard just begins to set.

4. Spread the Butter Crumble over the top of the pie and return to the oven for 20 to 25 minutes, or until the crumble is golden brown and the filling is set. Cool to room temperature before serving.

Buttermilk Pie

Buttermilk sounds a little scary, but it is not overpowering. It gives this pie a sweet and lightly tangy flavor.

INGREDIENTS | SERVES 8

1½ cups sugar
½ cup butter, melted
⅓ cup flour
4 eggs
1⅓ cups buttermilk
1 teaspoon vanilla
⅛ teaspoon salt
1 (9-inch) pastry crust, unbaked

1. Heat the oven to 375°F.

2. In a large bowl, whisk together the sugar, butter, flour, eggs, buttermilk, vanilla, and salt until smooth.

3. Pour the mixture into the prepared pastry crust and place on a baking sheet. Bake in the lower third of the oven for 15 minutes, then reduce the heat to 325°F and bake for an additional 30 to 40 minutes, or until the pie is a rich golden brown on the top. Cool completely before slicing.

Mocha Pie

A sweet, gooey custard meets the coffee shop in this chocolatey pie. Serve it slightly warm for a special treat.

INGREDIENTS | SERVES 8

2 tablespoons all-purpose flour
½ cup sugar
2 eggs
1 cup corn syrup
2 ounces semisweet chocolate, melted
2 tablespoons cocoa powder
1 teaspoon instant espresso powder
¼ teaspoon salt
2 tablespoons butter, melted
1 teaspoon vanilla
½ cup semisweet chocolate chips
1 (9-inch) pastry crust

1. Heat the oven to 350°F.

2. In a large bowl, whisk together the flour and sugar. Add the eggs, corn syrup, melted chocolate, cocoa powder, espresso powder, salt, butter, and vanilla. Whisk until smooth.

3. Spread the chocolate chips onto the crust in an even layer. Pour the filling over the chocolate chips and tap the pie gently on the counter to release any air bubbles.

4. Bake for 50 to 60 minutes, or until the filling is puffed all over and set. Cool to room temperature before serving.

Butternut Squash Pie

Butternut squash has a mild, naturally sweet flavor and is an excellent substitute for pumpkin.

1 medium butternut squash
1 cup packed light brown sugar
1 teaspoon cinnamon
½ teaspoon salt
¼ teaspoon fresh grated nutmeg
2 eggs
12 ounces evaporated milk
½ teaspoon vanilla
1 (9-inch) pastry crust, unbaked

Timesaving Trick

Butternut squash purée is available in most grocery stores in the frozen section. Be sure to fully thaw the purée before use. If you cannot find butternut squash purée, you can replace it with pumpkin purée or mashed sweet potatoes.

1. Heat the oven to 425°F.

2. Cut the top and bottom off the butternut squash, then cut the squash in half length-wise and scrape out the seeds. Place the squash cut side down on a parchment-lined baking sheet and roast for 45 to 55 minutes, or until a paring knife slips easily through the flesh. Cool to room temperature, scoop out the flesh, and purée in a blender until smooth. It should yield approximately 1½ cups. Supplement with pumpkin purée, if needed.

3. In a large bowl, whisk together the light brown sugar, cinnamon, salt, and nutmeg until well combined.

4. Add the squash purée, eggs, evaporated milk, and vanilla. Whisk until smooth.

5. Pour the mixture into the prepared pastry crust and place on a baking sheet. Bake in the lower third of the oven for 15 minutes, then reduce the heat to 350°F and bake for an additional 40 to 45 minutes, or until the filling is set at the edges and just slightly wobbly in the center. Cool for 3 hours on a wire rack before slicing.

Zucchini Pie

No one will ever guess the secret vegetable in this pie . . . unless you tell them!

INGREDIENTS | SERVES 8

4 medium zucchini, peeled, seeded, and sliced 1-inch thick

2 eggs

1½ cups sugar

¼ cup all-purpose flour

½ teaspoon salt

¼ cup butter

2 cups evaporated milk

1 teaspoon vanilla

½ teaspoon cinnamon

¼ teaspoon fresh grated nutmeg

1 (9-inch) pastry crust, unbaked

1. Boil the zucchini until it is fork-tender. Drain well and allow to cool.

2. Heat the oven to 375°F.

3. Place the zucchini in a blender or food processor and blend until smooth.

4. Pour the mixture into a large bowl and add the eggs, sugar, flour, salt, and butter and whisk until smooth.

5. Add the milk, vanilla, cinnamon, and nutmeg and whisk until well combined.

6. Carefully pour the mixture into the pastry crust. Place the pie on a baking sheet and bake in the lower third of the oven for 20 minutes. Reduce the heat to 350°F and cook for an additional 35 to 45 minutes, or until the pie is set and a thin knife inserted into the center of the pie comes out mostly clean. Cool completely before serving.

Martha Washington Pie

*Inspired by the chocolate-coated coconut Martha Washington candy,
this dense coconut pie has a chocolate ganache topping.*

INGREDIENTS | SERVES 8

¾ cup milk

4 tablespoons butter, softened

2 tablespoons all-purpose flour

¾ cup sugar

1 egg

1 egg yolk

¼ teaspoon salt

1 teaspoon vanilla

1½ cups sweetened shredded coconut

1 (9-inch) pastry crust, unbaked

¼ cup heavy cream

1 tablespoon butter

4 ounces semisweet chocolate, chopped

1. Heat the oven to 425°F.

2. In a medium saucepan, bring the milk to a simmer over medium heat. Remove from the heat and cool slightly.

3. In a large bowl, whisk together the butter, flour, and sugar until well combined.

4. Add the egg and egg yolk and beat well. Slowly pour in the milk, whisking constantly, then add the salt and vanilla. Fold in the coconut.

5. Pour the mixture into the prepared pastry crust and place on a baking sheet. Bake in the lower third of the oven for 10 minutes. Reduce the heat to 325°F and bake for an additional 25 to 35 minutes, or until the filling is set at the edges and just slightly wobbly in the center. Cool for 1 hour before making the topping.

6. In a small saucepan, bring the cream to a bare simmer. Remove from the heat and add the butter and chocolate. Let stand 1 minute, then whisk until smooth. Cool the mixture for 10 minutes, then carefully spread over the pie. Chill until the topping is set, about 30 minutes.

CHAPTER 8

Nut Pies

Caramel Pecan Pie

Nutty pecans combine with caramel for a pie that has a similar flavor to pralines!

INGREDIENTS | SERVES 8

1 (9-inch) pastry crust, unbaked

1 cup sugar, divided

2 cups whole milk

½ cup flour

½ teaspoon salt

2 egg yolks, beaten

1 tablespoon butter

1 teaspoon vanilla

1 cup chopped pecans, toasted

2 egg whites

¼ teaspoon cream of tartar

¼ cup sugar

Cooling Pies

The idea of warm pie fresh from the oven is enticing, but in most cases cutting into a pie before it has a chance to cool is not a good idea. The filling needs time to set, and it can only do that if it has a chance to cool all the way down. If you want a warm slice of pie, try reheating it in the oven for 5 minutes or in the microwave for 10 to 20 seconds.

1. Heat the oven to 375°F.

2. Line the pie crust with parchment paper or a double layer of aluminum foil and add pie weights or dry beans. Bake for 15 minutes, then remove the paper and weights and bake for an additional 10 to 12 minutes, or until the crust is golden brown all over. Remove from the oven and set aside to cool. Leave the oven on.

3. In a medium saucepan, add ¼ cup sugar over medium-low heat. Cook, swirling occasionally but not stirring, until the sugar melts and becomes light amber in color. Gradually whisk in the milk and cook until the caramel is dissolved. Remove from the heat.

4. In a large bowl, combine the remaining sugar, flour, and salt. Gradually whisk in the milk mixture. Once smooth, return to the saucepan and cook, stirring constantly, over medium heat until bubbling and thick, about 8 minutes.

5. Whisk the egg yolks in a small bowl. Combine ½ cup of the hot milk mixture into the eggs, then immediately whisk the tempered egg yolks into the saucepan. Cook for 2 minutes, whisking constantly.

6. Remove from the heat and add the butter, vanilla, and pecans. Pour into the prepared pastry shell.

7. In a large, clean bowl, whip the egg whites and cream of tartar until they are very frothy. Gradually add in the sugar, beating constantly, until the whites form stiff peaks. Spread over the pie and bake for 8 to 10 minutes, until golden. Cool completely to room temperature before serving.

Chocolate Hazelnut Pie

This pie is like chocolate hazelnut fudge baked in a pastry crust.

INGREDIENTS | SERVES 8

2 ounces unsweetened chocolate, chopped
2 tablespoons butter
2 eggs
2 egg yolks
½ cup sugar
½ cup corn syrup
¼ cup chocolate hazelnut spread
1 teaspoon vanilla
1 tablespoon cocoa powder
¾ cup toasted hazelnuts, chopped
1 (9-inch) pastry crust, unbaked

1. Heat the oven to 375°F.

2. In a double boiler, melt the chocolate and butter. Remove from the heat.

3. In a large bowl, combine the eggs, egg yolks, sugar, corn syrup, and chocolate hazelnut spread. Add in the melted chocolate, vanilla, and cocoa powder.

4. Spread the hazelnuts onto the bottom of the pastry crust, then pour the mixture over the top. Place on a baking sheet and cook for 40 to 50 minutes, or until the filling is just set. Serve slightly warm.

Macadamia Nut Pie

Macadamia nuts are native to Australia and were planted in Hawaii in the 1920s.

INGREDIENTS | SERVES 8

1 stick unsalted butter, melted
¾ cup sugar
¾ cup dark corn syrup
2 tablespoons dark rum
1 teaspoon vanilla
3 eggs
1¼ cup chopped macadamia nuts, lightly toasted
1 (9-inch) pastry crust, unbaked

1. Heat the oven to 350°F.

2. In a large bowl, whisk together the butter, sugar, corn syrup, rum, vanilla, and eggs until well combined.

3. Spread the chopped macadamia nuts evenly on the bottom of the pastry crust then pour the egg mixture over the top. Tap the pie gently on the counter to release any air bubbles.

4. Place the pie on a baking sheet and bake for 50 to 60 minutes, or until the filling is puffed all over and set. Cool to room temperature before serving.

Chocolate Macadamia Nut Pie

This no-bake pie is creamy, fluffy, and a hit with macadamia nut lovers.

8 ounces cream cheese, room temperature

1 egg yolk

⅓ cup sugar

1 teaspoon vanilla

3 ounces semisweet chocolate, melted

1 egg white

2 tablespoons sugar

⅓ cup heavy cream

4 ounces chopped macadamia nuts

1 (9-inch) Chocolate Cookie Crust, baked and cooled (See Chapter 2)

How to Fold

Folding is the process of carefully incorporating two mixtures together without deflating them. There are two tricks to make this easier. First, always bring your spatula straight down and then sweep it up over the top of the mixture. Second, rotate the bowl ¼ turn after each sweep. The less strokes you use, the less likely you will be to lose any volume.

1. Cream together cream cheese, egg yolk, sugar, and vanilla until smooth. Whisk in the melted chocolate and set aside.

2. In a clean bowl, whisk the egg white until it is very frothy. Slowly add in the sugar and beat until it forms medium peaks.

3. In a separate bowl, whip the cream until it holds firm peaks.

4. Gently fold the egg whites into the cream cheese mixture. Once no streaks of egg white remain, fold in the cream along with the chopped nuts. Spoon into the prepared crust and chill overnight.

Almond Pie

This pie is similar in texture to a pecan pie, but uses toasted almonds combined with almond liqueur for a nutty treat.

INGREDIENTS | SERVES 8

1 stick unsalted butter, melted

¾ cup packed light brown sugar

¾ cup light corn syrup

2 tablespoons almond liqueur

¼ teaspoon almond extract

1 teaspoon vanilla

3 eggs

1 cup sliced almonds, lightly toasted

1 (9-inch) pastry crust, unbaked

Almonds

Almond trees are native to the Middle East. While most people consider almonds to be nuts, they are in fact drupes, or fruit-covered seeds. Recent research indicates that almonds may help lower cholesterol and be beneficial for people who suffer from heart disease.

1. Heat the oven to 350°F.

2. In a large bowl, whisk together the butter, light brown sugar, corn syrup, almond liqueur, almond extract, vanilla, and eggs until well combined.

3. Spread the sliced almonds evenly on the bottom of the pastry crust, then pour the egg mixture over the top. Tap the pie gently on the counter to release any air bubbles.

4. Place the pie on a baking sheet and bake for 50 to 60 minutes, or until the filling is puffed all over and set. Cool to room temperature before serving.

Salted Peanut Pie

The salty and sweet flavor of this pie makes it almost addictive. If you prefer, you can use unsalted peanuts if you do not like the combination.

INGREDIENTS | SERVES 8

¾ stick unsalted butter, melted

¼ cup creamy peanut butter

¾ cup packed light brown sugar

½ cup light corn syrup

1 teaspoon vanilla

3 eggs

1 cup salted peanuts

1 (9-inch) pastry crust, unbaked

1. Heat the oven to 350°F.

2. In a large bowl, whisk together the butter, peanut butter, light brown sugar, corn syrup, vanilla, and eggs until well combined.

3. Spread the peanuts evenly on the bottom of the pastry crust, then pour the egg mixture over the top. Tap the pie gently on the counter to release any air bubbles.

4. Place the pie on a baking sheet and bake for 50 to 60 minutes, or until the filling is puffed all over and set. Cool to room temperature before serving.

Maple Walnut Pie

The warm flavors of this pie make it a nice treat on a cold winter's day.

INGREDIENTS | SERVES 8

1¼ cups pure maple syrup

2 tablespoons unsalted butter, melted

¾ cup heavy cream

¼ cup sugar

½ teaspoon cinnamon

1 tablespoon all-purpose flour

3 eggs

¼ teaspoon salt

1¼ cup chopped walnuts

1 (9-inch) pastry crust, unbaked

1. Heat the oven to 350°F.

2. In a large bowl, whisk together the maple syrup, butter, cream, and sugar until well combined. Add the cinnamon, flour, eggs, and salt. Whisk until smooth.

3. Spread the walnuts onto the bottom of the pastry crust. Carefully pour the filling over the top. Place on a baking sheet and bake for 45 to 55 minutes, or until the filling is puffed all over and set. Cool to room temperature before slicing.

Banana Macadamia Nut Pie

This pie can also be made with walnuts and a dash of cinnamon.
Toasted coconut makes a delicious garnish.

INGREDIENTS | SERVES 8

1 envelope unflavored powdered gelatin

2 tablespoons cold water

¾ cups half-and-half

¾ cup packed light brown sugar

4 egg yolks

¼ teaspoon salt

1 teaspoon vanilla

3 ripe bananas, peeled and mashed

4 egg whites

¼ teaspoon cream of tartar

¼ cup sugar

½ cup heavy cream

1 cup chopped, toasted macadamia nuts, divided

1 (9-inch) Traditional Graham Cracker Crust, baked and cooled

1 recipe Stabilized Whipped Cream (See Chapter 3)

Toasting Nuts

When making a pie where the filling is not baked or when nuts are used as a garnish, it is a good idea to toast them before use. Toasting releases the nuts' natural oils, gives the nuts a robust flavor, and helps them become crisp. Nuts that are baked in pies do not require toasting, but they can be. The nuts are insulated in the filling and should not burn.

1. In a small bowl, combine the gelatin with the cold water. Allow to stand for 10 minutes.

2. In a double boiler, combine the half-and-half, light brown sugar, and egg yolks. Cook, whisking constantly, until the mixture thickens, about 8 to 10 minutes. Remove from the heat and stir in the salt and vanilla. Fold in the mashed bananas. Set aside.

3. Melt the gelatin in the microwave for 10 seconds. Set aside to cool.

4. In a very clean bowl, combine the egg whites with the cream of tartar. Whip until the whites are very frothy then slowly add in the sugar. Whip until medium peaks are formed.

5. Stir the melted gelatin into the banana mixture, then fold the egg whites into the mixture in 3 additions until only a few streaks of white remain. Set aside.

6. In a medium bowl, whip the cream to firm peaks. Fold the cream, along with ¾ cup of the macadamia nuts, into the banana mixture, then carefully spread the mixture into the prepared crust. Chill for 4 hours or overnight.

7. Once chilled, top with Stabilized Whipped Cream and garnish with the remaining macadamia nuts. Chill for 30 minutes before serving.

Praline Pecan Pie

Looking for a different kind of pecan pie? Give this creamy version a try!

INGREDIENTS | SERVES 8

8 ounces cream cheese, room temperature

1 egg

⅓ cup sugar

1 teaspoon vanilla

1 (9-inch) pastry crust, unbaked

1 cup chopped pecans

2 eggs, beaten

¼ cup sugar

⅔ cup light corn syrup

1 teaspoon vanilla

1. Heat the oven to 350°F.

2. In a medium bowl, cream together the cream cheese, egg, sugar, and vanilla until creamy and smooth. Pour into the prepared shell. Top with the chopped pecans.

3. In a separate bowl, whisk together the eggs, sugar, corn syrup, and vanilla. Carefully pour this mixture over the cream cheese mixture.

4. Bake for 45 to 55 minutes, or until the filling is set. Cool to room temperature before serving.

Chocolate Chip Pecan Pie

Feel free to add a little extra chocolate or pecans to this pie. Chopped white chocolate would also be lovely here.

INGREDIENTS | SERVES 8

2 tablespoons salted butter, melted and cooled

½ cup sugar

⅔ cup corn syrup

2 tablespoons coffee liqueur

1 teaspoon vanilla

2 tablespoons flour

¼ teaspoon cinnamon

2 eggs

1 cup whole pecans

½ cup mini chocolate chips

1 (9-inch) pastry crust, unbaked

1. Heat the oven to 350°F.

2. In a medium bowl, combine the butter, sugar, corn syrup, coffee liqueur, vanilla, flour, and cinnamon. Whisk until smooth. Add the eggs and mix well.

3. On the bottom of the pastry crust, evenly layer the pecans and chocolate chips. Pour the filling over the pecans and chocolate.

4. Place the filled pie on a baking sheet and bake for 50 to 60 minutes, or until the filling is golden and puffed all over. Allow to cool for 2 hours before serving.

Coconut Walnut Pie

If you prefer, you can use semisweet chocolate chips rather than white chocolate chips in this pie.

1. Heat the oven to 425°F.

2. In a large bowl, whisk together the flour, sugar, milk, and eggs until completely combined.

3. Add the corn syrup, salt, butter, and vanilla and blend well.

4. Fold in the coconut, walnuts, and white chocolate chips.

5. Pour the mixture into the prepared pastry crust and place on a baking sheet. Bake in the lower third of the oven for 10 minutes, then reduce the heat to 350°F and bake for an additional 35 to 45 minutes, or until the filling is set at the edges and just slightly wobbly in the center. Cool completely before slicing.

Walnuts

According to the California Walnut Commission, walnuts are the oldest tree food. Walnuts originated in Persia and were brought to England by traders and soldiers. Walnuts were brought to California in 1867, and today California walnut growers produce as much as two-thirds of the walnuts sold worldwide.

Bourbon Pecan Pie

Bourbon-laced fluffy cream cheese filling and crunchy pecans fill a nutty pecan crust.

INGREDIENTS | SERVES 8

8 ounces cream cheese, softened

1 cup powdered sugar, divided

1 cup heavy cream

1 teaspoon vanilla

1½ cups chopped pecans, toasted, plus more for garnish

1 (9-inch) Graham Pecan Crust, baked and cooled (See Chapter 2)

1 recipe Salted Caramel Sauce (See Chapter 3)

1. In a large bowl, cream together the cream cheese and ½ cup of the powdered sugar. Set aside.

2. In a separate bowl, whip the heavy cream with the remaining powdered sugar and vanilla until it forms medium peaks.

3. Beat the whipped cream into the cream cheese mixture until almost combined, then add chopped pecans and fold until evenly mixed.

4. Pour into the prepared crust and chill overnight. Serve with a drizzle of Salted Caramel Sauce.

Mocha Walnut Pie

This pie provides a lot of flavor per slice. If you want to reduce the chocolate flavor, omit 1 ounce of the melted chocolate.

INGREDIENTS | SERVES 8

2 tablespoons all-purpose flour

½ cup packed light brown sugar

2 eggs

1 cup corn syrup

2 ounces semisweet chocolate, melted

2 tablespoons cocoa powder

1 teaspoon instant espresso powder

¼ teaspoon salt

2 tablespoons butter, melted

1 teaspoon vanilla

1 cup chopped walnuts, toasted

1 (9-inch) pastry crust, unbaked

1. Heat the oven to 350°F.

2. Whisk together the flour and light brown sugar. Add the eggs, corn syrup, melted chocolate, cocoa powder, espresso powder, salt, butter, and vanilla and mix well.

3. Spread the walnuts onto the crust in an even layer. Pour the filling over the walnuts and tap the pie gently on the counter to release any air bubbles.

4. Place the pie on a baking sheet and bake for 50 to 60 minutes, or until the filling is puffed all over and set. Cool to room temperature before serving.

CHAPTER 9

Citrus Pies

Lemon Cheese Pie

A lemony cream cheese filling is topped with a tart lemon topping. This is for lemon lovers!

INGREDIENTS | SERVES 8

8 ounces cream cheese, room temperature

1 (14-ounce) can condensed milk

½ cup fresh lemon juice, divided

1 teaspoon lemon zest

1 teaspoon vanilla

¼ teaspoon salt

1 (9-inch) Traditional Graham Cracker Crust, baked and cooled (See Chapter 2)

⅓ cup sugar

3 teaspoons cornstarch

½ cup water

1 egg yolk

1 tablespoon butter

1. In a medium bowl, cream together the cream cheese and condensed milk until smooth.

2. Add ¼ cup lemon juice, lemon zest, vanilla, and salt and blend until well combined. Spread into the prepared crust.

3. In a medium saucepan, combine ¼ cup lemon juice, sugar, cornstarch, water, and egg yolk. Cook over medium heat, stirring constantly, until the mixture simmers and thickens.

4. Remove from the heat and add the butter. Stir until melted.

5. Pour the warm lemon mixture over the cream cheese. Chill the pie for 4 hours or overnight before serving.

Frozen Concentrates

It is easy to turn a citrus pie into a lemonade pie by substituting the fresh juice with thawed lemonade concentrate. Since the concentrates contain extra sugar, you may want to reduce the sugar in the recipe by 2 tablespoons. Pink lemonade and limeade work well, too.

Orange Marmalade Pie

The little bits of sugary orange rind in the marmalade add an extra burst of flavor with each bite.

INGREDIENTS | SERVES 8

1 (9-inch) pastry crust
4 tablespoons butter, softened
½ cup sugar
2 eggs
2 tablespoons orange liqueur
½ cup orange marmalade

1. Heat the oven to 375°F.

2. Line the pie crust with parchment paper or a double layer of aluminum foil and add pie weights or dry beans. Bake for 8 minutes, then remove the paper and weights and bake for an additional 10 minutes, or until the crust is golden brown all over. Remove from the oven and set aside to cool.

3. Reduce the oven temperature to 350°F.

4. In a large bowl, cream together the butter and sugar until light and fluffy.

5. Add in the eggs, one at a time, and beat well. Add the orange liqueur and marmalade and mix until well combined.

6. Pour the mixture into the prepared crust and bake for 25 to 30 minutes, or until the top of the pie is golden brown. Cool to room temperature before serving.

Chocolate Lime Pie

Tart lime and rich chocolate make for a delicious dessert.

INGREDIENTS | SERVES 8

8 ounces cream cheese, room temperature

1 (14-ounce) can condensed milk

1 cup semisweet chocolate chips, melted

¼ cup fresh lime juice

1 teaspoon lime zest

1 teaspoon vanilla

¼ teaspoon salt

1 (9-inch) Traditional Graham Cracker Crust, baked and cooled (See Chapter 2)

1 recipe Stabilized Whipped Cream (See Chapter 3)

1. In a medium bowl, cream together the cream cheese, condensed milk, and melted chocolate until smooth.

2. Add the lime juice, lime zest, vanilla, and salt and blend until well combined. Spread into the prepared crust.

3. Top the pie with the prepared whipped cream and chill for 3 hours before serving.

Lime Cream Pie

This pie is similar to Key Lime Pie, but is made with regular lime juice and a little extra sugar.

INGREDIENTS | SERVES 8

4 egg yolks

1 cup sweetened condensed milk

½ cup fresh lime juice

1 teaspoon lime zest

1 tablespoon sugar

1 (9-inch) Traditional Graham Cracker Crust, baked and cooled (See Chapter 2)

1. Heat the oven to 350°F.

2. Whisk the egg yolks in a large bowl until lighter in color.

3. Whisk in the condensed milk, lime juice, lime zest, and sugar. Mix until well combined, then allow to stand for 5 minutes.

4. Pour the filling into the prepared crust and bake for 15 to 20 minutes, or until the pie is set. Chill overnight before serving.

Margarita Pie

This pie is wonderful after a spicy Mexican meal.

INGREDIENTS | SERVES 8

¼ cup lime juice

¼ cup orange juice

2 tablespoons tequila, optional

2 teaspoons lime zest

1 (14-ounce) can sweetened condensed milk

8 ounces cream cheese, softened

1 recipe Stabilized Whipped Cream (See Chapter 3), divided

1 (9-inch) Pretzel Crust, baked and cooled (See Chapter 2)

1. In a large bowl, whisk together the lime juice, orange juice, tequila, and lime zest.

2. Add in the sweetened condensed milk and cream cheese and whisk until smooth. Let stand for 10 minutes.

3. Fold 1 cup of the Stabilized Whipped Cream into the lime mixture, then spoon the mixture into the prepared crust. Top with the remaining whipped cream and chill for 4 hours before serving.

Dreamsicle Pie

This pie tastes just like the beloved ice cream treat.

INGREDIENTS | SERVES 8

1 (3-ounce) box orange-flavored gelatin

⅔ cup boiling water

½ cup cold water

1 cup ice cubes

1 cup heavy cream

3 tablespoons powdered sugar

½ teaspoon vanilla

1 (9-inch) Traditional Graham Cracker Crust, baked and cooled (See Chapter 2)

Whipped cream, for garnish

1. In a large bowl, dissolve the gelatin in the hot water.

2. In a measuring cup, combine the cold water with the ice cubes until there is 1¼ cups of ice and water. Pour the ice water into the hot gelatin and stir until the gelatin starts to thicken. Remove any unmelted ice.

3. In a medium bowl, whip the cream with the powdered sugar and vanilla until it forms medium peaks. Fold the cream into the gelatin, then chill for 15 to 20 minutes, or until the mixture is very thick.

4. Spoon the mixture into the prepared pie crust. Chill for 3 hours or until set. Garnish with whipped cream.

Orange Mousse Pie

If you like, you can add a few dark chocolate curls to the top of the pie.

INGREDIENTS | SERVES 8

1 (9-inch) pastry crust, unbaked
1¼ cups milk
¼ cup orange juice
1 tablespoon orange zest
½ cup sugar
3 tablespoons cornstarch
2 egg yolks
¼ teaspoon salt
1 tablespoon butter
1 teaspoon vanilla
½ teaspoon unflavored powdered gelatin
1 tablespoon cold water
1 cup heavy cream
3 tablespoons powdered sugar
1 teaspoon vanilla

1. Heat the oven to 375°F.

2. Line the pie crust with parchment paper or a double layer of aluminum foil and add pie weights or dry beans. Bake for 15 minutes, then remove the paper and weights and bake for an additional 10 to 12 minutes, or until the crust is golden brown all over. Remove from the oven and set aside to cool.

3. In a medium saucepan, combine the milk, orange juice, orange zest, sugar, cornstarch, egg yolks, and salt. Whisk until smooth, then cook over medium heat, stirring constantly, until it begins to simmer and thicken.

4. Remove from the heat and add the butter and vanilla. Stir until melted. Pour through a strainer into a separate bowl. Place a layer of cling film directly on the custard and chill for 1 hour.

5. In a small bowl, mix the powdered gelatin with the cold water. Let stand 10 minutes, then melt in the microwave for 10 seconds. Allow to cool for 5 minutes or until cool to the touch.

6. In a medium bowl, add the cream, powdered sugar, and vanilla. Whip on medium-high speed until it starts to thicken. Slowly pour in the cooled gelatin and whip until the cream forms medium peaks. Cover and chill for 30 minutes.

7. Add half of the whipped cream to the orange mixture and gently fold to incorporate. Pour into the prepared crust and garnish the top with the remaining whipped cream. Chill for 4 hours before serving.

Triple Citrus Meringue Pie

This pie is a fun twist on a traditional lemon meringue pie.

INGREDIENTS | SERVES 8

1 (9-inch) pastry crust, unbaked

4 egg yolks

⅓ cup cornstarch

1½ cups water

1¼ cups sugar

¼ teaspoon salt

3 tablespoons butter

1 tablespoon lemon juice

1 tablespoon lime juice

2 tablespoons orange juice

1 recipe Foolproof Meringue (See Chapter 3)

Cutting Clean Slices

Want to cut attractive, sharp-looking pie slices? Use a thin-bladed knife dipped in hot water and wiped dry for each cut. The warm knife trick is also good for cutting very cold pies, such as ice cream or frozen fluff pies. The heat from the knife will make each slice look picture perfect!

1. Heat the oven to 375°F.

2. Line the pie crust with parchment paper or a double layer of aluminum foil and add pie weights or dry beans. Bake for 12 minutes, then remove the paper and weights and bake for an additional 10 minutes, or until the crust is golden brown all over. Remove from the oven and set aside to cool. Leave the oven on.

3. In a medium saucepan, whisk together the egg yolks, cornstarch, water, sugar, and salt. Cook the mixture over medium heat, whisking constantly, until it comes to a boil. Boil for 1 minute, then remove from the heat and whisk in the butter and citrus juices. Pour through a strainer into a separate bowl, then pour directly into the prepared crust.

4. Spread the meringue onto the filling while it is still hot, making sure the meringue completely covers the filling and the inside edge of the crust. Bake for 10 to 12 minutes, or until the meringue is golden brown. Remove from the oven and cool to room temperature, uncovered, before slicing.

Orange Raspberry Pie

Fresh raspberries are a must for this pie. Frozen raspberries are too watery.

1. Heat the oven to 375°F.

2. Line the pie crust with parchment paper or a double layer of aluminum foil and add pie weights or dry beans. Bake for 15 minutes, then remove the paper and weights and bake for an additional 10 to 12 minutes, or until the crust is golden brown all over. Remove from the oven and set aside to cool.

3. In a medium saucepan, combine the sugar, lemon juice, and orange juice and stir until the sugar is melted.

4. Whisk in the egg yolks and cornstarch. Cook over medium heat, whisking constantly, until bubbling and thick. Reduce the heat to low and stir in the butter until melted. Remove from the heat to cool slightly.

5. Spread the raspberries onto the bottom of the prepared crust. Pour the curd through a strainer into the prepared crust. Cover the pie with plastic and chill for 4 hours.

6. Spread the chilled pie with the Spiked Whipped Cream. Serve immediately.

Lemon Chiffon Pie

This light and refreshing pie is the perfect end to a barbecue or picnic.

INGREDIENTS | SERVES 8

1 tablespoon unflavored powdered gelatin

¼ cup cold water

4 egg yolks

⅓ cup sugar

1 tablespoon lemon zest

½ cup lemon juice

4 egg whites

¼ teaspoon salt

¼ cup sugar

1 (9-inch) pastry crust, baked and cooled

1 recipe Stabilized Whipped Cream (See Chapter 3)

Does Your Pastry Crust Shrink?

If you notice that after baking your pastry crust shrinks significantly or the sides of the crust collapse, you may be overworking the dough. Use a light touch when mixing and rolling out pastry dough. Also, a good long chill in the refrigerator once the crust is in the pan will prevent shrinking.

1. In a small bowl, combine the gelatin and the water. Allow to stand until completely bloomed, about 10 minutes.

2. In a double boiler, combine the egg yolks, sugar, lemon zest, and lemon juice. Cook the mixture, whisking constantly, until thickened and lighter in color, about 10 minutes. Remove from the heat and add the bloomed gelatin. Whisk until dissolved. Allow to cool until it starts to thicken.

3. In a large, clean bowl, whip the egg whites with the salt until they are very frothy. Gradually add in the sugar, beating constantly, until the whites form medium peaks.

4. Working in thirds, fold the egg whites into the lemon mixture, making sure no large streaks of egg white remain. Pour the mixture into the prepared crust and chill until firm, about 4 hours.

5. Once chilled, prepare the Stabilized Whipped Cream. Top the pie and chill for 30 minutes before serving.

Lemon Chess Pie

Lemon adds a refreshing zip to the traditional chess pie.

INGREDIENTS | SERVES 8

4 eggs
¼ cup butter, melted
2 cups sugar
1 tablespoon yellow cornmeal
1 tablespoon all-purpose flour
1 teaspoon vanilla
¼ cup milk
¼ cup fresh lemon juice
1 (9-inch) pastry crust, unbaked

1. Heat the oven to 350°F.

2. In a large bowl, whisk together the eggs, butter, and sugar until smooth.

3. Add the cornmeal, flour, vanilla, milk, and lemon juice. Whisk until well combined.

4. Pour the mixture into the pastry crust and place on a baking sheet. Bake for 50 to 55 minutes, or until the filling is set and the top is golden brown. Allow to cool to room temperature before serving.

Frozen Lemon Pie

This pie is perfect on a hot afternoon served with a little whipped cream.

INGREDIENTS | SERVES 8

4 eggs, separated
¾ cup sugar, divided
½ cup fresh lemon juice
1 tablespoon lemon zest
1 cup whipping cream
1 (9-inch) Traditional Graham Cracker Crust, baked and cooled (See Chapter 2)

1. In a large bowl, combine the egg yolks with ½ cup of the sugar until lighter in color. Whisk in the lemon juice and lemon zest.

2. In another large bowl, whip the egg whites until very frothy. Gradually add in the remaining sugar and whip until the egg whites hold firm peaks.

3. In a medium bowl, whip the cream until it becomes fluffy and holds soft peaks. Fold in the egg whites, then fold in the egg yolk mixture until no streaks of white remain.

4. Pour the mixture into the prepared crust and freeze overnight. Remove from the freezer and thaw slightly before serving.

Blood Orange Curd Pie

Blood oranges are in season during winter. If they are not available, clementines also work well.

INGREDIENTS | SERVES 8

1 cup sugar

1 tablespoon lime juice

1 cup blood orange juice

8 egg yolks

2 tablespoons cornstarch

8 tablespoons unsalted butter

1 (9-inch) Traditional Graham Cracker Crust, baked and cooled (See Chapter 2)

1 recipe Foolproof Meringue (See Chapter 3)

Juicing Fresh Citrus

When juicing citrus fruit for pies, there are a few things you can do to make it easier. Roll the citrus to release the juices. Putting the fruit in the microwave for 8 to 10 seconds also helps release the juices. Use a citrus reamer to help loosen all the juice over a small strainer to catch any pulp and seeds.

1. Heat the oven to 375°F.

2. In a medium saucepan, combine the sugar, lime juice, and blood orange juice and stir until the sugar is melted.

3. Whisk in the egg yolks and cornstarch. Cook over medium heat, whisking constantly, until bubbling and thick.

4. Reduce the heat to low and stir in the butter until melted. Pour the curd through a strainer into the prepared crust.

5. Spread the Foolproof Meringue onto the filling while it is still hot, making sure the meringue completely covers the filling and the inside edge of the crust. Bake for 10 to 12 minutes, or until the meringue is golden brown. Remove from the oven and chill for 3 hours, uncovered, before slicing.

Daiquiri Pie

If you prefer to omit the rum, substitute ½ teaspoon of rum extract.

INGREDIENTS | SERVES 8

8 ounces cream cheese, room temperature

1 (14-ounce) can condensed milk

1 tablespoon fresh lemon juice

¼ cup fresh lime juice

3 tablespoons silver rum

¼ teaspoon salt

¼ teaspoon unflavored powdered gelatin

1 teaspoon cold water

½ cup heavy whipping cream, cold

1 tablespoon powdered sugar

½ teaspoon vanilla

1 (9-inch) Pretzel Crust, baked and cooled (See Chapter 2)

Raw Egg White Warning

Raw or undercooked egg whites should not be consumed by children, pregnant women, the elderly, or those with compromised immune systems. Pasteurized egg whites are readily available in grocery stores and can be used in recipes for chiffon pies and meringues where raw egg whites are used, making them safe for everyone.

1. In a medium bowl, cream together the cream cheese and condensed milk until smooth. Add the lemon juice, lime juice, rum, and salt and blend until well combined.

2. In a small bowl, mix the powdered gelatin with the cold water. Let stand 10 minutes, then melt in the microwave for 10 seconds. Allow to cool for 5 minutes, or until cool to the touch.

3. In a medium bowl, add the cream, powdered sugar, and vanilla. Whip on medium-high speed until it starts to thicken. Slowly pour in the cooled gelatin and whip until the cream forms medium peaks.

4. Fold the whipped cream into the cream cheese mixture until no streaks of white remain. Pour into the prepared crust and chill for 4 hours, or overnight, before serving.

CHAPTER 10

Tarts

Apple Tarte Tatin

This tart is traditionally cooked in a cast-iron skillet and served while still warm.

INGREDIENTS | SERVES 8

1 recipe Blitz Puff Pastry (See Chapter 2)
1 cup sugar
¼ cup water
3 tablespoons unsalted butter
8 medium Granny Smith apples, peeled, cored, and sliced in half

Cake Pan Variation

If you do not have an ovenproof skillet, this tart can also be made in a traditional cake pan. Simply prepare the caramel on the stove and pour into a buttered 9-inch cake pan and cool to room temperature. Place the apples, cheek side down, into the caramel, top with the pastry, and bake for about 50 minutes. Cool for 5 minutes before turning out.

1. Heat the oven to 400°F.

2. Roll out the pastry until it is ⅛ inch thick and 12 inches wide. Cover with plastic and chill until ready to use.

3. In a 10-inch ovenproof skillet, add the sugar and water. Cook over medium heat, swirling occasionally but not stirring, until the sugar becomes golden amber colored, about 6 to 7 minutes. Add the butter and swirl until melted.

4. Carefully place the apples, cheek side down, into the pan as tightly as you can. Cook for 10 to 15 minutes, or until the apples have started to soften and the juices are thick. Remove the pan from the heat.

5. Place the pastry on top of the apples and carefully tuck the edges around the apples with a butter knife.

6. Bake for 25 to 35 minutes, or until the crust is golden brown and firm to the touch. Remove from the oven and cool on a rack about 5 minutes before carefully turning out onto a serving plate.

Chocolate Walnut Tart

Bittersweet chocolate and smoky bourbon make this tart taste very earthy and sophisticated.

INGREDIENTS | SERVES 10

1 (10-inch) Short Crust for Tarts, unbaked

6 tablespoons unsalted butter, melted

¾ cup packed light brown sugar

3 tablespoons cornstarch

2 eggs

2 tablespoons light corn syrup

¼ cup bourbon

1 teaspoon vanilla

1 cup chopped walnuts

5 ounces bittersweet chocolate, chopped

1 tablespoon cocoa powder

1. Heat the oven to 350°F.

2. Line the tart with parchment paper or a double layer of aluminum foil and add pie weights or dry beans. Bake for 12 minutes, then remove the paper and weights and bake for an additional 10 to 15 minutes, or until the crust is golden brown all over. Remove from the oven and set aside to cool. Leave the oven on.

3. In a medium bowl mix the butter, light brown sugar, cornstarch, and eggs until smooth.

4. Add the corn syrup, bourbon, and vanilla and mix well.

5. Fold in the walnuts and chocolate.

6. Pour the mixture into the prepared crust. Bake for 25 to 35 minutes, or until the filling is set. Cool to room temperature before serving.

Blackberry Cheese Tart

Sweet blackberries and a lemony cheese filling make this a surprisingly refreshing dessert.

INGREDIENTS | SERVES 8

1 (10-inch) Short Crust for Tarts, unbaked (See Chapter 2)

8 ounces cream cheese, room temperature

2 tablespoons sour cream

¼ cup sugar

1 teaspoon lemon zest

1 teaspoon vanilla

2 tablespoons flour

2 cups fresh blackberries

⅓ cup sugar

¼ teaspoon vanilla

1 teaspoon fresh lemon juice

2 tablespoons cornstarch

2 tablespoons water

Taking the Time

It may be tempting to try to warm up cold butter or cream cheese in the microwave to save time. Taking the time to slowly soften ingredients will ensure they are uniformly softened. The microwave can lead to hot pockets within the ingredient or ingredients becoming too warm and ruining your creation. Take the time to do it right, about 1 hour, because it is worth it!

1. Heat the oven to 350°F.

2. Line the tart with parchment paper or a double layer of aluminum foil and add pie weights or dry beans. Bake for 12 minutes, then remove the paper and weights and bake for an additional 10 to 15 minutes, or until the crust is golden brown all over. Remove from the oven and set aside to cool. Leave the oven on.

3. In the bowl of a food processor or stand mixer, add the cream cheese, sour cream, sugar, lemon zest, vanilla, and flour. Process until very smooth. Refrigerate until ready to use.

4. In a medium saucepan, combine the blackberries, sugar, vanilla, and lemon juice. Cook over medium heat until the berries have softened, about 10 minutes.

5. Combine the cornstarch with the water and stir into the berry mixture. Cook until thickened, about 3 minutes, then remove from the heat.

6. Spread the cheese mixture into the prepared crust. Place the tart pan on a baking sheet and bake for 30 to 35 minutes, or until the cheese mixture is lightly golden and puffed all over. Cool to room temperature, then spread the blackberry mixture on top. Chill for 1 hour before serving.

Bourbon Peach Tart

Maybe it's a southern thing, but nothing tastes better with peaches than a little bourbon. If bourbon is unavailable or you prefer not to use it, replace it with peach nectar.

INGREDIENTS | SERVES 8

6 peaches, peeled, pitted, and cut into ½-inch-thick slices

¼ cup sugar

2 tablespoons cornstarch

1 tablespoon bourbon

⅛ teaspoon nutmeg

1 (10-inch) Short Crust for Tarts, unbaked (See Chapter 2)

1 recipe Sour Cream Sauce (See Chapter 3)

1. Heat the oven to 350°F.

2. In a large bowl, combine the peaches with the sugar, cornstarch, bourbon, and nutmeg. Let stand for 10 minutes.

3. Pour the peaches into the prepared crust and place the tart pan on a baking sheet. Bake for 45 to 55 minutes, or until the fruit is bubbling and the crust is golden brown. Cool to room temperature. Serve with Sour Cream Sauce.

Peeling Peaches

There are two ways to peel peaches. The first involves blanching the peaches for about 1 minute in boiling water, then shocking them in ice water. This causes the skin to release and it is easily peeled away. Another way is to use a vegetable peeler to gently peel the peaches. They cannot be too ripe or the peeler will damage the fruit. Try them both and see which works best for you.

Chocolate Silk Tart

This smooth chocolate tart makes a perfect end to a dinner party. Give it extra chocolate punch by making it in a chocolate cookie crust.

INGREDIENTS | SERVES 8

1 (10-inch) Short Crust for Tarts, unbaked (See Chapter 2)

½ cup semisweet chocolate chips

4 tablespoons butter

½ cup sugar

1 tablespoon cocoa powder

1 egg

1 egg yolk

3 ounces evaporated milk

1 teaspoon vanilla

1. Heat the oven to 350°F.

2. Line the tart with parchment paper or a double layer of aluminum foil and add pie weights or dry beans. Bake for 10 minutes, then remove the paper and weights and bake for an additional 10 to 12 minutes, or until the crust is lightly golden brown all over. Remove from the oven and set aside to cool. Leave the oven on.

3. In a double boiler, combine the chocolate chips and butter. Cook, stirring occasionally, until melted and smooth. Remove from the heat and cool slightly.

4. In a large bowl, whisk together the sugar, cocoa powder, egg, egg yolk, evaporated milk, and vanilla until smooth. Pour in the chocolate mixture and mix well.

5. Pour the filling into the prepared crust and place the pan on a baking sheet. Bake for 30 to 40 minutes, or until the filling is just set, but still a little wobbly in the center. Cool to room temperature before serving.

Cherry Clafoutis

This French dessert is not a traditional tart in the sense that it does not have a separate crust. As it bakes, the bottom forms its own crust and it is absolutely delightful for breakfast or dessert!

INGREDIENTS | SERVES 8

Nonstick cooking spray
¾ cup milk
½ cup cream
⅔ cup sugar, divided
3 eggs
1 teaspoon vanilla
1 tablespoon brandy
⅛ teaspoon salt
½ cup flour
3 cups pitted cherries
Powdered sugar, for garnish

Pitting Cherries

There are various ways to pit cherries. The easiest way is to buy a cherry pitter, but unless you consume a lot of fresh cherries, they are not practical. An easier, less expensive way is to use a paring knife to slice the cherry open. You should be able to pop out the pit with your finger or the knife once it is open. Be sure to do this on a plastic cutting board. Cherry juice can stain wood and laminate counters.

1. Heat the oven to 350°F and spray a 10-inch ceramic tart pan with nonstick cooking spray.

2. In a large bowl, whisk together the milk, cream, ⅓ cup of the sugar, eggs, vanilla, brandy, salt, and flour until smooth.

3. In a medium bowl, combine the remaining sugar with the cherries.

4. Spread the cherry mixture into the bottom of the pan. Carefully pour the batter over the top. Bake for 40 to 50 minutes, or until golden brown and puffed. Serve warm with a dusting of powdered sugar.

Walnut Tart

Try this tart with white chocolate chips, or a mixture of white and semisweet, for a delicious change of pace.

INGREDIENTS | SERVES 8

1 cup packed light brown sugar
3 tablespoons unsalted butter, softened
2 eggs
2 tablespoons all-purpose flour
½ teaspoon cinnamon
1½ cups chopped walnuts
1 (10-inch) Short Crust for Tarts, unbaked (See Chapter 2)
2 tablespoons heavy cream
¼ cup semisweet chocolate chips

1. Heat the oven to 350°F.

2. In a large bowl, cream together the light brown sugar and butter until light in color. Beat in the eggs, one at a time, until well blended. Add in the flour and cinnamon and mix until smooth, then fold in the walnuts.

3. Spread the mixture into the pastry crust and place the pan on a baking sheet. Bake for 40 to 45 minutes, or until the tart is golden brown. Cool to room temperature.

4. In a small pan, heat the cream until it simmers. Remove from the heat and add the chocolate. Let stand for 1 minute, then whisk until smooth. Drizzle over the cooled tart.

Lemon Curd Tart

This bright, refreshing tart is perfect for a baby shower or bridal shower.

INGREDIENTS | SERVES 8

1 (10-inch) Short Crust for Tarts, unbaked (See Chapter 2)

¾ cup sugar

¾ cup lemon juice

1 teaspoon lemon zest

6 egg yolks

1 tablespoon cornstarch

6 tablespoons unsalted butter

½ recipe Stabilized Whipped Cream (See Chapter 3)

Cooling Lemon Curd

Lemon curd can be made in advance and stored in an airtight jar for up to a week. If you are planning to make it ahead, be sure to cool the mixture properly to prevent the growth of harmful bacteria. Once the curd is cooked, immediately place it in a metal bowl resting in an ice bath. Cool the mixture, stirring constantly, until chilled. Transfer to the fridge until ready to use.

1. Heat the oven to 350°F.

2. Line the tart with parchment paper or a double layer of aluminum foil and add pie weights or dry beans. Bake for 10 minutes, then remove the paper and weights and bake for an additional 10 to 12 minutes, or until the crust is golden brown all over. Remove from the oven and set aside to cool.

3. In a medium saucepan, combine the sugar and lemon juice and stir until the sugar is melted. Whisk in the lemon zest, egg yolks, and cornstarch. Cook over medium heat, whisking constantly, until bubbling thick. Reduce the heat to low and stir in the butter until melted. Pour the curd through a strainer into the prepared crust. Chill for 4 hours.

4. Once the tart has chilled, prepare the Stabilized Whipped Cream. Pipe the whipped cream around the edge of the tart. Chill for 30 minutes before serving.

Blueberry Sour Cream Tart

Blueberries have enough natural flavors to stand up to tangy sour cream.
If using frozen berries, be sure to thaw and drain them well.

INGREDIENTS | SERVES 8

1 (10-inch) Short Crust for Tarts, unbaked (See Chapter 2)

2½ cups blueberries

1 cup water, divided

¾ cup sugar

2 tablespoons cornstarch

1 cup sour cream

⅓ cup sugar

2 eggs

1 teaspoon vanilla

1. Heat the oven to 350°F.

2. Line the tart with parchment paper or a double layer of aluminum foil and add pie weights or dry beans. Bake for 10 minutes, then remove the paper and weights and bake for an additional 10 to 12 minutes, or until the crust is golden brown all over. Remove from the oven and set aside to cool. Reduce the heat to 325°F.

3. In a medium saucepan, combine the blueberries, ½ cup water, and sugar. Cook over medium heat until the berries burst, about 10 minutes.

4. Combine the remaining water with the cornstarch, then stir into the blueberries. Cook until thickened, about 3 minutes.

5. In a large bowl, whisk together the sour cream, sugar, eggs, and vanilla. Spread into the prepared crust and put the tart pan on a baking sheet. Bake for 20 to 25 minutes, or until the custard is set. Cool to room temperature, then top with the blueberry mixture. Chill for 1 hour before serving.

Macadamia Nut Caramel Tart

Adding a few flakes of sea salt to the caramel layer before adding the macadamia nuts adds a flavorful twist.

INGREDIENTS | SERVES 8

1 (10-inch) Short Crust for Tarts, unbaked (See Chapter 2)

⅔ cup heavy cream

⅔ cup sugar

3 tablespoons unsalted butter

1½ cups chopped macadamia nuts, toasted

1 recipe Stabilized Whipped Cream (See Chapter 3)

Why Not Stir the Caramel?

Stirring sugar as it cooks into a caramel can cause the mixture to become grainy. For some recipes, like pralines, that is fine, but if you desire a smooth, silky caramel, it is best to put the spatula away and just swirl. That will mix the sugar, preventing burning, but will not form any crystals.

1. Heat the oven to 350°F.

2. Line the tart with parchment paper or a double layer of aluminum foil and add pie weights or dry beans. Bake for 12 minutes, then remove the paper and weights and bake for an additional 12 to 15 minutes, or until the crust is golden brown all over. Remove from the oven and set aside to cool.

3. In a medium saucepan, bring the cream to a simmer over low heat.

4. In another medium saucepan over high heat, add the sugar. Cook, swirling but not stirring, until the sugar melts and turns golden brown, about 8 minutes. Remove from the heat and slowly whisk in the hot cream. Stir in the butter and cool for 3 minutes.

5. Spread the caramel into the prepared tart crust. Top with the macadamia nuts and cool to room temperature. Prepare the Stabilized Whipped Cream and spread over the top. Chill for 30 minutes before serving.

Cherry Almond Tart

You could also make this tart with an almond pastry crust for extra flavor.
A scoop of good vanilla ice cream does not hurt either.

INGREDIENTS | SERVES 8

1 (10-inch) Short Crust for Tarts, unbaked (See Chapter 2)

1 egg

1 egg yolk

½ cup sugar

6 tablespoons unsalted butter, softened

1 cup ground almonds

1 teaspoon vanilla

3 cups pitted cherries

½ cup powdered sugar

1–2 tablespoons amaretto or lemon juice

1. Heat the oven to 350°F.

2. Line the tart with parchment paper or a double layer of aluminum foil and add pie weights or dry beans. Bake for 10 minutes, then remove the paper and weights and bake for an additional 10 to 12 minutes, or until the crust is golden brown all over. Remove from the oven and set aside to cool. Leave the oven on.

3. Beat the egg, egg yolk, and sugar until light and fluffy. Add the butter, almonds, and vanilla and beat until well blended.

4. Spread the mixture into the prepared tart crust and arrange the cherries on top.

5. Bake for 35 to 45 minutes, or until golden brown. Cool to room temperature.

6. In a small bowl, combine the powdered sugar with enough amaretto or lemon juice to make a thick glaze. Drizzle the top of the tart with glaze. Let stand 1 hour before serving.

Pear Walnut Tarte Tatin

Walnuts add a buttery nuttiness to this caramelized tart. Pecans, hazelnuts, or almonds would also be lovely here.

INGREDIENTS | SERVES 8

1 recipe Blitz Puff Pastry (See Chapter 2)

½ cup sugar

½ cup packed light brown sugar

¼ cup water

3 tablespoons unsalted butter

8 medium Bosc pears, peeled, cored, and sliced in quarters

¼ teaspoon cinnamon

⅔ cup chopped walnuts

Making Tarte Tatin Ahead

Tarte tatin can be made a few hours in advance and reheated just before serving. Once out of the oven, carefully invert the tart into a plate. Line the skillet with foil, then buttered parchment paper, and put the tart back into the pan apple side down. When you are ready to serve, simply put it into a hot oven for about 10 minutes. Turn it out on a plate and serve.

1. Heat the oven to 400°F.

2. Roll out the pastry until it is ⅛ inch thick and 12 inches wide. Cover with plastic and chill until ready to use.

3. In a 10-inch ovenproof skillet, add the sugar, light brown sugar, and water. Cook over medium heat, swirling occasionally but not stirring, until the sugar becomes golden amber colored, about 6 to 7 minutes. Add the butter and swirl until melted.

4. Carefully place the pears, cheek side down, into the pan as tightly as you can. Cook for 10 to 15 minutes, or until the pears have started to soften and the juices are thick. Remove the pan from the heat and sprinkle the cinnamon and walnuts evenly over the top.

5. Place the pastry on top of the pears and carefully tuck the edges around the fruit with a butter knife.

6. Bake for 25 to 35 minutes, or until the crust is golden brown and firm to the touch. Remove from the oven and cool on a rack for about 5 minutes before carefully turning out onto a serving plate.

Peach Crumb Tart

Buttery crumble and juicy spiced peaches make this tart irresistible!

INGREDIENTS | SERVES 8

4 peaches, peeled, pitted, and cut into ½-inch slices

¾ cup packed light brown sugar

¼ tablespoon cornstarch

2 tablespoons heavy cream

¼ teaspoon salt

½ teaspoon cinnamon

¼ teaspoon mace

½ teaspoon vanilla

2 tablespoons butter, melted and cooled

1 (10-inch) Short Crust for Tarts, unbaked (See Chapter 2)

1 recipe Butter Crumble (See Chapter 3)

1. Heat the oven to 375°F.

2. In a large bowl, combine the peaches, light brown sugar, cornstarch, cream, salt, cinnamon, mace, vanilla, and butter. Gently toss until the fruit is evenly coated.

3. Arrange the peaches into the prepared crust and spread the Butter Crumble mixture evenly over the top. Place the tart on a baking sheet and bake, in the lower third of the oven, for 40 to 50 minutes, or until the crumble is golden brown and the tart is bubbling. Cool to room temperature before serving.

Raspberry Linzer Tart

Warm spices and raspberry jam make this tart especially lovely at the holidays.

INGREDIENTS | SERVES 8

6 tablespoons unsalted butter

⅓ cup sugar

1½ teaspoons cinnamon

¼ teaspoon cloves

¼ teaspoon fresh grated nutmeg

3 egg yolks

¾ cup almond meal

1½ cups all-purpose flour

2–3 tablespoons ice water

10 ounces raspberry jam

Linzer Tart

Linzer tarts are originally from Linz, Austria. In Europe these tarts are filled with red currant jam and are a favorite holiday treat. In America raspberry jam is used since currant is less popular. According to some historians, the Linzer Tart is one of the oldest-known confections, with some recipes dating back as far as 1653!

1. Heat the oven to 350°F.

2. In a large bowl, cream the butter and sugar until well combined. Add cinnamon, cloves, and nutmeg and mix well. Add egg yolks, one at a time, and blend thoroughly.

3. In a medium bowl, combine the almond meal and flour. Mix the flour mixture into the butter mixture until the dough forms a smooth ball. Wrap in plastic and chill for 30 minutes.

4. Remove the dough from the refrigerator and divide in half. Roll out each half on a lightly floured surface to a ⅛-inch-thick, 12-inch circle, turning the dough often to make sure it does not stick. Dust the surface with additional flour if needed.

5. Roll one of the dough circles around the rolling pin and unroll it into a 10-inch tart pan. Carefully press the dough into the pan. Press your fingers against the rim of the pan to trim the dough. Cut the second circle into ½-inch strips.

6. Spread the jam on the bottom of the tart pan. Lay out 5 strips of spiced dough on top of the filling about ½ inch apart. Starting ½ inch from the edge of the tart, fold back every other strip and lay down 1 strip of spiced pastry. Fold the pastry back down and fold back the other pieces. Lay down a second strip about ½ inch from the first strip. Repeat this process until all the strips are used. Press your fingers against the rim of the pan to trim the dough. Use your thumb to press the edges of the lattice into the sides of the bottom crust.

7. Bake for 30 to 40 minutes, or until golden brown and firm. Cool to room temperature before serving.

Strawberry Custard Tart

This fresh tart has a similar flavor to strawberry shortcake. Raspberries or blueberries would be a good substitute if fresh strawberries are not available.

INGREDIENTS | SERVES 8

1 (10-inch) Short Crust for Tarts, unbaked (See Chapter 2)

1 cup whole milk

⅓ cup sugar

2 tablespoons cornstarch

2 egg yolks

⅛ teaspoon salt

1 teaspoon vanilla

2 tablespoons butter

1 cup strawberries, sliced

½ recipe Stabilized Whipped Cream (See Chapter 3)

1. Heat the oven to 375°F.

2. Line the tart crust with parchment paper or a double layer of aluminum foil and add pie weights or dry beans. Bake for 12 minutes, then remove the paper and weights and bake for an additional 12 to 15 minutes, or until the crust is golden brown all over. Remove from the oven and set aside to cool.

3. In a medium saucepan, combine the milk, sugar, cornstarch, egg yolks, and salt. Whisk until smooth, then cook over medium heat, stirring constantly, until it begins to simmer and thicken.

4. Remove from the heat and add the vanilla and the butter. Stir until melted. Pour through a strainer into a separate bowl, then pour directly into the prepared crust. Place a layer of cling film directly on the custard and chill for at least 4 hours, or overnight.

5. Once the tart has chilled, layer the sliced strawberries on the top. Decorate with the Stabilized Whipped Cream. Chill for 30 minutes before serving.

Mushroom Tart

Dried wild mushrooms are often available in the produce section,
but 4 ounces of fresh mushrooms can be substituted.

INGREDIENTS | SERVES 8

1 (10-inch) Parmesan Pastry Crust, unbaked (See Chapter 2)

½ ounce dry wild mushrooms

1 cup boiling water

2 tablespoons olive oil, not extra-virgin

1 medium onion, sliced

1 pound button mushrooms, sliced

2 cloves garlic, minced

2 tablespoons all-purpose flour

2 tablespoons lemon juice

2 egg yolks

½ teaspoon salt

½ teaspoon fresh thyme, chopped

1 tablespoon fresh parsley, chopped

Washing Mushrooms

Did you know it is okay to wash your mushrooms? Despite the dire warnings that washing mushrooms will make them soggy, a quick wash will do no harm. Use a colander and just give the mushrooms a quick rinse in cool water, then turn them out onto towels and dry well.

1. Heat the oven to 350°F.

2. Line the tart with parchment paper or a double layer of aluminum foil and add pie weights or dry beans. Bake for 12 minutes, then remove the paper and weights and bake for an additional 10 to 15 minutes, or until the crust is golden brown all over. Remove from the oven and set aside to cool.

3. Combine the dry mushrooms with the water. Let stand for 10 minutes, or until rehydrated. Drain the mushrooms, reserving the liquid, and chop well.

4. In a large skillet over medium heat, add the olive oil. Once the oil shimmers, add the onions and cook until softened, about 5 minutes. Add the button mushrooms and cook until tender, about 5 minutes. Add the garlic and rehydrated mushrooms and cook until fragrant, about 30 seconds.

5. Add the flour to the mushrooms and cook for 1 minute. Stir in ½ cup of the reserved mushroom liquid with the lemon juice and cook, stirring constantly, until thickened. Reduce the heat to low.

6. Whisk together ¼ cup of the reserved mushroom liquid with the egg yolks. Whisk the mixture into the mushrooms. Increase the heat to medium and cook until the liquid coats the back of a spoon. Stir in the salt, thyme, and parsley. Pour into the tart shell. Serve warm.

Onion Tart

Tender onions and smoky bacon make this a delicious brunch, lunch, or dinner tart.

1. Heat the oven to 350°F.

2. Roll out the pastry to a ⅛-inch-thick, 12-inch circle, turning the dough often to make sure it does not stick. Dust the surface with additional flour if needed.

3. Fold the dough in half and place it into a 10-inch tart pan. Unfold and carefully push the dough into the pan, making sure not to pull or stretch the dough. Press the dough against the edge of the tart pan to trim. Use a fork and dock the bottom and sides of the dough well. Cover with plastic and place in the refrigerator to chill.

4. Heat a medium skillet over medium-high heat. Add the onions and chicken stock and cook until the onions are soft and the liquid has reduced, about 30 minutes. Drain off any excess liquid, then transfer the onions to a bowl and allow to cool.

5. In the same skillet over medium heat, cook the bacon until crisp and the fat has rendered. Drain the excess fat, then combine the cooked bacon with the onions. Stir in the cream and add the salt and pepper.

6. Pour the mixture into the crust and place the tart pan on a baking sheet. Bake in the lower third of the oven for 30 to 40 minutes, or until golden brown and the crust is set. Cool slightly before serving.

CHAPTER 11

Rustic Tarts

Apple Brûlée Tart

Brûlée is French for burned, and it refers to the sugar topping, which is deeply caramelized under a broiler or with a torch.

INGREDIENTS | SERVES 8

1 recipe Blitz Puff Pastry (See Chapter 2)

1 egg, beaten

4 medium Granny Smith apples, peeled, cored, and sliced ⅛ inch thick

⅓ cup sugar, divided

1 tablespoon cornstarch

¼ teaspoon cinnamon

¼ teaspoon allspice

1. Roll out the pastry until it is ⅛ inch thick and trim it so that it is a 13-inch square. Brush the beaten egg along the edge of the pastry, about a ½-inch border, and fold the edges of the pastry in making a ½-inch lip around the edge of the pastry. Using a fork, pierce the center of the pastry. Cover with plastic and chill for 30 minutes.

2. In a medium bowl, combine the apples, ¼ cup of the sugar, cornstarch, cinnamon, and allspice. Toss so that all the apples are coated and let stand for 5 minutes.

3. Heat the oven to 450°F and line a baking sheet with parchment paper. Once the pastry has chilled, layer the apples onto the pastry, pouring over any juices from the bowl, and bake for 20 minutes.

4. Reduce the oven to 375°F and bake for 25 to 35 minutes more, or until the apples are soft and the pastry is puffed and crisp.

5. Once the tart has cooled slightly, sprinkle the remaining sugar evenly over the top of the tart. Using a kitchen torch, melt the sugar over the tart. If you do not have a torch, place the sugared tart under a heated broiler. Watch it carefully as it can burn easily. Cool to room temperature before serving.

Fig Tart

Fresh figs have a beautiful, subtle flavor that is perfect with a slightly sweet cheese filling.

INGREDIENTS | SERVES 8

¾ cup mascarpone cheese

2 teaspoons orange zest

1 teaspoon vanilla

3 tablespoons honey

2 tablespoons sugar

1 egg yolk

¼ teaspoon salt

1 (10-inch) Cornmeal Tart Crust, chilled (See Chapter 2)

10 mission figs, quartered

2 tablespoons apricot jam

Buying Figs

Figs are available mid to late summer in the produce department. When buying figs, look for stems that are firmly attached to the fruit and flesh that is only slightly soft. Figs are very perishable, so store them in the refrigerator and use them within 3 days of purchasing them.

1. In a large bowl, whisk together the mascarpone, orange zest, vanilla, honey, sugar, egg yolk, and salt. Cover and chill for 30 minutes.

2. Heat the oven to 350°F and line a baking sheet with parchment paper.

3. Place the chilled pastry on the prepared baking sheet. Spread the mascarpone mixture onto the pastry leaving a ½-inch border. Fold the pastry at the edge so that it is just covering the cheese filling.

4. Bake for 30 to 40 minutes, or until the crust is golden brown and the cheese filling has just set. Cool to room temperature.

5. To serve, top the tart with the sliced figs. In a small bowl, add the apricot jam. Heat in the microwave, using 10-second bursts, until the jam is melted. Brush the jam over the figs. Serve immediately.

Blueberry Ricotta Tart

This tart has a lemon-and-honey-flavored ricotta cheese base. The ricotta filling provides a creamy counterpoint to the juicy berries.

INGREDIENTS | SERVES 8

1 cup ricotta cheese
2 teaspoons lemon zest
1 teaspoon vanilla
2 tablespoons honey
2 tablespoons sugar
1 egg yolk
¼ teaspoon salt
1 (12-inch) round pastry crust, chilled
1 cup fresh blueberries
½ recipe Butter Crumble (See Chapter 3)

1. In a large bowl, whisk together the ricotta, lemon zest, vanilla, honey, sugar, egg yolk, and salt. Cover and chill for 30 minutes.

2. Heat the oven to 350°F and line a baking sheet with parchment paper.

3. Place the chilled pastry on the prepared baking sheet. Spread the ricotta mixture onto the pastry leaving a ½-inch border. Arrange the blueberries over the ricotta mixture, then fold the pastry just over the edge of the filling. Top with the Butter Crumble.

4. Bake for 45 to 55 minutes, or until the fruit is bubbling and both the crumble and pastry are golden brown. Cool to room temperature before serving.

Peach-Raspberry Galette

Galette is a French term for freeform tarts. This tart features the seasonal pair of raspberries and peaches.

INGREDIENTS | SERVES 8

3 medium peaches, peeled, pitted, and sliced ¼-inch thick

1 cup fresh raspberries

½ cup sugar

½ teaspoon vanilla

1 tablespoon cornstarch

¼ teaspoon cinnamon

1 (12-inch) round pastry crust, chilled

2 tablespoons butter

1. Heat the oven to 425°F and line a baking sheet with parchment paper.

2. Combine the peaches, raspberries, sugar, vanilla, cornstarch, and cinnamon in a large bowl, mix well, and then let stand 5 minutes.

3. Place pastry on the prepared baking sheet. Arrange the fruit on the pastry leaving a 2-inch border around the edge. Fold the pastry over the fruit, then dot butter.

4. Bake for 10 minutes, then reduce the heat to 350°F and bake for 40 to 50 minutes, or until the fruit is tender and the crust is golden brown. Cool to room temperature before serving.

Nectarine Tart

Nectarines are available from the summer through the fall, and this tart is a great way to showcase them.

INGREDIENTS | SERVES 8

¼ cup packed light brown sugar

¼ teaspoon mace or nutmeg

1 tablespoon cornstarch

4 nectarines, pitted and sliced ¼-inch thick

1 (12-inch) round pastry crust, chilled

2 tablespoons butter

1. Heat the oven to 425°F and line a baking sheet with parchment paper.

2. In a large bowl, combine the light brown sugar, nutmeg, cornstarch, and nectarines. Let stand for 10 minutes.

3. Place the pastry on the prepared baking sheet. Arrange the nectarines on the pastry, leaving a 1-inch border. Pour over any juices. Carefully fold the pastry over the nectarines, then dot the top of the fruit with butter.

4. Bake for 10 minutes, then reduce the heat to 350°F and bake for an additional 30 to 40 minutes, or until the pastry is golden brown and the fruit is tender. Cool to room temperature before serving.

Apple Galette

This is a freeform version of an apple pie. If you want to give this tart a twist, add some raisins or walnuts.

INGREDIENTS | SERVES 8

2 Granny Smith apples, peeled, cored, and sliced ¼ inch thick

2 Crispin apples, peeled, cored, and sliced ¼ inch thick

½ cup packed light brown sugar, divided

1 teaspoon orange zest

1 tablespoon orange juice

2 tablespoons cornstarch

½ teaspoon cinnamon

¼ teaspoon allspice

⅛ teaspoon nutmeg

1 (12-inch) round pastry crust, chilled

2 tablespoons butter

Even Baking

Most home ovens do not heat as evenly as they should, causing your baked goods to cook unevenly. You can do a few things to help. First, rotate your baked goods halfway through to ensure even browning. Second, heat the oven with a pizza stone or unglazed tiles on the bottom rack. This will help even out the heat.

1. Heat the oven to 425°F and line a baking sheet with parchment paper.

2. In a large bowl, combine the apples, ¼ cup light brown sugar, orange zest, orange juice, cornstarch, cinnamon, allspice, and nutmeg. Toss until evenly coated, then allow to stand for 5 minutes.

3. Place the pastry crust on the prepared baking sheet. Carefully arrange the apples in the center of the pastry, leaving a 2-inch border of pastry around the apples. Pour over any juices from the bowl. Fold the edges of the pastry over the apples and sprinkle the remaining brown sugar over the top.

4. Bake the tart for 15 minutes, then reduce the heat to 350°F for 35 to 45 additional minutes, or until the pastry is golden and the apples are tender. Serve slightly warm.

Caramelized Onion and Gruyère Tart

Sweet caramelized onions pair well with the earthy cheese in this tart. It is perfect for lunch or dinner along with a cup of creamy soup.

INGREDIENTS | SERVES 8

3 strips thick-cut bacon, chopped

3 large, or 4 medium, yellow onions, peeled and sliced ¼-inch thick

2 teaspoons sugar

½ cup water

3 cloves garlic, minced

1 teaspoon apple cider vinegar

¼ teaspoon fresh grated nutmeg

1 teaspoon hot sauce

1 recipe Blitz Puff Pastry (See Chapter 2)

1 egg, beaten

1 cup shredded Gruyère cheese

¼ teaspoon smoked paprika

Make Them Mini

If you want, you can transform your large tart into individual tarts very simply. First, cut the dough into 4-inch circles. Divide the filling between the circles, fold, and bake. You will need to check the tarts starting at 20 minutes to avoid overcooking. Individual tarts are great for bake sales, tea parties, and cocktail parties.

1. In a large sauté pan over medium heat, cook the bacon until crisp. Remove the bacon from the pan and allow to drain. Reserve the fat.

2. Add the onions to the pan along with the sugar and cook for 1 minute, then reduce the heat to medium-low and add ¼ cup of the water. Cook, stirring constantly, until the onions are well caramelized, about 30 minutes. If the pan becomes too dry or the onions begin to stick, add the additional water.

3. Once the onions are caramelized, add in the garlic, vinegar, nutmeg, and hot sauce and cook for 1 minute. Remove from the heat and allow to cool.

4. Heat the oven to 425°F and line a baking sheet with parchment paper.

5. Roll out the pastry to ⅛ inch thick, then use a pizza wheel to cut out a 12-inch circle. Place on the prepared baking sheet and brush the edge of the pastry with beaten egg, about a ½-inch border. Fold the pastry in, forming a ½-inch rim. Dock the center of the pastry, cover with plastic, and chill for 30 minutes.

6. Once chilled, spread the caramelized onions over the pastry. Top with the cooked bacon and the shredded cheese, and dust the top with the paprika. Bake for 15 minutes, then reduce the heat to 350°F and bake for an additional 30 to 40 minutes, or until the pastry is crisp and golden. Serve warm.

Ginger Pear Tart

This is a wonderful fall dessert. Make this with very ripe pears for the best flavor.

INGREDIENTS | SERVES 8

4 Bosc pears, peeled, cored, and sliced ¼-inch thick
1 teaspoon grated fresh ginger
½ cup packed light brown sugar
¼ teaspoon cinnamon
1 tablespoon cornstarch
½ cup crushed gingersnap cookies
2 tablespoons butter, melted
1 (12-inch) round pastry crust, chilled

1. Heat the oven to 425°F and line a baking sheet with parchment paper.

2. In a large bowl, combine the pears, ginger, light brown sugar, cinnamon, and cornstarch. Toss until the fruit is evenly coated, then set aside for 5 minutes.

3. In a small bowl, combine the gingersnap crumbs with the butter until the crumbs are evenly coated.

4. Place the pastry in the prepared baking sheet. Arrange the pears on the pastry, leaving a 2-inch border. Pour any juices over the top. Carefully fold the pastry over the pears, then spread the gingersnap crumbs over the top.

5. Bake for 10 minutes, then reduce the heat to 350°F and bake for an additional 30 to 40 minutes, or until the pastry is golden and the fruit is tender. Cool to room temperature before serving.

Cherry Frangipane Tart

Almond paste is available in the baking aisle in most markets. It often comes in small cans, but can also be sold in tubes.

INGREDIENTS | SERVES 8

1 cup (7 ounces) almond paste

¼ cup all-purpose flour

⅓ cup sugar

6 tablespoons unsalted butter, room temperature

2 eggs

1 (12-inch) round pastry crust, chilled

1 cup pitted cherries, thawed and drained well if frozen

Almond Paste

Almond paste is a mixture of blanched almonds, sugar, and sometimes butter or eggs. Other uses for almond paste include filling pastries and cakes, and as an ingredient in cookies. Extra almond paste can be stored in the freezer for up to 3 months.

1. Heat the oven to 425°F and line a baking sheet with parchment paper.

2. In a large bowl, beat together the almond paste, flour, and sugar until well combined. Add the butter and mix well, then add the eggs, one at a time, beating well after each addition.

3. Place the chilled pastry on the prepared baking sheet. Spread the almond mixture onto the pastry leaving a ½-inch border. Arrange the cherries over the almond mixture, then fold the pastry over the cherries.

4. Bake for 10 minutes, then reduce the heat to 350°F and bake for an additional 25 to 35 minutes, or until the pastry is golden and the fruit is tender. Cool to room temperature before serving.

Fresh Summer Fruit and Cream Tart

Buttery puff pastry is baked into a crisp, thin sheet and topped with sweet cream cheese and fresh fruit. This is the perfect way to celebrate summer berries.

INGREDIENTS | SERVES 8

1 recipe Blitz Puff Pastry (See Chapter 2)

8 ounces cream cheese, room temperature

½ cup powdered sugar, plus more for garnish

1 teaspoon vanilla

1 teaspoon lemon zest

½ cup fresh strawberries, hulled and sliced

½ cup fresh blueberries

½ cup fresh raspberries

½ cup fresh blackberries

¼ cup apricot jelly

1. Heat the oven to 400°F and line a baking sheet with parchment paper.

2. Roll the pastry out to ½ inch thick and trim the pastry into a 12-inch square. Place the pastry on the prepared baking sheet and pierce with a fork. Top the pastry with a second sheet of parchment paper, then place a second baking sheet on top of the pastry. Bake for 12 to 15 minutes, or until the pastry is firm, then remove the top baking sheet and parchment paper and bake for an additional 12 to 15 minutes, or until the pastry is golden brown and crisp. Allow to cool completely to room temperature.

3. In a medium bowl, beat the cream cheese with the powdered sugar, vanilla, and lemon zest until fluffy and smooth. Carefully spread the cream cheese mixture over the pastry, leaving a 1-inch border around the edge. Arrange the fruit on the cream cheese.

4. In a small saucepan, melt the apricot jelly until thin. With a pastry brush, glaze the fruit with the melted jelly. Dust the edges of the pastry with powdered sugar, if desired.

Rhubarb-Cherry Tart

If you find this tart a little too sharp in flavor, add a little more sugar. The sweet and tangy flavor of cherries is a natural match for the tart rhubarb.

INGREDIENTS | SERVES 8

1 pound rhubarb, washed and cut into 1-inch pieces

2 cups dry cherries

1 cup packed light brown sugar

1 teaspoon vanilla

1 (12-inch) round pastry crust, chilled

Shiny Glaze

If you want to give your fruit tarts a professional-looking finish and a lot of shine, try an apricot glaze. Simply melt apricot jam either in the microwave or in a pot on the stove until it is thoroughly melted.

1. Combine the rhubarb, cherries, and light brown sugar in a medium saucepan over medium heat. Cook, covered with a lid, until the rhubarb is softened, about 10 minutes. Uncover and cook, stirring constantly, until thick about 15 to 20 minutes.

2. Turn off the heat and stir in the vanilla. Set aside to cool.

3. Heat the oven to 375°F and line a baking sheet with parchment paper.

4. Place the pastry on the prepared baking sheet. Spoon the rhubarb filling in the center, leaving a 1-inch border around the edge. Carefully fold the pastry over the filling.

5. Bake for 35 to 45 minutes, or until the pastry is golden brown and the filling is bubbling. Cool to room temperature before serving.

Pear-Berry Tart

If you prefer, you may substitute dry cherries, or even golden raisins, for the cranberries.

INGREDIENTS | SERVES 8

1 cup orange juice

1 cup dry cranberries

4 Bosc pears, peeled, cored, and cut ¼ inch thick

½ cup sugar

1 tablespoon orange zest

1 tablespoon cornstarch

1 (12-inch) round pastry crust, chilled

1 recipe Butter Crumble (See Chapter 3)

Soggy Tart Crust

If you find that your tart crusts are a little soggy on the bottom after baking, here is a tip that may help. Lay a fine layer of crushed cookie or cake crumbs under the fruit filling. The crumbs will absorb the juices and help prevent sogginess.

1. In a small saucepan, bring the orange juice to a boil. Remove from the heat and add the cranberries. Allow to stand 10 minutes, then drain well.

2. Heat the oven to 375°F and line a baking sheet with parchment paper.

3. In a large bowl, combine the cranberries, pears, sugar, orange zest, and cornstarch. Mix until the fruit is well coated, then let stand for 5 minutes.

4. Place the pastry on the prepared baking sheet. Arrange the fruit in the center, leaving a 1-inch border around the edge. Pour over any juices, then spread the crumble over the top.

5. Bake for 45 to 55 minutes, or until the crumble and pastry are golden brown and the fruit is tender. Cool to room temperature before serving.

Plum Tart

Plums can be fairly tart, so test the fruit for sweetness before baking. If it is too tart, add additional sugar; if they are very sweet, you may need to reduce it.

INGREDIENTS | SERVES 8

1 recipe Blitz Puff Pastry

1 cup (7 ounces) almond paste

¼ cup all-purpose flour

⅓ cup sugar

6 tablespoons unsalted butter, room temperature

2 eggs

5 large plums, pitted and cut in half

2 tablespoons sugar

Dried Plums and Prunes

Due to changes in marketing, prunes are now more commonly called dried plums, but did you know that there is a specific variety of plum called a prune? They are the variety most commonly sold dried, but the fresh prune is smaller than other plums and has a freestone pit.

1. Heat the oven to 375°F and line a baking sheet with parchment paper.

2. Roll the pastry out to ½ inch thick and trim the pastry into a 12-inch square. Place the pastry on the prepared baking sheet and pierce well with a fork. Cover and chill.

3. In a large bowl, beat together the almond paste, flour, and sugar until well combined. Add the butter and mix well, then add the eggs, one at a time, beating well after each addition.

4. Spread the almond mixture over the chilled pastry, leaving a ½-inch border around the edge. Arrange the plums over the top, cut side down. Dust the top of the tart with sugar.

5. Bake for 40 to 45 minutes, or until the pastry is golden brown and the fruit is tender. Cool to room temperature before serving.

Pear Gorgonzola Tart

*Gorgonzola is a blue cheese from Italy. If you find the flavor too pungent,
feel free to substitute cream cheese for part of the cheese.*

INGREDIENTS | SERVES 8

3 Bosc pears, peeled, cored, and sliced
¼-inch thick
¼ teaspoon cayenne pepper
1 (12-inch) round pastry crust, chilled
2 ounces cream cheese, room
temperature
¼ cup fig jam
2 ounces Gorgonzola cheese, crumbled

1. Heat the oven to 425°F and line a baking sheet with parchment paper.

2. In a large bowl, combine the pears and cayenne pepper until evenly coated. Set aside.

3. Place the pastry crust on the prepared baking sheet. Spread the cream cheese in the center of the pastry, leaving a 2-inch border around the edge. Spread the fig jam over the top of the cream cheese, then arrange the pear slices over the top. Carefully fold the edges of the pastry over the fruit and top with the crumbled Gorgonzola cheese.

4. Bake for 10 minutes, then reduce the heat to 350°F and bake for an additional 30 to 40 minutes, or until the pastry is golden brown and the fruit is tender. Serve warm.

Apple, Brie, and Bacon Tart

Cut the rind off the Brie before baking for a smoother tart.
If you like the flavor of the rind, feel free to leave it on.

INGREDIENTS | SERVES 8

1 recipe Blitz Puff Pastry (See Chapter 2)

1 egg, beaten

6 strips thick-cut bacon, chopped

¼ cup apple butter

6 ounces Brie cheese, cut into ¼-inch slices

2 Granny Smith apples, cored, and sliced ¼ inch thick

2 tablespoons fresh grated Parmesan cheese

Brie

Brie is a cow's milk cheese that is allowed to age and ripen for a few months to as long as a few years. Brie is best when served at room temperature and can also be baked. Brie baked in a pastry crust is called brie en croute. Jam, fruit, and crackers are popular accompaniments for the soft cheese.

1. Heat the oven to 400°F and line a baking sheet with parchment paper.

2. Roll the pastry out to ½ inch thick and trim the pastry into a 12-inch square. Place the pastry on the prepared baking sheet. Brush the beaten egg along the edge of the pastry, about a ½-inch border, and fold the edges of the pastry in, making a ½-inch lip around the edge of the pastry. Using a fork, pierce the center of the pastry. Cover with plastic and chill for 30 minutes.

3. In a medium skillet over medium heat, cook the bacon until it just begins to brown. Remove from the pan and drain well.

4. Spread the apple butter over the center of the puff pastry. Arrange the Brie cheese, apples, and bacon over the apple butter and dust the top with Parmesan cheese.

5. Bake for 30 to 40 minutes, or until the pastry is golden and the apples are tender. Cool for 5 minutes before serving.

Ham and Cheese Tart

*Serve this tart warm for breakfast with some fresh fruit or for lunch with
a crisp salad. Turkey can be substituted for the ham if desired.*

INGREDIENTS | SERVES 8

1 recipe Blitz Puff Pastry (See Chapter 2)

1 egg beaten

4 ounces cream cheese

4 ounces sour cream

1 egg yolk

1 cup sharp Cheddar cheese

1 cup diced ham

2 tablespoons fresh grated Parmesan cheese

1. Heat the oven to 400°F and line a baking sheet with parchment paper.

2. Roll the pastry out to ½ inch thick and trim the pastry into a 12-inch square. Place the pastry on the prepared baking sheet. Brush the beaten egg along the edge of the pastry, about a ½-inch border, and fold the edges of the pastry in, making a ½-inch lip around the edge of the pastry. Using a fork pierce the center of the pastry. Cover with plastic and chill for 30 minutes.

3. In a large bowl, beat together the cream cheese and sour cream until smooth. Add in the egg yolk and beat until well blended. Fold in the Cheddar cheese.

4. Spread the cheese mixture into the pastry. Arrange the ham over the top and dust the top with the grated Parmesan cheese.

5. Bake for 15 minutes, then reduce the heat to 350°F and bake for an additional 30 to 40 minutes, or until the filling is puffed and golden brown. Serve warm.

Goat Cheese and Roasted Red Pepper Tart

Fresh goat cheese has a slightly tangy flavor and is delicious with the slightly charred flavor of roasted peppers.

INGREDIENTS | SERVES 8

6 ounces goat cheese

2 ounces cream cheese, room temperature

1 clove garlic, minced fine

¼ teaspoon fresh chopped thyme

¼ teaspoon fresh oregano

½ teaspoon salt

1 cup frozen spinach, thawed and drained

3 roasted red peppers packed in water, drained

1 (12-inch) round pastry crust, chilled

1 egg, beaten

1. Heat the oven to 425°F and line a baking sheet with parchment paper.

2. In a large bowl, beat together the goat cheese, cream cheese, garlic, thyme, oregano, and salt until smooth. Fold in the spinach, then cover and chill until ready to bake.

3. Slice the roasted peppers into 1-inch pieces. Set aside.

4. Place the pastry on the prepared baking sheet. Brush the beaten egg ½ inch around the edge of the pastry, then fold over to form a border. Spread the cheese mixture into the center of the tart, then arrange the red pepper slices on the top.

5. Bake for 10 minutes, then reduce the heat to 350°F and bake for an additional 30 to 40 minutes, or until the pastry is golden brown and the cheese is bubbling and starting to brown. Serve warm.

Sun-Dried Tomato, Pesto, and Mozzarella Tart

*For the best flavor, use the pesto that is sold in the refrigerated
cases at the grocery store or make your own!*

INGREDIENTS | SERVES 8

1 (12-inch) round pastry crust, chilled

1 egg beaten

4 ounces fresh mozzarella balls, sliced
¼ inch thick

½ cup sun-dried tomatoes, sliced thin

¼ cup fresh grated Parmesan cheese

¼ cup prepared pesto sauce

¼ teaspoon salt

¼ teaspoon fresh cracked pepper

Pesto in the Blender

Fresh, homemade pesto is a snap to make.
Add 2 cups of fresh basil to your blender
along with ⅓ cup fresh grated Parmesan
cheese, ⅓ cup of toasted walnuts or pine
nuts, and 2 cloves garlic. Purée and slowly
add ⅓ to ½ cup of olive oil. Season with
salt to taste.

1. Heat the oven to 425°F and line a baking sheet with
   parchment paper.

2. Place the pastry on the prepared baking sheet. Brush
   the beaten egg ½ inch around the edge of the pastry,
   then fold over to form a border. Cover and chill for 30
   minutes.

3. Arrange the mozzarella slices over the pastry. Place the
   sun-dried tomato strips and Parmesan cheese over the
   mozzarella. Drizzle the pesto over the top, then season
   with the salt and pepper.

4. Bake for 10 minutes, then reduce the heat to 350°F and
   bake for an additional 30 to 40 minutes, or until the
   pastry is golden brown and the cheese is bubbling and
   starting to brown. Serve warm.

CHAPTER 12

Holiday Traditions

Pumpkin Pecan Pie

If you like pecan pie and pumpkin pie, you must try this. It is the best of both worlds!

INGREDIENTS | SERVES 8

3 eggs, divided
1 cup pumpkin purée
1 cup sugar, divided
1 teaspoon cinnamon
½ teaspoon salt
½ teaspoon ground ginger
¼ teaspoon ground cloves
1 (9-inch) Mealy Pie Crust, unbaked
(See Chapter 2)
⅔ cup light corn syrup
2 tablespoons melted butter
1 teaspoon vanilla
1 cup whole pecans

1. Heat the oven to 375°F.

2. In a medium bowl, mix together 1 egg, pumpkin purée, ⅓ cup sugar, cinnamon, salt, ginger, and cloves until smooth. Spread into the bottom of the pie crust. Set aside.

3. In a medium bowl, whisk the remaining eggs until just blended, then whisk in the corn syrup, ⅔ cup sugar, melted butter, and vanilla until well combined. Stir in the pecans. Pour over the pumpkin mixture in the crust.

4. Bake for 50 to 60 minutes, or until filling is set in the center of the pie. Cool the pie to room temperature before serving.

Pumpkin Eggnog Pie

*During the fall, eggnog can be found in the dairy case of most markets.
Eggnog has a rich flavor that is delicious with pumpkin!*

INGREDIENTS | SERVES 8

⅓ cup packed light brown sugar
½ teaspoon salt
1 teaspoon cinnamon
¼ teaspoon fresh grated nutmeg
⅛ teaspoon allspice
⅛ teaspoon ground cloves
2 eggs
1 (15-ounce) can pumpkin purée
12 ounces eggnog
1 (9-inch) pastry crust, unbaked

1. Heat the oven to 425°F.

2. In a large bowl, whisk together light brown sugar, salt, cinnamon, nutmeg, allspice, and cloves until combined.

3. Add the eggs, pumpkin, and eggnog and whisk until smooth.

4. Pour the mixture into the pastry crust and place on a baking sheet. Bake in the lower third of the oven for 15 minutes, then reduce the heat to 350°F and bake for an additional 40 to 45 minutes, or until the filling is set at the edges and just slightly wobbly in the center. Cool for 3 hours on a wire rack before slicing.

Eggnog Chiffon Pie

The classic eggnog is transformed into a fluffy, light pie that is perfect after a hearty meal.

INGREDIENTS | SERVES 8

1 envelope unflavored powdered gelatin

¼ cup cold water

⅓ cup sugar

2 tablespoons cornstarch

¼ teaspoon salt

4 egg yolks

2 cups eggnog

1 teaspoon vanilla

4 egg whites

¼ teaspoon salt

2 tablespoons sugar

1 (9-inch) Traditional Graham Cracker Crust, baked and cooled

1 recipe Spiked Whipped Cream (See Chapter 3)

1. In a small bowl, combine the gelatin and the water. Allow to stand until completely bloomed, about 10 minutes.

2. In a medium saucepan, combine the sugar, cornstarch, salt, egg yolks, and eggnog. Cook over medium heat, whisking constantly, until thickened, about 10 minutes.

3. Remove from the heat and add the gelatin and vanilla. Mix until well blended, then allow it to cool until slightly warm.

4. In a large, clean bowl, whip the egg whites with the salt until they are very frothy. Gradually add in the sugar, beating constantly, until the whites form medium peaks.

5. Working in thirds, fold the egg whites into the eggnog mixture, making sure no large streaks of egg white remain. Pour the mixture into the prepared crust and chill until firm, about 4 hours.

6. Once chilled, prepare the Spiked Whipped Cream. Top the pie and serve immediately.

Brandied Sweet Potato Pie

Brandy, warm spices, and creamy sweet potato create a pie that is perfect to celebrate the season!

INGREDIENTS | SERVES 8

3 medium sweet potatoes, peeled and cut into 1-inch pieces

¾ cup packed light brown sugar

1 teaspoon cinnamon

¼ teaspoon salt

¼ teaspoon allspice

⅛ teaspoon fresh grated nutmeg

2 tablespoons brandy

2 eggs

12 ounces evaporated milk

1 (9-inch) pastry crust, unbaked

Canned Sweet Potatoes

Most canned sweet potatoes come in a sugary syrup. If you decide to use a canned sweet potato in a pie recipe, you may need to adjust the amount of sugar you add to the filling since the sweet potatoes will absorb some of the sweet syrup. Start by adding half of the sugar, then test to see if more is needed.

1. Heat the oven to 425°F.

2. Steam the sweet potatoes until they are fork-tender. Remove from the steamer and mash or purée in a food processor until smooth. Set aside to cool.

3. In a large bowl, whisk together the light brown sugar, cinnamon, salt, allspice, and nutmeg until well combined.

4. Add the brandy, eggs, sweet potato, and evaporated milk and whisk until smooth.

5. Pour the mixture into the pastry crust and place on a baking sheet. Bake in the lower third of the oven for 15 minutes, then reduce the heat to 350°F and bake for an additional 40 to 45 minutes, or until the filling is set at the edges and just slightly wobbly in the center. Cool for 3 hours on a wire rack before slicing.

Cranberry Crunch Pie

This pie has three delicious layers and makes a big impact!

INGREDIENTS | SERVES 8

1 (9-inch) pastry crust, unbaked

1 (16-ounce) can whole cranberry sauce, divided

8 ounces cream cheese, room temperature

1 egg yolk

⅓ cup sugar

½ teaspoon vanilla

2 tablespoons cornstarch, divided

1 Granny Smith apple, peeled, cored, and finely diced

1 recipe Pecan Streusel (See Chapter 3)

1. Heat the oven to 375°F.

2. Line the pie crust with parchment paper or a double layer of aluminum foil and add pie weights or dry beans. Bake for 10 minutes, then remove the paper and weights and bake for an additional 10 to 12 minutes, or until the crust is golden brown all over. Remove from the oven and set aside to cool. Leave the oven on.

3. In a large bowl, beat together ½ cup of the cranberry sauce with the cream cheese, egg yolk, sugar, vanilla, and 1 tablespoon of the cornstarch. Spread into the bottom of the prepared crust.

4. In a separate bowl, combine the remaining cornstarch with the apples and remaining cranberry sauce. Spread over the cream cheese mixture, then spread the Pecan Streusel over the top.

5. Place the pie on a baking sheet and bake for 25 to 30 minutes, or until the streusel has turned golden brown. Cool to room temperature before serving.

Peppermint Patty Pie

Feel free to add more peppermint patties to this pie if you like it really minty.
A few crumbled chocolate mint cookies would also be really good here.

INGREDIENTS | SERVES 8

6 ounces cream cheese, softened

¼ teaspoon mint extract

1 cup powdered sugar

1 cup heavy cream

1 teaspoon vanilla

12 mini, or 4 regular, peppermint patties, cut into ½-inch pieces

1 (9-inch) Chocolate Cookie Crust, baked and cooled (See Chapter 2)

1. In a large bowl, cream together the cream cheese, mint extract, and powdered sugar. Mix until smooth, then set aside.

2. In a separate bowl, whip the cream with the vanilla until it forms medium peaks. Fold the whipped cream and chopped peppermint patties into the cream cheese mixture until no streaks of cream remain.

3. Pour the mixture into the prepared crust. Chill for 4 hours before serving.

Candy Cane Pie

This creamy, minty pie is studded with crunchy bits of peppermint candy. If you like,
you can fold in ½ cup of miniature chocolate chips for extra flavor.

INGREDIENTS | SERVES 8

6 ounces cream cheese, softened

½ teaspoon mint extract

1 cup powdered sugar

1 cup heavy cream

½ teaspoon vanilla

1 (9-inch) Chocolate Cookie Crust, baked and cooled (See Chapter 2)

½ cup crushed peppermint candy, divided

1. In a large bowl, cream together the cream cheese, mint extract, and powdered sugar. Mix until smooth, then set aside.

2. In a separate bowl, whip the cream with the vanilla until it forms medium peaks. Fold the cream into the mint mixture along with ⅓ cup of the crushed peppermint candy until no streaks of cream remain.

3. Pour the mixture into the prepared crust and garnish with the remaining candy. Chill for 4 hours before serving.

Powdered Sugar Decorations

When serving pies decorated with powdered sugar, it is best to dust them just before serving.

Cranberry Walnut Pie

If you prefer, you can use pecans or almonds for the walnuts in this pie, or even use peanuts.

INGREDIENTS | SERVES 8

1 (9-inch) pastry crust, unbaked
1½ cups chopped walnuts
4 cups fresh cranberries
1½ cups packed light brown sugar
2 tablespoons cornstarch
½ teaspoon cinnamon
2 teaspoons orange zest
1 tablespoon orange juice

1. Heat the oven to 375°F.

2. Line the pie crust with parchment paper or a double layer of aluminum foil and add pie weights or dry beans. Bake for 10 minutes, then remove the paper and weights and bake for an additional 10 to 12 minutes, or until the crust is golden brown all over. Remove from the oven and set aside to cool. Leave the oven on.

3. Line a baking sheet with parchment paper, then spread the chopped walnuts evenly over the sheet. Bake for 8 to 10 minutes, or until the nuts become fragrant. Cool to room temperature.

4. In a medium saucepan, combine the cranberries and light brown sugar over medium heat. Cook, stirring constantly until the berries burst and the mixture thickens. Cool to room temperature, then stir in the cornstarch, cinnamon, orange zest, orange juice, and walnuts. Pour the mixture into the prepared crust.

5. Bake for 35 to 45 minutes, or until the filling is bubbly and thickened. Cool to room temperature before serving.

Cranberry Chiffon Pie

Tangy, sweet, and light as a cloud, this pie is sure to please your holiday guests!

INGREDIENTS | SERVES 8

2 cups cranberry juice

1 tablespoon powdered gelatin

¼ cup cold water

4 egg yolks

⅓ cup sugar

1 teaspoon orange zest

2–3 drops red food coloring

4 egg whites

¼ teaspoon salt

¼ cup sugar

1 (9-inch) pastry crust, baked and cooled

1 recipe Stabilized Whipped Cream (See Chapter 3)

Cranberries

Cranberries are the fruit of an evergreen shrub common to the northern United States and southern Canada. Cranberries are primarily harvested by flooding the bogs in which they grow. Once flooded, a harvester removes the berries, which float to the surface of the water. Once floating, they are scooped or pumped to trucks and taken to be processed.

1. In a medium saucepan over medium heat, add the cranberry juice. Bring to a boil, then reduce to a simmer and cook, stirring occasionally, until reduced to ½ cup, about 15 minutes. Cool to room temperature.

2. In a small bowl, combine the gelatin and the water. Allow to stand until completely bloomed, about 10 minutes.

3. In a double boiler, combine the egg yolks, sugar, orange zest, and cranberry reduction. Cook the mixture, whisking constantly, until thickened and lighter in color. Remove from the heat and add the food coloring and bloomed gelatin. Whisk until dissolved. Allow to cool until it starts to thicken.

4. In a large, clean bowl, whip the egg whites with the salt until they are very frothy. Gradually add in the sugar, beating constantly, until the whites form medium peaks.

5. Working in thirds, fold the egg whites into the cranberry mixture, making sure no large streaks of egg white remain. Pour the mixture into the prepared crust and chill until firm, about 4 hours.

6. Once chilled, prepare the Stabilized Whipped Cream. Top the pie and chill for 30 minutes before serving.

Eggnog Cream Pie

Eggnog made into custard and topped with whipped cream is a fun twist on the traditional holiday beverage. Dust the top of the pie with a little fresh grated nutmeg for a special touch.

INGREDIENTS | SERVES 8

1 (9-inch) pastry crust, unbaked
2 cups eggnog
¼ cup sugar
1 tablespoon bourbon or rum
¼ cup cornstarch
3 egg yolks
¼ teaspoon salt
½ teaspoon fresh grated nutmeg
½ teaspoon vanilla
2 tablespoons butter
1 recipe Stabilized Whipped Cream (See Chapter 3)

1. Heat the oven to 375°F.

2. Line the pie crust with parchment paper or a double layer of aluminum foil and add pie weights or dry beans. Bake for 15 minutes, then remove the paper and weights and bake for an additional 10 to 12 minutes, or until the crust is golden brown all over. Remove from the oven and set aside to cool.

3. In a medium saucepan, combine the eggnog, sugar, bourbon or rum, cornstarch, egg yolks, salt, and nutmeg. Whisk until smooth, then cook over medium heat, stirring constantly, until it begins to simmer and thicken.

4. Remove from the heat and add the vanilla and butter. Stir until melted. Pour through a strainer into a separate bowl, then pour directly into the prepared crust. Place a layer of cling film directly on the custard and chill for at least 6 hours or overnight.

5. Once the pie has chilled, prepare the Stabilized Whipped Cream and top the pie. Chill for 30 minutes before serving.

Quick Mincemeat Pie

Traditionally mincemeat takes as long as a week to prepare while the fruit soaks in the brandy and fruit juice. In this recipe, you cook the mincemeat to speed up the process without losing the flavor.

INGREDIENTS | SERVES 8

2 Granny Smith apples, peeled, cored, and finely chopped

1 cup dark raisins

½ cup golden raisins

½ cup dry currants

4 tablespoons butter, melted

½ cup sugar

¼ cup brandy

2 tablespoons orange juice

1 tablespoon orange zest

¼ teaspoon cinnamon

¼ teaspoon allspice

⅛ teaspoon cloves

⅛ teaspoon fresh grated nutmeg

1 (9-inch) Mealy Pie Crust, unbaked (See Chapter 2)

1 egg, beaten

1 (9-inch) Flaky Pie Crust, chilled (See Chapter 2)

Decorative Top Crusts

For a special winter touch to your double-crusted pies, why not consider making your top crust a snowflake? Simply fold the dough for the top crust into quarters on a lightly dusted work surface. With a sharp paring knife cut small slits and holes into the folded edges and center of the pastry. When you unfold it, you will have a unique snowflake design!

1. In a large saucepan, combine the apples, dark raisins, golden raisins, currants, butter, sugar, brandy, orange juice, orange zest, cinnamon, allspice, cloves, and nutmeg. Cook over medium heat until it comes to a simmer. Turn off the heat and let the mixture cool to room temperature.

2. Heat the oven to 425°F.

3. Fill the Mealy Pie Crust with the cooled mincemeat mixture. Brush the edge of the bottom pie crust with the beaten egg so that the top crust will adhere. Top with the Flaky Pie Crust and trim the dough to 1 inch of the pan's edge. Tuck the edge of the top crust under the edge of the bottom crust. Crimp the dough using your fingers or a fork. Brush the entire top crust with the beaten egg and cut 4 or 5 slits in the top to vent steam.

4. Place the pie on a baking sheet and bake for 30 minutes, then reduce the heat to 350°F for an additional 30 to 40 minutes, or until the pie is bubbling and the juices are thick. Cool to room temperature before slicing.

Raisin Pie

You can substitute dried cranberries, dried cherries, or chopped dates in this pie.

INGREDIENTS | SERVES 8

1 egg

⅓ cup sugar

2 tablespoons cornstarch

¼ teaspoon salt

½ teaspoon cinnamon

¼ teaspoon cloves

¼ teaspoon fresh grated nutmeg

½ cup molasses

½ cup buttermilk

1 cup dark raisins, chopped

1 (9-inch) Mealy Pie Crust, unbaked (See Chapter 2)

1 (9-inch) Flaky Pie Crust, cut into 10 (1-inch) strips (See Chapter 2)

1 egg, beaten

Gritty Raisins

Ever buy a box of raisins that taste a little gritty? That is due to the natural sugars in the raisins crystallizing. Crystallized raisins are usually fine to eat and bake with, and you can remove the gritty texture by quickly blanching the raisins in boiling water or apple juice.

1. Heat the oven to 425°F.

2. Mix the egg, sugar, cornstarch, salt, cinnamon, cloves, nutmeg, molasses, and buttermilk until smooth. Stir in the chopped raisins until well mixed.

3. Pour the raisin mixture into the Mealy Pie Crust and top with the pastry strips. Lay out 5 strips of pie dough on top of the filling about ½ inch apart. Starting ½ inch from the edge of the pie, fold back every other strip and lay down 1 strip of pastry. Fold the pastry back down and fold back the other pieces. Lay down a second strip about ½ inch from the first strip. Repeat this process until all the strips are used. Trim the dough to 1 inch of the pan's edge. Tuck the edge of the top crust under the edge of the bottom crust. Crimp the dough using your fingers or a fork. Brush the lattice with the beaten egg.

4. Bake for 40 to 45 minutes, or until the filling is bubbly in the center and the lattice is golden brown. Cool for 30 minutes before serving.

Pumpkin Chiffon Pie

After a big meal, this fluffy pie packs in the flavor without being heavy.

INGREDIENTS | SERVES 8

1 envelope unflavored powdered gelatin

¼ cup cold water

1 cup sugar

4 egg yolks

2 tablespoons cornstarch

¼ teaspoon salt

½ teaspoon cinnamon

¼ teaspoon allspice

¼ teaspoon ground cloves

⅛ teaspoon fresh grated nutmeg

1½ cups pumpkin purée

1 teaspoon vanilla

4 egg whites

¼ teaspoon salt

2 tablespoons sugar

1 (9-inch) Traditional Graham Cracker Crust, baked and cooled

1 recipe Spiked Whipped Cream (See Chapter 3)

1. In a small bowl, combine the gelatin and the water. Allow to stand until completely bloomed, about 10 minutes.

2. In a medium saucepan, combine the sugar, egg yolks, cornstarch, salt, cinnamon, allspice, cloves, nutmeg, and pumpkin. Cook over a double boiler, whisking constantly, until thickened, about 12 minutes.

3. Remove from the heat and add the gelatin and vanilla. Mix until well blended, then allow to cool until slightly warm.

4. In a large, clean bowl, whip the egg whites with the salt until they are very frothy. Gradually add in the remaining sugar, beating constantly, until the whites form medium peaks.

5. Working in thirds, fold the egg whites into the pumpkin mixture, making sure no large streaks of egg white remain. Pour the mixture into the prepared crust and chill until firm, about 4 hours.

6. Once chilled, prepare the Spiked Whipped Cream. Top the pie and serve immediately.

Sweet Potato Pie

This pie is excellent when it is still just a little warm. Try it with a little cinnamon whipped cream!

INGREDIENTS | SERVES 8

4 medium sweet potatoes, baked until fork-tender

6 ounces cream cheese, room temperature

2 eggs

½ cup packed light brown sugar

2 tablespoons maple syrup

½ teaspoon cinnamon

¼ teaspoon nutmeg

¼ teaspoon cloves

¼ teaspoon allspice

¼ teaspoon ginger

1 teaspoon vanilla

1 (9-inch) pastry crust, unbaked

1. Heat the oven to 425°F.

2. Peel the sweet potatoes and place the flesh into a large bowl. Add the cream cheese and beat until smooth.

3. Add the eggs, light brown sugar, maple syrup, cinnamon, nutmeg, cloves, allspice, ginger, and vanilla and mix until well blended.

4. Pour the sweet potato mixture into the pastry crust and place the pie on a baking sheet. Bake for 10 minutes, then reduce the heat to 350°F and bake for an additional 30 to 40 minutes, or until the filling is puffed and set at the edges, but a little jiggly in the center. Cool to room temperature before serving.

Yams and Sweet Potatoes

While many people use the terms *yam* and *sweet potato* interchangeably, the 2 tubers are very different. Sweet potatoes come in many different varieties. Many stores label sweet potatoes as yams, but yams are a tropical tuber common in Latin cooking and are not commonly sold in most markets.

Sweet Potato Meringue Pie

If you have never had a sweet potato meringue pie, then you are missing out! The rich filling pairs so well with the fluffy meringue, it is hard to resist a second slice!

INGREDIENTS | SERVES 8

3 medium sweet potatoes, baked until fork-tender

¾ cup sugar

1 teaspoon cinnamon

¼ teaspoon salt

¼ teaspoon allspice

¼ teaspoon ground cloves

⅛ teaspoon fresh grated nutmeg

2 eggs

12 ounces evaporated milk

1 (9-inch) pastry crust, unbaked

1 recipe Foolproof Meringue (See Chapter 3)

1. Heat the oven to 425°F.

2. Peel the sweet potatoes and add the flesh to a large bowl. Add the sugar, cinnamon, salt, allspice, cloves, and nutmeg. Whisk until well combined.

3. Add the eggs and evaporated milk and whisk until smooth.

4. Pour the mixture into the pastry crust and place on a baking sheet. Bake in the lower third of the oven for 10 minutes, then reduce the heat to 350°F and bake for an additional 40 to 45 minutes, or until the filling is set at the edges and just slightly wobbly in the center. Remove the pie and increase the oven to 450°F.

5. Prepare the Foolproof Meringue and spread over the top of the hot pie. Return to the oven for 10 to 12 minutes, or until the meringue is golden brown. Cool to room temperature before serving.

Orange Honey Pecan Pie

Sweet honey and fragrant orange give this pecan pie a warm holiday twist.

INGREDIENTS | SERVES 8

2 tablespoons all-purpose flour

½ cup packed light brown sugar

2 eggs

¾ cup honey

¼ teaspoon salt

2 tablespoons butter, melted

1 teaspoon vanilla

1 tablespoon orange zest

1½ cups coarsely chopped pecans

1 (9-inch) Mealy Pie Crust, unbaked
(See Chapter 2)

1. Heat the oven to 350°F.

2. Whisk together the flour and light brown sugar. Add the eggs, honey, salt, butter, vanilla, and orange zest. Whisk until smooth.

3. Spread the pecans into the crust in an even layer. Pour the filling over the pecans and tap the pie gently on the counter to release any air bubbles.

4. Place the pie on a baking sheet and bake for 50 to 60 minutes, or until the filling is puffed all over and set. Cool to room temperature before serving.

Honey and Allergies

Eating locally harvested honey may help reduce your seasonal allergy symptoms. While there is no actual scientific proof that eating local honey can help alleviate allergy symptoms, there is a theory that eating local honey is similar to getting a flu shot. Your body develops a sort of immunity to local pollen, thereby reducing your allergic response.

Gingerbread Custard Pie

The filling of this pie has all the warm spices of gingerbread,
as well as some coconut and chopped walnuts.

INGREDIENTS | SERVES 8

1⅓ cups milk

2 tablespoons all-purpose flour

¾ cup packed dark brown sugar

¼ cup molasses

½ teaspoon cinnamon

¼ teaspoon nutmeg

¼ teaspoon ginger

6 tablespoons butter, softened

2 eggs

¼ teaspoon salt

1 teaspoon vanilla

½ cup chopped walnuts, toasted

½ cup sweetened shredded coconut

1 (9-inch) pastry crust, unbaked

1. Heat the oven to 425°F.

2. In a medium saucepan, bring the milk to a simmer over medium heat. Remove from the heat and cool slightly.

3. In a large bowl, whisk together the flour, dark brown sugar, molasses, cinnamon, nutmeg, ginger, and butter until completely combined.

4. Add the eggs, salt, and vanilla and mix well. Slowly whisk in the warm milk until smooth. Fold in the walnuts and coconut.

5. Pour the mixture into the pastry crust and place on a baking sheet. Bake in the lower third of the oven for 10 minutes, then reduce the heat to 325°F and bake for an additional 30 to 40 minutes, or until the filling is set at the edges and just slightly wobbly in the center. Do not overbake or the custard will become watery. Cool completely before slicing.

CHAPTER 13

Potpies

Sausage and Cheese Potpie

You can use almost any sausage you like here, but hot Italian sausage give this pie a spicy kick!

Bulk Sausage

If your market does not sell bulk or uncased sausage, you have 2 options. First, buy raw link sausage and, with a paring knife, slit the cases down one side and push out the filling. Second, buy ground pork and add your own seasonings. For Italian sausage, add 2 tablespoons of Italian seasoning and crushed red pepper to taste.

1. Heat the oven to 425°F.

2. In a large skillet over medium heat, add the sausage and cook until well browned. Add the salt, paprika, onions, and mushrooms and cook until the vegetables begin to soften, about 5 minutes. Add the garlic and cook until fragrant, about 1 minute.

3. Add the butter and stir until melted, then add the flour evenly over the top and stir until no raw flour remains. Reduce the heat to medium-low.

4. In a small bowl, whisk together the chicken stock and egg yolk. Add the stock to the sausage mixture, stirring constantly, until the liquid begins to thicken.

5. Remove the pan from the heat and add the cheese. Stir until completely melted. Cool for 10 minutes at room temperature.

6. Transfer the sausage mixture into the Mealy Pie Crust. Brush the edge of the Mealy Pie Crust with the beaten egg so that the top crust will adhere. Top with the Flaky Pie Crust and trim the dough to 1 inch of the pan's edge. Tuck the edge of the top crust under the edge of the bottom crust. Crimp the dough using your fingers or a fork. Brush the entire top crust with the beaten egg and cut 4 or 5 slits in the top to vent steam.

7. Place the pie on a baking sheet and bake for 30 minutes, then reduce the heat to 350°F for an additional 30 to 40 minutes, or until the pie is bubbling and the crust is golden brown. Cool for 30 minutes before slicing.

Roasted-Vegetable Potpie

Winter vegetables are perfect for roasting. The roasting process brings out the natural sweetness in the hardy vegetables and makes them wonderfully tender.

INGREDIENTS | SERVES 8

1 butternut squash, peeled, seeded, and cut into ½-inch cubes

4 parsnips, peeled and cut into ½-inch pieces

2 large onions, peeled and cut into ½-inch pieces

4 large carrots, peeled and cut into ½-inch pieces

2 tablespoons olive oil

½ teaspoon salt

¼ teaspoon cinnamon

½ teaspoon fresh cracked black pepper

½ teaspoon thyme

3 tablespoons butter

1 pint button mushrooms, sliced

2 cloves garlic, minced

⅓ cup all-purpose flour

4 cups vegetable broth

½ cup white wine

1 Flaky Pie Crust, rolled out 12" x 15" (See Chapter 2)

1. Heat the oven to 425°F and line a baking sheet with parchment paper.

2. In a large bowl, combine the butternut squash, parsnips, onions, and carrots. Drizzle with the olive oil, salt, cinnamon, pepper, and thyme and mix until the vegetables are evenly coated. Spread on the prepared baking sheet and bake for 50 to 60 minutes, or until the vegetables are fork-tender. Remove from the oven to cool.

3. In a medium saucepan over medium heat, melt the butter until it foams. Add the mushrooms and cook, stirring frequently, until they are tender and golden brown. Add the garlic and cook until fragrant, about 30 seconds.

4. Sprinkle the flour over the top and cook until no raw flour remains, then stir in the vegetable broth and wine and bring to a simmer, stirring constantly. Add the roasted vegetables and cook for 3 minutes.

5. Pour the mixture into a 2½-quart baking dish and top with the Flaky Pie Crust, tucking the edges into the pan. Cut 2 or 3 slits to vent steam, then bake for 35 to 45 minutes, or until the pastry is golden and the filling is bubbling. Cool for 30 minutes before serving.

Cheeseburger Pie

All the best flavors of a cheeseburger can be found in this tasty pie. Garnishing with a drizzle of ketchup and mustard gives this meal a whimsical touch!

INGREDIENTS | SERVES 8

1 (9-inch) pastry crust, unbaked

1 tablespoon butter

1 pound lean ground beef, 85/15 preferred

1 medium onion, chopped

¼ cup dill pickle relish

½ teaspoon salt

½ teaspoon fresh cracked black pepper

2 tablespoons all-purpose flour

½ cup milk

1½ cups shredded Cheddar cheese, divided

¼ cup yellow mustard

¼ cup ketchup

Playing with Flavor

Here are a few easy ways to add extra flavor to your potpies. First, marinate chicken or beef before cooking. Marinating will tenderize the meat and flavor it from the inside out. Second, add a teaspoon or so of a preferred seasoning blend to your potpie in addition to the seasonings in the recipe. Tex-Mex flavored pies are good with taco seasoning, and lemon pepper is always good with chicken!

1. Heat the oven to 375°F.

2. Line the pie crust with parchment paper or a double layer of aluminum foil and add pie weights or dry beans. Bake for 10 to 12 minutes, then remove the paper and weights and bake for an additional 10 to 12 minutes, or until the crust is golden brown all over. Remove from the oven and set aside to cool. Leave the oven on.

3. In a medium skillet over medium heat, melt the butter until it foams. Add the ground beef and cook until well browned. Drain off the excess fat.

4. Return the pan to the heat and add the onion, relish, salt, and pepper. Cook until the onions begin to soften, about 3 minutes, then add the flour and stir until no raw flour remains.

5. Stir in the milk and cook until the mixture begins to thicken. Remove from the heat and allow to cool for 10 minutes.

6. Spread 1 cup of the shredded cheese into the bottom of the prepared crust. Pour the meat mixture over the top, then top the pie with the remaining cheese.

7. Place the pie on a baking sheet and bake for 25 to 35 minutes, or until the cheese is melted and lightly browned. Remove from the oven and let stand for 20 to 30 minutes before serving. Drizzle each slice with a little mustard and ketchup.

Shrimp Gumbo Pie

If you like, you may add ½ cup of frozen okra to this pie. The okra adds an earthy flavor and will thicken the filling slightly.

INGREDIENTS | SERVES 8

2 strips bacon, chopped

1 tablespoon butter

½ teaspoon salt

1 medium onion, diced

1 celery stalk, diced

½ green bell pepper, diced

1 clove garlic, minced

1 teaspoon Cajun seasoning blend

2 tablespoons all-purpose flour

½ cup seafood or chicken broth

1 (10-ounce) can diced tomatoes with green chilies

1 cup frozen sliced okra

1 pound peeled, deveined shrimp

1 (9-inch) Mealy Pie Crust, unbaked (See Chapter 2)

1 egg, beaten

1 (9-inch) Flaky Pie Crust (See Chapter 2)

1. Heat the oven to 425°F.

2. In a large skillet, cook the bacon over medium heat until crisp. Add the butter and melt until it foams, then add the salt, onion, celery, and bell pepper. Cook, stirring frequently, until the vegetables are tender, about 8 minutes.

3. Add the garlic and Cajun seasoning and cook until fragrant, about 30 seconds.

4. Sprinkle the flour over the top of the vegetable mixture and mix until no raw flour remains. Stir in the broth and diced tomatoes with green chilies. Bring to a simmer and cook until the mixture thickens.

5. Add the okra and shrimp and cook for 2 minutes.

6. Pour the shrimp mixture into the Mealy Pie Crust. Brush the edge of the bottom pie crust with the beaten egg so that the top crust will adhere. Top with the Flaky Pie Crust and trim the dough to 1 inch of the pan's edge. Tuck the edge of the top crust under the edge of the bottom crust. Crimp the dough using your fingers or a fork. Brush the entire top crust with the beaten egg and cut 4 or 5 slits in the top to vent steam.

7. Place the pie on a baking sheet and bake for 30 minutes, then reduce the heat to 350°F for an additional 30 to 40 minutes, or until the pie is bubbling and the crust is golden brown. Cool for 30 minutes before slicing.

Steak and Potato Pie

Hearty meat and potato dishes will stick to your ribs, and the leftovers make a satisfying lunch!

INGREDIENTS | SERVES 8

2 pounds chuck roast, cut into 1-inch cubes

1 teaspoon salt

1 teaspoon fresh cracked pepper

½ cup all-purpose flour

4 tablespoons vegetable oil, divided

3 cups beef stock

1 cup water

2 russet potatoes, peeled and cut into ½-inch cubes

2 carrots, peeled and cut into ½-inch pieces

4 tablespoons butter

1 medium onion, diced

2 cloves garlic, minced

2 teaspoons fresh rosemary, chopped

1 teaspoon fresh thyme, chopped

⅓ cup all-purpose flour

1 Flaky Pie Crust, rolled out 12" x 15" (See Chapter 2)

Reverse Potpies

Here is a fun way to serve your potpies. Prepare the fillings on the stove, letting them simmer slowly for about a half hour, until they are thickened. While they simmer, use a large biscuit cutter to create large crust circles. Bake at 350°F until they are golden brown and crisp. When ready to serve, just spoon the filling over the crust.

1. In a large bowl, combine the chuck roast, salt, pepper, and flour until all the meat is evenly coated.

2. In a large pot, heat 2 tablespoons of the vegetable oil over medium-high heat until it shimmers. Add half of the beef to the pot and brown well on all sides. Remove from the pot and add the remaining vegetable oil. Brown the remaining meat, then add the first addition of meat back to the pot.

3. Add the beef stock and water to the pot and bring the mixture to a boil. Reduce the heat to medium-low and cook the meat, covered, for 40 minutes.

4. Add the potatoes and cook for 10 minutes, then add the carrots and cook for 10 additional minutes, or until the potatoes and carrots are tender. Strain the meat and vegetables from the cooking liquid to cool. Reserve the cooking liquid.

5. In a large skillet over medium heat, melt the butter until it foams. Add onion and cook until tender Add the garlic, rosemary, and thyme. Cook until fragrant, about 1 minute. Sprinkle the flour over the top of the mixture and cook until no raw flour remains.

6. Add 1 cup of the reserved cooking liquid to the onion mixture and cook, stirring constantly, until thick. Remove from heat and add the steak and vegetables.

7. Heat the oven to 425°F. Pour the meat mixture into a 2½-quart casserole dish. Top with the pastry crust, tucking the edges of the pastry into the pan, and cut 2 or 3 slits into the pastry to vent steam. Bake for 20 minutes, then reduce the heat to 350°F and bake for an additional 30 to 40 minutes. Cool for 30 minutes before serving.

Chili Pie with a Corn Bread Topping

Thick beef chili is perfect with corn bread, so this all-in-one corn bread–topped chili is perfect for a cold night or the big game!

INGREDIENTS | SERVES 8

¾ pound ground beef, 85/15 preferred
1 tablespoon olive oil
1 medium onion, diced
2 cloves garlic, crushed
1½ cups beef broth
1½ cups vegetable broth
¼ cup chili powder
2 tablespoons smoked paprika
1 teaspoon cumin
½ teaspoon coriander
1 teaspoon ground red pepper
1 chipotle pepper in adobo, chopped
½ cup cold water
⅓ cup masa harina
1 (9-inch) pastry crust, unbaked
½ cup all-purpose flour
½ cup yellow cornmeal
2 tablespoons sugar
1 teaspoon baking powder
¼ teaspoon salt
1 egg, beaten
⅔ cup buttermilk
4 tablespoons butter, melted
½ cup shredded sharp Cheddar cheese

1. In a large pot over medium heat, add the ground beef. Cook, stirring occasionally, until the meat is thoroughly browned. Drain off the excess fat.

2. Add the olive oil, onion, and garlic and cook until the onions are tender and soft, about 10 minutes.

3. Add the beef broth, vegetable broth, chili powder, smoked paprika, cumin, coriander, red pepper, and chipotle pepper. Bring the mixture to a boil, then reduce the heat to medium-low and cook, partially covered, for 1 hour, stirring occasionally.

4. In a small bowl, combine the water and masa harina and mix until smooth. Pour into the chili and whisk until smooth. Increase the heat to medium and bring to a boil. Cook until thick, about 10 minutes.

5. Heat the oven to 375°F.

6. Line the pie crust with parchment paper or a double layer of aluminum foil and add pie weights or dry beans. Bake for 10 to 12 minutes, then remove the paper and weights and bake for an additional 10 to 12 minutes. Remove from the oven and set aside to cool. Leave the oven on.

7. In a medium bowl, whisk together the flour, cornmeal, sugar, baking powder, and salt. In a separate bowl, mix together the egg, buttermilk, and butter. Combine wet ingredients into the dry and mix until just combined.

8. Pour the chili into the prepared crust. Spread the corn bread topping on the chili and sprinkle the shredded cheese over the top. Place on a baking sheet and bake for 30 to 40 minutes. Cool for 30 minutes before serving.

Roast Chicken Potpie

This potpie uses rotisserie chicken from the grocery store to save time, but you can roast your own or use roasted chicken breasts or thighs if you prefer.

INGREDIENTS | SERVES 8

2 tablespoons butter
1 large onion, diced
2 stalks celery, diced
2 carrots, peeled and diced
1 bay leaf
1 teaspoon fresh thyme
½ teaspoon salt
½ teaspoon fresh cracked black pepper
3 cups chicken stock, divided
½ cup all-purpose flour
½ cup heavy cream
1 cooked rotisserie chicken, shredded
1 Flaky Pie Crust, rolled out 12" x 15"
(See Chapter 2)

Chicken, Turkey, Beef, and Ham

Most potpies that call for chicken can be made with any leftover cooked meat you have on hand. Around the holidays, left-over turkey, beef, and ham are common and you can easily substitute them for chicken. When using beef, substitute any chicken broth with beef broth for a richer flavor, and if you are using ham, you may want to reduce the salt in the filling since hams can be quite salty.

1. Heat the oven to 425°F.

2. In a medium saucepan over medium heat, melt the butter until it foams. Add the onion, celery, and carrots and cook until they begin to soften, about 5 minutes.

3. Add the bay leaf, thyme, salt, and pepper and cook for 3 minutes more, or until the herbs are fragrant.

4. Add 1 cup of the chicken stock and bring to a simmer. Cook, covered, for 10 minutes.

5. In a medium bowl, whisk together the remaining chicken stock, flour, and cream until smooth. Slowly pour it into the simmering vegetables, whisking constantly, and cook until it begins to thicken. Turn off the heat and add the shredded chicken. Allow to cool to room temperature.

6. Transfer the chicken mixture into a 2½-quart baking dish. Top with the Flaky Pie Crust, tucking the edges of the crust into the pan, and cut 4 or 5 slits in the top to vent steam.

7. Place the dish on a baking sheet and bake for 20 minutes, then reduce the heat to 350°F for an additional 35 to 45 minutes, or until the pie is bubbling and the crust is golden brown. Cool for 30 minutes before slicing.

Turkey Potpie

This is a great way to use up leftover turkey meat, and the puff pastry top makes this fancy enough for company.

INGREDIENTS | SERVES 8

2 tablespoons butter
1 medium onion, diced
1 stalk celery, diced
1 teaspoon salt
1 teaspoon fresh cracked black pepper
1 bay leaf
½ cup flour
3 cups chicken stock
½ cup half-and-half
1 pound bag frozen peas and carrots
4 cups shredded turkey meat
1 recipe Blitz Puff Pastry, rolled out 12" x 15" (See Chapter 2)

1. Heat the oven to 425°F.

2. In a medium saucepan over medium heat, melt the butter until it foams. Add the onion, celery, salt, and pepper and cook until they begin to soften, about 5 minutes.

3. Add the bay leaf and cook for 10 minutes more. Sprinkle the flour over the top and cook until no raw flour remains.

4. Add the stock and half-and-half and bring to a boil, stirring constantly, then reduce the heat to medium-low and simmer until thickened. Remove the bay leaf and stir in the peas and carrots and the shredded turkey. Cook for 3 minutes, then remove from the heat.

5. Pour the turkey mixture into a 2½-quart casserole dish and cover with the puff pastry, tucking the edges of the pastry into the pan. Bake for 20 minutes, then reduce the heat to 350°F and bake for an additional 30 to 40 minutes, or until the pastry is golden brown and the filling is bubbling. Cool for 30 minutes before serving.

Chicken and Green Chili Potpie

Take a trip to the Southwest with this delicious potpie. Green chilies are not spicy; they just add mellow earthy flavor.

INGREDIENTS | SERVES 8

4 tablespoons butter

1 medium onion, chopped

2 cloves garlic, minced

½ teaspoon cumin

½ teaspoon chili powder

1 (4-ounce) can diced green chilies

½ teaspoon salt

½ teaspoon fresh cracked black pepper

1 medium tomato, seeded and diced

½ cup flour

2 cups chicken broth

1 cup milk, 2% or whole

3 cups cooked shredded chicken

2 cups shredded Monterey jack cheese, divided

1 Flaky Pie Crust, rolled out 12" x 15" (See Chapter 2)

1. Heat the oven to 425°F.

2. In a medium saucepan over medium heat, melt the butter until it foams. Add the onion and cook until it begins to soften, about 5 minutes.

3. Add the garlic, cumin, chili powder, green chilies, salt, pepper, and tomato and cook for 3 minutes more, or until the garlic and spices are fragrant. Sprinkle the flour over the top and cook until no raw flour remains.

4. Add the chicken broth and bring to a simmer. Cook, uncovered, for 10 minutes stirring often.

5. Whisk in the milk and bring back to a simmer, then turn off the heat and add the shredded chicken and 1½ cups of the shredded cheese. Stir well.

6. Transfer the chicken mixture into a 2½-quart baking dish. Top with the pastry crust, tucking the edges into the pan, and cut 2 or 3 slits into the top to vent steam. Place the dish on a baking sheet and bake for 20 minutes, then reduce the heat to 350°F, top the pie with the remaining shredded cheese, and bake for an additional 35 to 45 minutes, or until the pie is bubbling. Cool for 30 minutes before slicing.

Hearty Vegetable Potpie

Who says you need to have meat to make a hearty potpie? This pie delivers satisfying flavors and is guaranteed to fill you up!

INGREDIENTS | SERVES 8

4 tablespoons butter or olive oil

1 pint button mushrooms, cut in half

1 pint crimini mushrooms, cut in half

1 large onion, diced

½ teaspoon salt

½ teaspoon freshly cracked black pepper

2 russet potatoes, peeled and cut into ½-inch pieces

2 carrots, peeled and diced

2 cups broccoli florets, cut into ½-inch pieces

2 cups cauliflower florets, cut into ½-inch pieces

4 cups vegetable broth

½ cup all-purpose flour

1 recipe Blitz Puff Pastry, rolled out 12" x 15" (See Chapter 2)

1. Heat the oven to 425°F.

2. In a large skillet over medium heat, melt the butter or oil until it foams. Add the mushrooms, onions, salt, and pepper. Cook until softened, about 10 minutes.

3. Add the potatoes and carrots and cook, stirring frequently, until the carrots and potatoes become tender, about 10 minutes.

4. Add the broccoli, cauliflower, and 3 cups of the vegetable broth. Bring to a boil, then reduce to a simmer and cook for 5 minutes.

5. Mix the remaining vegetable broth with the flour until smooth. Stir into the vegetable mixture and cook until it thickens.

6. Pour the vegetable mixture into a 2½-quart casserole dish and cover with the puff pastry, tucking the edges of the pastry into the pan. Bake for 20 minutes, then reduce the heat to 350°F and bake for an additional 30 to 40 minutes, or until the pastry is golden brown and the filling is bubbling. Cool for 30 minutes before serving.

Creamy Seafood Pie

Feel free to use any combination of shellfish you prefer in this recipe.
This pie would also be lovely with flaked white fish or salmon.

INGREDIENTS | SERVES 8

2 strips bacon, chopped

4 tablespoons butter

1 medium russet potato, peeled and cut into ½-inch pieces

1 medium onion, diced

1 cup sliced mushrooms

2 cloves garlic, minced

½ teaspoon thyme

½ teaspoon smoked paprika

½ teaspoon salt

½ teaspoon fresh cracked black pepper

⅓ cup all-purpose flour

2 cups milk

1 cup half-and-half

1 pound peeled, deveined shrimp

1 pound fresh bay scallops

12 ounces lump crabmeat, picked through for shells

1 recipe Biscuit Topping (See Chapter 3)

2 tablespoons melted butter

Buying Seafood

Here are some tips for selecting the best seafood. First, smell it. Fresh seafood has a neutral smell. If there is even a hint of fishiness, select something else. Second, touch it. It should feel firm and plump. If the seafood feels mushy, soft, or watery, discard. Finally, look at it. Seafood should be glossy but not wet and be pale in color. If there is any slime or off colors, it is not fresh.

1. Heat the oven to 375°F.

2. In a medium saucepan, cook the chopped bacon over medium heat until crisp. Drain the bacon on paper towels.

3. Return the pan to the heat and add the butter. Once the butter foams, add the potatoes, onions, and mushrooms. Cook, stirring constantly, until the potatoes become tender, about 10 minutes.

4. Add the garlic, thyme, paprika, salt, and pepper and cook until fragrant, about 1 minute.

5. Sprinkle the flour over the vegetable mixture and cook until no raw flour remains. Slowly stir in the milk and half-and-half and bring the mixture to a simmer, stirring constantly, until it begins to thicken.

6. Once it thickens, stir in the shrimp, scallops, and crabmeat. Cook for 2 minutes, then remove the pan from the heat and cool slightly. Stir in the crisp bacon.

7. Pour the seafood filling into a 2½-quart baking dish. Top with the biscuit topping and brush the biscuits with the melted butter. Bake for 30 to 40 minutes, or until the biscuits are brown and the filling is bubbling. Cook for 30 minutes before serving.

Cheesy Hash Brown Beef Pie

This pie combines a creamy beef filling topped with a cheesy hash brown topping for a meal that will be a favorite with kids and adults.

INGREDIENTS | SERVES 8

1 Mealy Pie Crust, rolled out 12" x 15" (See Chapter 2)

1 tablespoon oil

1 pound ground beef

1 medium onion, chopped

2 cloves garlic, minced

½ teaspoon salt

½ teaspoon pepper

¼ cup flour

2 cups milk

½ teaspoon hot sauce

1 cup frozen hash brown potatoes, thawed

1 cup shredded Cheddar cheese

1. Heat the oven to 375°F.

2. Line a 2½-quart casserole dish with the pastry crust. Cover with plastic and chill until ready to bake.

3. In a medium skillet over medium heat, add the oil. Once the oil shimmers, add the ground beef and cook until well browned. Drain off any excess fat.

4. Add the onion to the pan and cook until it softens, about 5 minutes, then add the garlic and cook until fragrant, about 1 minute.

5. Season with salt and pepper, then sprinkle the flour evenly over the meat. Cook until no dry flour remains, about 3 minutes.

6. Slowly add the milk, stirring constantly, until smooth. Add the hot sauce and bring the mixture to a simmer. Once it thickens, remove from the heat to cool slightly.

7. Pour the meat mixture into the prepared dish and top with the hash browns and cheese. Bake for 35 to 45 minutes, or until the cheese and hash browns are bubbling and brown. Cool for 20 minutes before serving.

Cheesy Chicken Potpie

This cheesy chicken pie is a kid pleaser. Don't be fooled—it is not just for kids. It also pleases adults!

INGREDIENTS | SERVES 8

4 medium chicken breasts
½ teaspoon salt
½ teaspoon fresh cracked pepper
½ teaspoon smoked paprika
4 tablespoons butter
1 medium onion, diced
2 stalks celery, diced
2 carrots, peeled and diced
2 cloves garlic, minced
½ cup flour
3 cups milk
4 ounces cream cheese, room temperature
4 ounces shredded Cheddar cheese
1 Flaky Pie Crust, rolled out 12" x 15" (See Chapter 2)
2 tablespoons Parmesan cheese

The Ease of the Freezer

Take advantage of all your freezer has to offer. Double your potpie filling, then cool half and freeze in a large container. When you are ready to use it, just thaw it overnight in the refrigerator. Then all you have to do is prepare a crust, fill, and bake! Also, save time later by chopping extra onions, carrots, and celery. You can freeze them in plastic bags for up to 3 months, saving time on busy days!

1. Heat the oven to 425°F and line a baking sheet with aluminum foil.

2. Season the chicken breast with the salt, pepper, and paprika. Place the chicken on the prepared baking sheet and roast for 25 to 35 minutes, when the juices run clear when cut or until the chicken reaches an internal temperature of 160°F. Rest for 10 minutes, then chop the chicken into ½-inch pieces. Set aside.

3. In a medium saucepan over medium heat, melt the butter until it foams. Add the onion, celery, and carrots. Cook until the vegetables are tender, about 8 minutes.

4. Add the garlic and cook until fragrant, about 30 seconds. Sprinkle the flour over the top of the mixture and cook until no raw flour remains.

5. Stir in the milk and bring to a simmer, stirring constantly, until it begins to thicken. Reduce the heat to low and add the cream cheese. Stir until melted, then add the Cheddar cheese. Shut off the heat and stir until melted. Stir in the chicken.

6. Pour the chicken mixture into a 2½-quart baking dish. Top with the pastry crust, tucking the edges of the pastry into the pan. Sprinkle the top with Parmesan cheese and cut 2 or 3 slits into the pastry to vent steam. Bake for 20 minutes, then reduce the heat to 350°F and bake for an additional 30 to 40 minutes, or until the pastry is golden brown and the filling is bubbling. Cool for 30 minutes before serving.

Personal Chicken Potpies

These individual pies are perfect for a party or anytime you want a little bowl of comfort.

INGREDIENTS | SERVES 4

1 tablespoon butter

1 medium onion, diced

1 stalk celery, diced

1 carrot, peeled and diced

1 bay leaf

¼ teaspoon fresh thyme

¼ teaspoon poultry seasoning

¼ teaspoon salt

¼ teaspoon fresh cracked black pepper

1½ cups chicken stock, divided

¼ cup all-purpose flour

½ cup sour cream

1 rotisserie chicken breast, shredded

1 egg, beaten

1 recipe Blitz Puff Pastry, cut into 4 squares (See Chapter 2)

1. Heat the oven to 425°F.

2. In a medium saucepan over medium heat, melt the butter until it foams. Add the onion, celery, and carrots and cook until they begin to soften, about 5 minutes.

3. Add the bay leaf, thyme, poultry seasoning, salt, and pepper and cook for 3 minutes more, or until the herbs are fragrant.

4. Add half of the chicken stock and bring to a simmer. Cook, covered, for 10 minutes.

5. In a medium bowl, whisk together the remaining chicken stock, flour, and sour cream until smooth. Slowly pour it into the simmering vegetables, whisking constantly, and cook until it begins to thicken. Turn off the heat and add the shredded chicken. Allow to cool to room temperature.

6. Transfer the chicken mixture into 4 oven-safe bowls. Brush the edge of each bowl with beaten egg and top with the pastry, letting the edges hang over the sides of the bowl.

7. Place the dishes on a baking sheet and bake for 10 minutes, then reduce the heat to 350°F for an additional 15 to 20 minutes, or until the pie is bubbling and the crust is golden brown and crisp. Cool for 10 minutes before serving.

Fruity Chicken Potpie

Golden raisins and apples add a bit of refreshing sweetness to this savory potpie.

INGREDIENTS | SERVES 8

2 Flaky Pie Crusts, rolled out 12" x 15" (See Chapter 2)

2 tablespoons butter

1 large onion, diced

1 medium Granny Smith apple, peeled, cored, and chopped

1 cup golden raisins

1 bay leaf

½ teaspoon fresh thyme

¼ teaspoon cinnamon

¼ teaspoon cayenne

½ teaspoon salt

½ teaspoon fresh cracked black pepper

3 cups chicken stock, divided

½ cup all-purpose flour

½ cup heavy cream

2 cooked chicken breasts, shredded

Chicken Bouillon

If you do not have chicken stock or broth on hand, you can substitute chicken bouillon and water. Since bouillon tends be fairly salty, do not season the filling with salt until it is ready to go into the oven. The last thing you want is a potpie so salty no one can eat it.

1. Heat the oven to 425°F.

2. Line a 2½-quart casserole dish with one pastry crust. Cover with plastic and chill until ready to bake.

3. In a medium saucepan over medium heat, melt the butter until it foams. Add the onion and apple and cook until they begin to soften, about 5 minutes.

4. Add the raisins, bay leaf, thyme, cinnamon, cayenne, salt, and pepper and cook for 3 minutes more, or until the herbs are fragrant. Add 1 cup of the chicken stock and bring to a simmer. Cook, covered, for 10 minutes.

5. In a medium bowl, whisk together the remaining chicken stock, flour, and cream until smooth. Slowly pour it into the simmering vegetables, whisking constantly, and cook until it begins to thicken. Turn off the heat and add the shredded chicken. Allow to cool to room temperature.

6. Transfer the chicken mixture into the prepared baking dish. Top with the remaining pastry crust, tucking the edges of the crust into the pan, and cut 4 or 5 slits in the top to vent steam.

7. Place the dish on a baking sheet and bake for 20 minutes, then reduce the heat to 350°F for an additional 35 to 45 minutes, or until the pie is bubbling and the crust is golden brown. Cool for 30 minutes before slicing.

Tex-Mex Taco Pie

Queso quesadilla is a mild-flavored, white Mexican melting cheese. If it is not available, just double the Colby-Jack cheese or substitute Cheddar if you prefer.

INGREDIENTS | SERVES 8

1 Mealy Pie Crust, rolled out 12" x 15" (See Chapter 2)

1 tablespoon butter

1 medium onion, chopped

2 cloves garlic, minced

1 pound ground beef

1 packet taco seasoning

1 (10-ounce) can diced tomatoes with green chilies

½ teaspoon kosher salt

1 cup evaporated milk

1 egg

1 cup shredded Cheddar cheese, divided

½ cup shredded queso quesadilla cheese, divided

½ cup shredded Colby-Jack cheese, divided

½ cup crushed tortilla chips

1 cup sour cream, for garnish

1. Heat the oven to 375°F.

2. Line a 2½-quart casserole dish with the pastry crust. Cover with plastic and chill until ready to bake.

3. In a large skillet over medium heat, melt the butter until it foams. Add the onion and cook until tender, about 5 minutes.

4. Add the garlic and cook until fragrant, about 30 seconds.

5. Add the ground beef and cook until well browned. Stir in the taco seasoning, tomatoes with green chilies, and salt. Cook, stirring frequently, for 10 minutes, or until the mixture thickens and no liquid remains. Reduce the heat to medium-low.

6. In a small bowl, whisk together the evaporated milk and egg until well combined. Stir the egg mixture into the meat mixture and cook, stirring constantly, until the mixture thickens slightly and is hot.

7. Add ¾ cup of the Cheddar cheese along with ¼ cup each of the queso quesadilla and Colby-Jack cheese. Turn off the heat and stir until melted.

8. Pour the meat mixture into the prepared casserole dish. Top with the tortilla chips and remaining cheese. Bake for 35 to 45 minutes, or until the cheese is golden brown and the mixture is bubbling. Cool for 30 minutes before serving.

Tuna Noodle Potpie

*This pie takes the classic tuna noodle casserole to the next level
with a layer of crisp puff pastry baked on top!*

INGREDIENTS | SERVES 8

2 tablespoons butter

1 medium onion, chopped

1 carrot, peeled and chopped

1 stalk celery, chopped

¼ cup flour

2 cups milk

1 cup frozen peas

12 ounces canned tuna, drained

2 ounces egg noodles, cooked and cooled

1 egg, beaten

1 recipe Blitz Puff Pastry, rolled out 12" x 15" (See Chapter 2)

1. Heat the oven to 425°F.

2. In a medium skillet over medium heat, melt the butter until it foams. Add the onion, carrots, and celery and cook until softened, about 5 minutes. Sprinkle the flour over the top and cook, stirring constantly, until no raw flour remains.

3. Slowly add the milk, stirring constantly, until smooth. Bring the mixture to a simmer and allow it to thicken.

4. Once thick, add the peas, tuna, and cooked noodles. Remove the pan from the heat and allow it to cool slightly.

5. Transfer the mixture to a 2½-quart baking dish. Brush the beaten egg around the edge of the dish and lay the puff pastry over the top, trimming the edges so that they hang 1 inch over the side of the dish.

6. Bake for 20 minutes, then reduce the heat to 350°F for an additional 25 to 30 minutes, or until the filling is bubbling and the pastry is golden brown and crisp. Cool for 20 minutes before serving.

CHAPTER 14

International Flavors

Bánh Patê Sô (Hot Meat Pie)

This recipe is for delectable Vietnamese meat pies cooked in buttery puff pastry.

¼ ounce dry wood ear (black fungus) mushrooms

½ cup boiling water

¼ cup soaked bean thread noodles, lightly chopped

12 ounces ground pork

1 medium onion, chopped

1 tablespoon fish sauce or soy sauce

1 teaspoon fresh cracked black pepper

½ teaspoon sugar

2 recipes Blitz Puff Pastry (See Chapter 2), rolled out ⅛ inch thick and cut into 16 squares

1 egg, beaten

French Influences

The French occupation of Vietnam had a lasting influence on Vietnamese cuisine. The Bánh mì sandwich, for example, is served on baguette-style bread. French influences on Vietnamese cuisine can also be seen in a variety of stews and pastries made with puff pastry.

1. In a small bowl, combine the dry mushrooms with the hot water. Allow to stand for 10 minutes, then drain well and finely chop.

2. In a medium bowl, mix the chopped mushrooms with the noodles, then add the pork, onion, fish sauce, pepper, and sugar. Cover and chill for 1 hour.

3. Heat the oven to 400°F and line a baking sheet with parchment paper.

4. Evenly divide the filling among the pastry squares, then brush beaten egg along the edges. Fold over, making sure the filling does not come out of the pastry, and crimp with a fork to seal. With scissors or a sharp paring knife, snip a small vent in the top of each pastry, then brush the pastries lightly with egg.

5. Bake for 15 to 20 minutes, or until the pastry is puffed, golden brown on top and bottom, and the filling reaches 160°F. Cool slightly before serving.

Bakewell Tart

Creamy almond filling tops tart raspberry jam in this delicious teatime treat.

INGREDIENTS | SERVES 8

1 cup coarsely chopped almonds, blanched preferred

2 tablespoons all-purpose flour

⅔ cup sugar

9 tablespoons butter, room temperature

½ teaspoon almond extract

1 egg

1 egg white

1 (10-inch) Short Crust for Tarts, unbaked (See Chapter 2)

½ cup raspberry jam

Powdered sugar, for garnish

1. Add the almonds and flour to the work bowl of a food processor and pulse a few times to break up the almonds.

2. Mix in sugar, butter, and almond extract. Blend until smooth, then add the egg and egg white and blend well. Transfer filling to a bowl, then cover and chill for at least 3 hours.

3. Heat the oven to 350°F.

4. Line the tart pastry with parchment paper or a double layer of aluminum foil and add pie weights or dry beans. Bake for 12 minutes, then remove the paper and weights and bake for an additional 10 to 15 minutes, or until the crust is golden brown all over. Remove from the oven and set aside to cool. Leave the oven on.

5. Spread the jam over the base of the tart shell. Spoon the almond filling carefully over the jam and spread so that it is smooth. Place the tart on a baking sheet and bake for 40 to 50 minutes, or until golden and set in the center. Cool the tart completely on a rack before unmolding. Serve with a dusting of powdered sugar.

Banoffi Pie

This pie, the invention of Ian Dowding and the Hungry Monk restaurant in England, is a delicious blend of bananas, rich toffee, and whipped cream.

INGREDIENTS | SERVES 8

1 (14-ounce) can sweetened condensed milk
1 (9-inch) pastry crust, unbaked
1 pint heavy cream
1 teaspoon instant coffee
½ teaspoon vanilla
¼ cup powdered sugar
5 ripe bananas, sliced into ¼-inch slices

Toffee Shortcut

If you are unsure about boiling the can of sweetened condensed milk, there is another option. Many grocery stores carry, in their Mexican food sections, canned dolce de leche. It has all the delicious flavor of the kind you make yourself without all the work!

1. Heat the oven to 275°F.

2. In a deep, oven-safe pot, place the unopened can of sweetened condensed milk. Fill the pot with water so that the can is completely covered and bring the pot to a boil. Once boiling, cover with a tight-fitting lid and carefully transfer the pot to the oven. Be sure the can is still fully covered with water, and add more if needed. Bake for 3½ hours, then remove the can from the pot and cool to room temperature on a wire rack.

3. Heat the oven to 350°F.

4. Line the pastry crust with parchment paper or a double layer of aluminum foil and add pie weights or dry beans. Bake for 12 to 15 minutes, then remove the paper and weights and bake for an additional 12 to 15 minutes, or until the crust is golden brown all over. Remove from the oven and set aside to cool.

5. In a large bowl, add the cream, instant coffee, vanilla, and powdered sugar. Whip until the cream forms stiff peaks.

6. To assemble, begin by carefully spreading the condensed milk into the bottom of the crust. Layer the sliced bananas over the toffee, then spread the whipped cream over top. Chill for 1 hour before serving.

Cornish Pasties

If you are looking for a hearty, easy-to-transport meal look no further.
These filling pies are great for picnics, camping, or tailgating.

INGREDIENTS | SERVES 8

2 Lard Pie Crusts (See Chapter 2), rolled into 2⅛-inch thick, 12-inch squares

12 ounces lean sirloin steak, cut into ½-inch cubes

1 teaspoon salt

1 teaspoon fresh cracked pepper

1 small turnip, peeled and diced into ⅛-inch pieces

1 small russet potato, peeled and diced into ⅛-inch pieces

1 small onion, chopped

½ teaspoon fresh chopped thyme

1 tablespoon butter, melted

1 egg, beaten

Suet

Suet is raw beef or mutton fat from the kidneys and loin. In England suet is used for a variety of dishes such as Christmas puddings, mincemeat, and steak and kidney pie. If you can locate suet, you can use it for part or all of the fat in pastry crusts for savory British pies for a more authentic, robust flavor.

1. Cut each pastry into 4 squares, at least 6 inches square. Cover with plastic and chill for 10 minutes.

2. In a large bowl, combine the steak, salt, pepper, turnip, potato, onion, thyme, and melted butter. Mix well.

3. Heat the oven to 450°F and line a baking sheet with parchment paper.

4. Divide the filling evenly among the pastries. Brush the edges of the pastry with beaten egg, then fold over and crimp the edges with your fingers or a fork. Brush the tops of each pastry with the beaten egg.

5. Place the pastries on the prepared baking sheet and bake for 15 minutes, then turn the heat down to 350°F and bake for 40 to 50 minutes, or until the pastry is golden brown on the top and bottom. Serve warm or cold.

Pork Mince Pie

Traditional British pork pies are made with finely minced pork shoulder, bacon, and pork jelly. This version is streamlined with easy-to-find ingredients.

Talk to Your Butcher

Take advantage of your grocery store's meat and seafood department. Looking for a particular cut of meat that they do not have? Ask if they can special order it for you. The butcher can also grind roasts and steaks for soup and chili, cut and trim steaks, and even steam shellfish!

1. On a lightly floured surface, roll out one of the pastry circles until it is approximately 14 inches wide. Line an 8-inch springform pan with the pastry sheet. Do not trim away any excess pastry. Wrap with plastic and chill until ready to fill.

2. In the work bowl of a food processor, add the chopped bacon. Pulse until the bacon is finely minced. Add the ground pork, sage, mace, allspice, salt, and pepper. Pulse 10 times or until well mixed.

3. Spread the pork mixture into the lined pan. Brush the edge of the pastry with the beaten egg and lay the second pastry circle on the top. Trim the pastry so that it has a 1-inch border, then fold the border in toward the top of the pie and crimp well. With a 1-inch metal pastry cutter, punch a hole out of the center of the pastry. Remove the pastry, but leave the cutter in the top of the pie. Cover and chill for 1 hour.

4. Heat the oven to 400°F.

5. Once chilled, brush the top of the pie with beaten egg and place the pie on a baking sheet. Bake for 30 minutes, then reduce the heat to 350°F and bake for an additional 30 to 45 minutes, or until the pastry is golden brown and the pork filling reaches an internal temperature of 160°F. Remove from the oven, remove the metal cutter from the top of the pie, and cool for 2 hours.

Pork Mince Pie

(CONTINUED)

6. In a small bowl, combine the pork stock with the gelatin. Allow to sit for 10 minutes, then warm the mixture in a small pot or in the microwave until warm and thoroughly melted.

7. With a funnel, carefully pour the melted gelatin mixture into the vent in the center of the pie until the liquid fills the pie but does not overflow. You may have extra gelatin mixture. Refrigerate for 4 hours or overnight before serving. Serve cold or at room temperature.

Hong Kong–Style Egg Custard Tarts

*This dim sum favorite combines a puff pastry base with a creamy egg custard filling.
You can use a short crust tart pastry instead of puff pastry if you prefer.*

INGREDIENTS | SERVES 12

1 recipe Blitz Puff Pastry, rolled out
⅛-inch thick (See Chapter 2)

⅓ cup sugar

1 cup water

5 eggs

2 egg yolks

⅔ cup evaporated milk

½ teaspoon vanilla

1. Cut 12 (3-inch) circles from the pastry. If you cannot get 12 from the pastry, fold the scraps and reroll. Press the circles carefully into the cups of a standard cupcake pan. Cover with plastic and chill.

2. In a medium saucepan, combine the sugar and water. Bring to a boil, making sure the sugar is completely dissolved. Remove from the heat and cool to room temperature.

3. Heat the oven to 375°F.

4. In a large bowl, whisk the eggs and egg yolks until smooth. Add the sugar syrup, evaporated milk, and vanilla and mix until well combined.

5. Pour the egg mixture through a strainer into the chilled tart shells.

6. Bake for 15 to 20 minutes, or until the pastry is golden brown and the custard filling is puffed, but still slightly wobbly in the center. Cool to room temperature before serving.

Chinese Fried Beef Pancakes

While these are called pancakes, they more closely resemble a calzone or empanada that is griddled rather than baked or deep-fried.

INGREDIENTS | SERVES 8

2 cups all-purpose flour

1 cup water

½ teaspoon salt

¾ pound ground beef

1 egg, beaten

2 teaspoons cornstarch

1 tablespoon soy sauce

2 teaspoons Chinese cooking wine, or cooking sherry

1 teaspoon fresh grated ginger

2 green onions, finely chopped

½ teaspoon toasted sesame oil

1 clove garlic, minced

1 tablespoon water

¼ cup vegetable oil, divided

A Simple Dipping Sauce

Next time you serve an Asian-inspired meal and need a dipping sauce, give this recipe a try. Simply combine ½ cup soy sauce with ½ teaspoon toasted sesame oil, 1 tablespoon rice wine vinegar, 1 finely chopped green onion, 1 teaspoon each minced garlic and ginger, and ½ teaspoon sugar. Mix well and refrigerate for 1 hour before serving.

1. In a medium bowl, combine the flour, water, and salt until it forms a smooth ball. Knead on a lightly floured surface until smooth. Place the dough back in the bowl, cover with plastic, and allow it to rest for 1 hour.

2. In a medium bowl, combine the beef, egg, cornstarch, soy sauce, cooking wine, ginger, green onions, sesame oil, and garlic. Mix until combined, but do not overmix. Cover with plastic and chill for 30 minutes.

3. Divide the dough into 8 pieces. Roll each piece into an 8-inch circle.

4. Divide the filling between the wrappers. Brush half the edge of each wrapper with water and fold in half, pinching the edges until they are well sealed. Cover with plastic and rest at room temperature for 15 minutes.

5. Once rested, heat a large nonstick skillet over medium heat. Add half of the oil and once it shimmers, add 4 of the pies. Cover with a lid and cook for 2 to 3 minutes, or until the pies are golden brown. Turn the pies and cook, covered, for an additional 2 minutes. Remove the lid and cook for 2 to 3 minutes on each side again to crisp. The pies should reach an internal temperature of 160°F and the beef should not be pink.

6. Remove from the pan and transfer to a baking sheet in a warm oven. Repeat this process with the remaining pies. Enjoy warm.

Chinese Curry Beef Pie

This is an East-meets-West fusion of British meat pie and Chinese curried beef. It is popular in pubs and lovely with a tall glass of beer!

1. In a large bowl, combine the beef, soy sauce, and sugar.

2. Heat a large skillet over medium heat and heat the oil until it shimmers. Add the meat and cook until well browned. Remove the beef, reserving the drippings.

3. Add the onions and curry powder to the pan. Cook until the onions are softened, about 5 minutes, then add the potatoes and cook for 5 minutes, stirring constantly.

4. Add the water and bring to a boil. Cover with a lid and cook for 10 minutes. Remove the lid and cook until no water remains, about 3 minutes.

5. Return the beef to the pan along with the peas. Cook until the peas are tender. Remove the pan from the heat and cool to room temperature.

6. Heat the oven to 450°F.

7. Spoon the cooled filling into the pastry crust. Brush the edge of the bottom pie crust with the beaten egg so that the top crust will adhere. Top with the Flaky Pie Crust and trim the dough to 1 inch of the pan's edge. Tuck the edge of the top crust under the edge of the bottom crust. Crimp the dough using your fingers or a fork. Brush the entire top crust with the beaten egg and cut 4 or 5 slits in the top to vent steam.

8. Place the pie on a baking sheet and bake for 20 minutes, then reduce the heat to 350°F and bake for an additional 25 to 35 minutes, or until the pie is golden brown and the filling is bubbling. Cool for 30 minutes before serving.

Canadian Butter Tarts

These tarts have a buttery, somewhat runny filling that is studded with plump raisins.

INGREDIENTS | SERVES 6

Nonstick cooking spray

2 pastry crusts cut into 12 (4-inch) circles

⅔ cup dark raisins

¾ cup plus 2 tablespoons packed light brown sugar

2 tablespoons corn syrup

1 egg

1 tablespoon butter, melted

½ teaspoon vanilla

1. Heat the oven to 425°F and spray a standard cupcake pan with nonstick cooking spray.

2. Line each cup with the pastry circles, making sure not to pull the pastry. Divide the raisins evenly between the pastries. Cover with plastic and chill for 10 minutes.

3. In a medium bowl, whisk together the light brown sugar, corn syrup, egg, butter, and vanilla until smooth.

4. Fill each pastry cup ⅔ full with the brown sugar mixture. You may have extra.

5. Place the tarts on a baking sheet and bake for 5 minutes, then reduce the heat to 350°F and bake for 10 to 12 minutes, or until the pastry is golden and the tarts are browned on the top. Cool completely in the pan before serving.

Indian Chicken Korma Potpie

This pie is filled with a spicy chicken curry and topped with crisp, flaky pastry.
The warm spices and creamy curry sauce make this a hit!

INGREDIENTS | SERVES 8

1 pound boneless, skinless chicken thighs, cut into ½-inch pieces

2 tablespoons garam masala, divided

¼ cup vegetable oil

1 large onion, chopped

3 cloves garlic, minced

1 tablespoon fresh ginger, peeled and minced

1 teaspoon cumin

1 teaspoon coriander

½ teaspoon turmeric

½ teaspoon cardamom

1 teaspoon cinnamon

1 teaspoon red pepper flakes, or to taste

1 teaspoon kosher salt

1 cup Greek-style or strained yogurt

1 cup milk

1 tablespoon sugar

1 tablespoon lemon juice

¼ cup heavy cream

1 tablespoon chopped cilantro

1 (9-inch) Mealy Pie Crust, unbaked (See Chapter 2)

1 egg, beaten

1 (9-inch) Flaky Pie Crust (See Chapter 2)

1. In a medium bowl, combine the chicken and the garam masala. Toss to coat evenly, then allow it to stand at room temperature for 30 minutes.

2. In a large skillet, heat the oil over medium heat until it shimmers. Add half of the chicken to the pan and cook until golden brown on each side. Remove to a separate dish and repeat with the remaining chicken.

3. Add the onion, garlic, and ginger to the pan and cook until fragrant, about 2 minutes. Add the cumin, coriander, turmeric, cardamom, cinnamon, red pepper, and salt. Mix the spices with the onion mixture and cook about 5 minutes.

4. Return the chicken to the pan along with the yogurt, milk, and sugar. Stir well, then reduce the heat to medium-low and cook for 10 minutes, or until slightly thickened. Turn off the heat and stir in the lemon juice, cream, and cilantro. Cool for 10 minutes.

5. Heat the oven to 450°F.

6. Spoon the cooled filling into the Mealy Pie Crust. Brush the edge of the bottom pie crust with the beaten egg so that the top crust will adhere. Top with the Flaky Pie Crust and trim the dough to 1 inch of the pan's edge. Tuck the edge of the top crust under the edge of the bottom crust. Crimp the dough using your fingers or a fork. Brush the entire top crust with the beaten egg and cut 4 or 5 slits in the top to vent steam.

7. Place the pie on a baking sheet and bake for 20 minutes, then reduce the heat to 350°F and bake for an additional 25 to 35 minutes. Cool for 30 minutes before serving.

Butter Pie

This potato and onion pie originates in Lancashire, England, where it was traditionally served on Fridays when meat was not served.

INGREDIENTS | SERVES 8

3 large russet potatoes, peeled and cut into ¼-inch slices

1 (9-inch) Mealy Pie Crust, unbaked (See Chapter 2)

1 large onion, peeled, cut in half, and then cut into ¼-inch slices

4 tablespoons butter

1 teaspoon salt

½ teaspoon pepper

1 egg, beaten

1 (9-inch) Flaky Pie Crust (See Chapter 2)

1. Heat the oven to 375°F.

2. In a large pot, add the sliced potatoes. Fill the pot with water so that the potatoes are just covered. Bring the pot to the boil and cook for about 5 minutes, or until the potatoes are beginning to soften but are still firm in the center. Drain and cool.

3. In the bottom of the Mealy Pie Crust, layer in the potato slices. Break apart the onions and spread them over the potatoes. Dot the butter over the onions and season with the salt and pepper.

4. Brush the edge of the bottom pie crust with the beaten egg so that the top crust will adhere. Top with the Flaky Pie Crust and trim the dough to 1 inch of the pan's edge. Tuck the edge of the top crust under the edge of the bottom crust. Crimp the dough using your fingers or a fork. Brush the entire top crust with the beaten egg and cut 4 or 5 slits in the top to vent steam.

5. Place the pie on a baking sheet and bake for 35 to 45 minutes, or until the pie is golden brown and the filling is fork-tender. Cool for 30 minutes before serving.

Mexican Hot Chocolate Pie

Mexican hot chocolate is a blend of chilies, vanilla, chocolate, and spices.
This rich pie has all those flavors baked into a fudgy filling.

INGREDIENTS | SERVES 8

2 ounces unsweetened chocolate, chopped

2 tablespoons butter

2 eggs

2 egg yolks

½ cup sugar

¾ cup corn syrup

1 teaspoon vanilla

½ teaspoon chile powder

½ teaspoon cinnamon

1 tablespoon cocoa powder

1 (9-inch) pastry crust, unbaked

Chile Powder Versus Chili Powder

Chile powder refers to the dried, ground fruit of chili pepper plants that are not blended with other spices. Chili powder, on the other hand, is a blend of dried chilies along with other spices and herbs that is used primarily for making chili or as a seasoning on meats and chicken.

1. Heat the oven to 375°F.

2. In a double boiler, melt the chocolate and butter until smooth. Remove from the heat.

3. In a large bowl, combine the eggs, egg yolks, sugar, and corn syrup.

4. Add in the melted chocolate, vanilla, chile powder, cinnamon, and cocoa powder and whisk until well combined.

5. Pour the mixture into the pastry crust and place on a baking sheet. Bake for 30 to 35 minutes, or until the filling is just set. Serve slightly warm.

Zwiebelkuchen (German Onion Pie)

This creamy, oniony pie makes a delicious meal in itself but is also good with grilled bratwurst and red cabbage.

INGREDIENTS | SERVES 8

6 strips thick-cut bacon, chopped

2 large onions, peeled and cut into ¼-inch rings

1 cup sour cream

2 eggs

1 tablespoon flour

½ teaspoon salt

½ teaspoon fresh cracked black pepper

¼ teaspoon nutmeg

1 (9-inch) pastry crust, unbaked

1. Heat the oven to 425°F.

2. In a large skillet over medium heat, cook the bacon until crisp. Remove the bacon from the pan to drain and reserve the fat.

3. Add the onions to the pan and cook until they soften and become translucent. Do not brown. Remove the pan from the heat and cool slightly.

4. In a large bowl, whisk together the sour cream, eggs, flour, salt, pepper, and nutmeg until smooth. Stir in the onions and bacon, then pour into the pastry crust.

5. Place the pie on a baking sheet and bake for 10 minutes, then reduce the heat to 350°F and cook for an additional 35 to 45 minutes, or until the top of the pie is golden brown. Cool for 30 minutes before serving.

Shepherd's Pie

While this pie does not have a pastry crust, it is topped with a layer of fluffy mashed potato that gets slightly crisp on the top as it bakes.

INGREDIENTS | SERVES 8

3 pounds russet potatoes, peeled and cut into ½-inch cubes

2 tablespoons butter, melted

1 teaspoon salt

⅓ cup half-and-half, room temperature

½ cup sharp Cheddar cheese

2 tablespoons butter

2 ribs celery, chopped

1 medium onion, peeled and chopped

2 medium carrots, peeled and chopped

2 cloves garlic, minced

½ teaspoon thyme

½ teaspoon fresh cracked black pepper

2 pounds ground beef or lamb

2 tablespoons all-purpose flour

½ cup beef stock

1 tablespoon Worcestershire sauce

1 cup frozen peas

Nonstick cooking spray

The Meat Makes a Difference

Traditionally shepherd's pie is made with minced lamb, since lamb is a very popular and very affordable source of protein in the United Kingdom. In the United States, it is usually made with ground beef since beef is more readily available and more popular. What you may not know is that a shepherd's pie made with beef is called cottage pie in the United Kingdom!

1. In a large pot, add the sliced potatoes. Fill the pot with water so that the potatoes are just covered. Bring the pot to the boil and cook for about 10 minutes, or until the potatoes are fork-tender. Drain and return to the pot and mash with a potato masher until just smooth.

2. Add the melted butter, ½ teaspoon salt, and 3 tablespoons of the half-and-half, adding more if needed, and mix until creamy and smooth. Add the cheese and mix until melted. Set aside.

3. In a large skillet over medium heat, melt the butter until it foams. Add the celery, onions, and carrots and cook until they begin to soften, about 5 minutes. Add the garlic, thyme, ½ teaspoon salt, and pepper and cook until fragrant, about 1 minute.

4. Add the ground beef to the pan and cook until the beef is thoroughly browned, about 10 minutes.

5. Add the flour and cook until no raw flour remains. Stir in the beef stock and Worcestershire sauce. Cook until the sauce thickens slightly, then stir in the frozen peas. Cook until the peas thaw.

6. Heat the oven to 400°F and spray a 2-quart casserole dish with nonstick cooking spray.

7. Pour the filling into the prepared dish, then spread the mashed potatoes over the top. Drag a fork lightly over the top of the mashed potatoes. Bake for 20 to 25 minutes, or until the mashed potatoes are golden brown. Cool 10 minutes before serving.

Guinness Pub Pie

This pie is hearty and filling, and perfect with a good, stout beer on a cold night.

INGREDIENTS | SERVES 8

2 tablespoons butter

1 rib celery, chopped

1 medium onion, peeled and chopped

2 medium carrots, peeled and chopped

1 small russet potato, peeled and cut into ¼-inch cubes

1 tablespoon tomato paste

3 cloves garlic, minced

½ teaspoon thyme

½ teaspoon salt

½ teaspoon fresh cracked black pepper

1 pound beef or lamb roast, cut into ½-inch cubes

¼ cup all-purpose flour

1 cup Guinness stout

1 tablespoon Worcestershire sauce

1 cup frozen peas

1 (9-inch) Mealy Pie Crust, unbaked (See Chapter 2)

1 egg, beaten

1 (9-inch) Flaky Pie Crust (See Chapter 2)

1. Heat the oven to 425°F.

2. In a large skillet over medium heat, melt the butter until it foams. Add the celery, onions, carrots, and potatoes. Cook until they begin to soften, about 5 minutes.

3. Add the tomato paste and cook until the vegetables become very soft and the tomato paste has begun to brown slightly, about 5 minutes. Add the garlic, thyme, salt, and pepper and cook until fragrant, about 1 minute.

4. Add the beef or lamb to the pan and cook until the meat is thoroughly browned, about 10 minutes.

5. Add the flour and cook until no raw flour remains. Stir in the Guinness and Worcestershire sauce. Cook until the sauce thickens and is bubbling then stir in the frozen peas. Cook until the peas thaw. Remove from the heat to cool slightly.

6. Pour the meat mixture into the Mealy Pie Crust. Brush the edge of the bottom pie crust with the beaten egg so that the top crust will adhere. Top with the Flaky Pie Crust and trim the dough to 1 inch of the pan's edge. Tuck the edge of the top crust under the edge of the bottom crust. Crimp the dough using your fingers or a fork. Brush the entire top crust with the beaten egg and cut 4 or 5 slits in the top to vent steam.

7. Place the pie on a baking sheet and bake for 15 minutes, then reduce the heat to 350°F and bake for an additional 40 to 50 minutes, or until the crust is golden brown and the filling is bubbling. Cool for 30 minutes before serving.

Spanakopita (Greek Spinach Pie)

If you are not a fan of feta cheese, you can substitute strained ricotta cheese.

INGREDIENTS | SERVES 8

1 tablespoon olive oil

1 large onion, peeled and chopped

3 cloves garlic, minced

2 tablespoons fresh chopped parsley

10 ounces frozen chopped spinach, thawed, and thoroughly drained

2 eggs, beaten

8 ounces feta cheese, rinsed, drained, and crumbled

½ cup (8 tablespoons) unsalted butter, melted

18 sheets phyllo dough

Straining Cheese and Yogurt

Some recipes call for strained yogurt or ricotta cheese. Straining removes excess water, which can affect the texture of the finished dish. The easiest way to strain either yogurt or cheese is to line a colander with a coffee filter or cheesecloth and put over a bowl. Add the yogurt or cheese and allow to strain overnight.

1. Heat the oven to 350°F.

2. In a medium skillet over medium heat, add the olive oil. Once it shimmers, add the onions and cook until translucent, about 5 minutes.

3. Add the garlic and parsley and cook until fragrant, about 1 minute. Cool to room temperature.

4. In a large bowl, combine the onion mixture, spinach, and egg until well combined. Fold in the crumbled feta. Cover and chill for 30 minutes.

5. Brush the inside of a 9" × 13" pan lightly with butter. Lay 6 sheets of phyllo dough into the pan, brushing each sheet lightly with butter.

6. Carefully spread half of the spinach mixture over the dough, leaving a ½-inch space around the edges. Repeat this process, then top with the remaining phyllo sheets, brushing each sheet lightly with butter. Pour any remaining butter over the top of the phyllo dough.

7. Bake for 30 to 40 minutes, or until the pastry is golden brown all over. Cool for 10 minutes before cutting.

Tomato, Basil, and Mozzarella Tart

Red, green, and white are the colors of the Italian flag, and also the colors of the delicious ingredients in this simple, fresh tart.

INGREDIENTS | SERVES 8

1 Parmesan Pastry Crust in a 9-inch tart pan, unbaked (See Chapter 2)

1 egg, beaten

8 ounces fresh mozzarella, sliced ¼-inch thick

4 ripe Roma tomatoes, sliced ¼-inch thick

8 fresh basil leaves

3 tablespoons extra-virgin olive oil

½ teaspoon sea salt

½ teaspoon fresh cracked black pepper

Fresh Mozzarella

Fresh mozzarella is typically sold in a brine solution or vacuum sealed for freshness. Gourmet and specialty stores often make fresh mozzarella in house, but regular grocery stores may carry it as well in the deli department. The color of fresh mozzarella varies from pale white to slightly yellow depending on the diet of the buffalo or cow that produced the milk.

1. Heat the oven to 350°F.

2. Line the tart pastry with parchment paper or a double layer of aluminum foil and add pie weights or dry beans. Bake for 12 minutes, then remove the paper and weights, brush the inside of the part crust lightly with beaten egg, and bake for an additional 12 to 15 minutes, or until the crust is golden brown all over. Remove from the oven and cool to room temperature.

3. Layer the sliced cheese alternately with the sliced tomatoes onto the bottom of the tart. Tear the basil leaves and sprinkle them over the top of the tart.

4. Drizzle the olive oil over the cheese and tomatoes, then season with salt and pepper. Serve at room temperature.

Torta della Nonna (Italian Cheese Tart)

The name of this dish means "Grandma's Cake" in Italian. It's from the Tuscany region of Italy.

INGREDIENTS | SERVES 8

4 egg yolks

¾ cup sugar

⅔ cup all-purpose flour

1 tablespoon orange zest

2 cups milk

1½ cups ricotta cheese

¼ cup pine nuts

1 (10-inch) Short Crust for Tarts, molded and unbaked (See Chapter 2)

1 egg, beaten

Powdered sugar, for garnish

Homemade Ricotta

Making ricotta cheese at home is easy and tastes better than store-bought. Combine 1 quart whole milk, 2 cups heavy cream, ½ teaspoon salt, and ¼ cup lemon juice in a nonreactive saucepan. Gently heat the milk, stirring constantly, until it reaches a boil. Cook for about 2 minutes or until the mixture curdles, then remove from the heat and strain into cheese cloth. Allow the cheese to drain overnight in the refrigerator. It stays fresh for 2 days.

1. Heat the oven to 375°F.

2. In the bowl of a double boiler, whisk together the egg yolks and sugar until smooth.

3. Gradually whisk in the flour so that there are no lumps, then whisk in the orange zest.

4. Stream in the milk, whisking constantly, until smooth. Heat the double boiler until the water simmers. Cook, stirring constantly, until the custard thickens.

5. Remove from the heat and stir in the ricotta cheese and pine nuts.

6. Spread the filling into the molded tart crust. Lay the second crust over the top and use the edge of the pan to trim off any excess. Pinch the edges together and brush the top of the crust with beaten egg.

7. Place the tart on a baking sheet and bake for 50 to 55 minutes, or until the tart is golden brown. Cool to room temperature and dust with powdered sugar before serving.

Pomegranate
Cream Cheese Pie
(*Chapter 6*)

Cheeseburger Pie
(Chapter 13)

Lemon Chess Pie (*Chapter 9*)

Chocolate Chip Pecan Pie (*Chapter 8*)

Ham and Swiss Hand Pies (*Chapter 16*)

Apple Crumble Pie
(*Chapter 5*)

Coconut Custard Pie (*Chapter 7*)

Apple, Gruyère, and Caramelized Onion Quiche (*Chapter 18*)

Buttermilk Pie (*Chapter 7*)

Personal Chicken Potpies
(*Chapter 13*)

Strawberry Pie
(Chapter 5)

Peach Sour Cream Pie (*Chapter 5*)

Bánh Patê Sô (Hot Meat Pie)
(*Chapter 14*)

Home-Style Apple Pie (*Chapter 4*)

Lattice-Top Cherry Pie (*Chapter 4*)

Orange Mousse Pie (*Chapter 9*)

Tomato, Basil, and Mozzarella Tart (*Chapter 14*)

Blueberry Ricotta Tart (*Chapter 11*)

Salted Peanut Pie (*Chapter 8*)

CHAPTER 15

Ice Cream Pies

Peppermint Ice Cream Pie

Nothing is more refreshing than a chilly, mint-flavored ice cream pie studded with chocolate.

INGREDIENTS | SERVES 8

3 pints peppermint ice cream

½ cup mini chocolate chips

4 candy canes, or 10 round peppermint candies, crushed, divided

1 (9-inch) Chocolate Cookie Crust, baked and cooled (See Chapter 2)

1 (12-ounce) jar hot fudge sauce

1. In a large bowl, add the ice cream and stir until it begins to soften. Add the mini chocolate chips and half of the crushed peppermint candy. Stir until evenly incorporated.

2. Carefully spoon the ice cream mixture into the prepared crust. Spread so that it is even, then cover with plastic and place in the freezer for at least 4 hours or overnight.

3. To serve, set the pie out on the counter to warm up for 5 minutes. Warm the hot fudge sauce according to the directions on the jar. Serve with the warmed sauce and garnish with the reserved peppermint candy.

Chocolate Caramel Cookie Pie

This pie has a similar flavor to the popular Twix candy bar and could not be easier to prepare!

INGREDIENTS | SERVES 8

1 cup caramel ice cream topping

12 shortbread cookies, roughly crumbled

1 (9-inch) Traditional Graham Cracker Crust, baked and cooled (See Chapter 2)

1 quart chocolate ice cream

¼ cup milk chocolate ice cream topping

1. Into the bottom of the prepared crust, add ⅓ cup of the caramel topping and one-third of the crumbled cookies. Cover and freeze for 1 hour.

2. Spread half of the ice cream over the frozen caramel mixture, then top with ⅓ cup of the caramel topping and one-third of the cookies. Cover and freeze for 1 hour.

3. Spread the remaining ice cream over the pie. Drizzle the remaining caramel sauce, the remaining cookies, and the milk chocolate ice cream topping over the pie. Chill for 2 hours. Allow the pie to warm up on the counter for 5 minutes before serving.

Butter Pecan Pretzel Pie

This sweet and salty pie is a pecan lover's delight!

INGREDIENTS | SERVES 8

2 tablespoons butter

¼ cup packed light brown sugar

¼ teaspoon vanilla

1 quart butter pecan ice cream

1 (9-inch) Pretzel Crust, baked and cooled (See Chapter 2)

½ cup whole pecans, toasted

1. In a small saucepan, combine the butter and light brown sugar over medium heat. Bring the mixture to a boil and cook until the mixture smells nutty. Remove from the heat and stir in the vanilla. Set aside to cool.

2. Spread half of the butter pecan ice cream into the prepared crust. Drizzle the brown sugar sauce over the ice cream and arrange half of the toasted pecans over the top. Cover the pie and chill for 30 minutes.

3. Spread the remaining ice cream over the top and garnish the pie with the remaining pecans. Cover and chill for 2 hours. Allow the pie to warm up on the counter for 5 minutes before serving.

Tin Roof Sundae Ice Cream Pie

It is said the tin roof sundae got its name from the sound of peanuts hitting the metal canisters when they were scooped, which sounded like rain hitting a metal roof.

INGREDIENTS | SERVES 8

1 cup chocolate-covered peanuts, divided

1 quart vanilla ice cream

⅔ cup chocolate fudge ice cream topping

1 (9-inch) Chocolate Cookie Crust, baked and cooled (See Chapter 2)

½ cup caramel ice cream topping

1. In a large bowl, combine ¾ cup of the chocolate-covered peanuts and the vanilla ice cream. Drizzle in the fudge, but do not overmix.

2. Spoon the ice cream into the prepared crust, then wrap and freeze for 2 hours.

3. Once chilled, drizzle the caramel topping on the pie and arrange the reserved peanuts on the top. Let the pie stand for 5 minutes before serving.

Brownie a la Mode Pie

In this pie vanilla ice cream is studded with chunks of freshly baked fudge brownies.

INGREDIENTS | SERVES 8

Nonstick cooking spray

6 tablespoons butter, divided

1 ounce bittersweet chocolate, chopped

1 cup sugar

1 egg

1 egg yolk

½ teaspoon vanilla

½ cup all-purpose flour

1 tablespoon Dutch-processed cocoa powder

½ teaspoon salt

1 quart vanilla ice cream

1 (9-inch) Chocolate Cookie Crust, baked and cooled (See Chapter 2)

½ cup chocolate syrup

1. Heat the oven to 350°F. Spray an 8" × 8" square baking pan with nonstick spray, line the pan with parchment paper, then spray the paper with nonstick spray.

2. In a small bowl, combine 3 tablespoons butter and chopped chocolate. Melt in the microwave using 30-second bursts, stirring well in between, until smooth. Set aside to cool.

3. In a medium bowl, combine the remaining butter, sugar, egg, egg yolk, and vanilla until smooth. Add the melted chocolate mixture and whisk to combine.

4. Sift in the flour, cocoa powder, and salt. Whisk until no large lumps of flour remain, then spread it evenly in the prepared pan.

5. Bake for 20 to 30 minutes, or until the brownies are set in the center. Remove from the oven and allow to cool completely in the pan. Once cooled, cut into ¼-inch pieces.

6. In a large bowl, combine the ice cream with 2 cups of the chopped brownies. Once mixed well, spread the ice cream into the prepared crust. Garnish the top of the pie with additional brownie pieces, pressing them slightly into the ice cream. Cover and chill for 2 hours.

7. Allow the pie to warm up on the counter for 5 minutes before serving. Top each slice with a drizzle of chocolate syrup.

Vanilla Almond Crunch Pie

Toasted almond gives this simple pie a lot of great, nutty flavor. If you like, you can substitute the caramel sauce for fudge or omit altogether.

INGREDIENTS | SERVES 8

1 cup blanched almonds

⅓ cup sugar

2 tablespoons water

1 quart vanilla ice cream

1 (9-inch) Traditional Graham Cracker Crust, baked and cooled (See Chapter 2)

½ cup Salted Caramel Sauce (See Chapter 2)

1. Heat the oven to 325°F and line a shallow baking sheet with parchment paper.

2. In a small bowl, combine the almonds, sugar, and water. Toss to coat. Spread the almonds on the prepared baking sheet and bake until golden brown, about 16 to 20 minutes. Cool completely on the pan, then break up into small pieces.

3. In a large bowl, combine the ice cream with the almonds until evenly distributed. Spread into the prepared crust and drizzle the top with the caramel sauce.

4. Freeze for 2 hours to set. Allow to stand for 5 minutes before serving.

Rocky Road Pie

Created in 1929, rocky road ice cream can be made with any kind of toasted nut you prefer.

INGREDIENTS | SERVES 8

1 (9-inch) Chocolate Cookie Crust, baked and cooled (See Chapter 2)

½ cup mini chocolate chips

1 cup mini marshmallows

½ cup flaked almond, toasted

1 quart chocolate ice cream, slightly softened

¼ cup heavy cream

4 ounces milk chocolate, chopped

2 teaspoons butter

¼ teaspoon vanilla

1. In the bottom of the prepared crust, spread 2 tablespoons of the chocolate chips, half of the marshmallows, and 2 tablespoons of the almonds.

2. Spread half of the ice cream over the crust, then top with half of the remaining chocolate chips, half of the remaining marshmallows, and half of the remaining almonds. Spread the remaining ice cream over the top, then cover with plastic and chill for 2 hours.

3. In a small saucepan, bring the cream to a simmer. Shut off the heat and add the chopped milk chocolate, butter, and vanilla. Let stand for 1 minute, then whisk until smooth. Cool to room temperature.

4. Once the pie has chilled, spread the chocolate sauce over the top. Top with the remaining chocolate chips, marshmallows, and almonds. Allow the pie to stand at room temperature for 5 minutes before serving.

Chocolate Chip Cookie Dough Pie

This pie uses egg-free cookie dough pieces, making it not only extra tasty but safe for everyone to eat.

INGREDIENTS | SERVES 8

1 cup all-purpose flour

⅓ cup packed light brown sugar

3 tablespoons sugar

4 tablespoons butter, softened

¼ teaspoon vanilla

1 tablespoon cream cheese, softened

½ cup mini chocolate chips

1 quart vanilla ice cream

1 (9-inch) Traditional Graham Cracker Crust, baked and cooled (See Chapter 2)

½ cup chocolate fudge ice cream topping, for garnish

1. In a medium bowl, combine the flour, light brown sugar, sugar, butter, vanilla, and cream cheese until smooth. Stir in the chocolate chips.

2. Scoop the dough out onto a parchment-lined baking sheet by rounded teaspoons. Freeze for 2 hours. Once frozen, cut the cookie dough pieces in half.

3. In a large bowl, combine all but ½ cup of the chopped cookie dough with the vanilla ice cream until evenly distributed. Spoon the ice cream into the prepared crust.

4. Garnish the top of the pie with the reserved cookie dough pieces. Cover and chill for 3 hours.

5. Allow the pie to warm up on the counter for 5 minutes before serving. Drizzle the chocolate topping on each slice to garnish.

Peanut Butter Ripple Pie

This pie is made with vanilla ice cream, but you can make it with chocolate ice cream in a chocolate crust for a more peanut-butter-cup-like experience.

INGREDIENTS | SERVES 8

1 cup peanut butter, creamy or chunky

1 tablespoon butter

¼ teaspoon vanilla

1 quart vanilla ice cream

1 (9-inch) Pretzel Crust, baked and cooled (See Chapter 2)

National Ice Cream Pie Day

It may be an unrecognized holiday, but you will want to celebrate Ice Cream Pie Day! August 18 is the (unofficial) day to celebrate chilly, frosty ice cream pies and share them with friends and family!

1. In a medium microwave-safe bowl, add the peanut butter and butter. Microwave until the butter melts. Mix well, then stir in the vanilla. Cool to room temperature.

2. Spread one-quarter of the ice cream into the prepared crust. Drizzle one-third of the peanut butter over the ice cream. Cover and put in the freezer for 30 minutes. Repeat this process twice more, then spread the remaining ice cream over the top of the pie.

3. Cover and freeze for 2 hours. Let stand for 5 minutes before slicing.

Cookies and Cream Pie

Chocolate sandwich cookies, chocolate chip ice cream, and a chocolate cookie crust make this pie extra rich and very chocolaty!

INGREDIENTS | SERVES 8

20 chocolate sandwich cookies, crushed lightly

1 quart chocolate chip ice cream

1 (9-inch) Chocolate Cookie Crust, baked and cooled (See Chapter 2)

¼ cup heavy cream

4 ounces white chocolate, chopped

2 teaspoons butter

1. In a large bowl, combine the crushed cookies with the ice cream until evenly distributed. Spread into the prepared crust, then cover and chill for 2 hours.

2. In a small saucepan over medium heat, bring the cream to a simmer. Remove the pan from the heat and add the chopped chocolate and butter. Let stand for 1 minute, then stir until smooth. Cool to room temperature.

3. Once the pie has frozen, drizzle the white chocolate mixture over the top. Let stand for 5 minutes before slicing.

Strawberry Salted-Caramel Pie

Sweet strawberries and salty caramel sauce are a match made in dessert heaven.

INGREDIENTS | SERVES 8

1 recipe Salted Caramel Sauce, divided (See Chapter 3)

1 (9-inch) Traditional Graham Cracker Crust, baked and cooled (See Chapter 2)

1 pint strawberries, hulled and sliced

3 cups strawberry ice cream

1. Spread half of the Salted Caramel Sauce into the prepared crust. Cover and freeze for 30 minutes.

2. In a large bowl, combine the strawberries and ice cream. Spread the mixture into the crust. Cover and chill for 2 hours.

3. Let stand for 5 minutes before slicing. Drizzle the remaining caramel sauce over each slice to garnish.

Blueberries and Cream Pie

Fresh blueberries are cooked into a thick syrup that is marbled into vanilla ice cream. Fresh cherries would also be good in this recipe.

INGREDIENTS | SERVES 8

1¼ cups fresh blueberries, divided

1 teaspoon lemon zest

1 teaspoon lemon juice

2 tablespoons cornstarch

¼ cup white sugar

¼ teaspoon cinnamon

Pinch fresh grated nutmeg

1 tablespoon unsalted butter

1 quart vanilla ice cream

1 (9-inch) Traditional Graham Cracker Crust, baked and cooled (See Chapter 2)

1. In a medium saucepan, combine 1 cup of blueberries, lemon zest, lemon juice, cornstarch, sugar, cinnamon, and nutmeg. Cook over medium heat until the berries pop and the juices are thick. Remove from the heat and stir in the butter until melted. Cool to room temperature.

2. In a medium bowl, combine half of the ice cream with the blueberry mixture.

3. Scoop half of the blueberry ice cream alternately with half of the vanilla ice cream into one layer into the crust. Use a butter knife to swirl the ice cream, then repeat with the remaining ice cream. Garnish the top of the pie with the reserved blueberries. Cover and chill for 2 hours. Let stand for 5 minutes before slicing.

Lemon Ice Cream Pie

Luscious lemon curd is topped with an oh-so-easy-to-make ice cream topping. Lime and orange curd would also be great here.

INGREDIENTS | SERVES 8

½ cup sugar

½ cup fresh lemon juice

4 egg yolks

1 tablespoon cornstarch

4 tablespoons unsalted butter

1 (9-inch) Traditional Graham Cracker Crust, baked and cooled (See Chapter 2)

1 pint vanilla ice cream

1 cup heavy cream

2 tablespoons powdered sugar

½ teaspoon vanilla

Why Warm It Up?

Ice cream pies are easier to slice and taste better if you let them sit out on the counter for 5 to 10 minutes before serving. It also helps to use a serrated knife dipped into hot water and dried for serving. Serrated knives will slice through the cold ice cream and crust more easily than a straight blade.

1. In a medium saucepan, combine the sugar and lemon juice, and stir until the sugar is melted.

2. Whisk in the egg yolks and cornstarch. Cook over medium heat, whisking constantly, until bubbling and thick. Reduce the heat to low and stir in the butter until melted.

3. Pour the curd through a strainer into the prepared crust. Cover and freeze for 1 hour.

4. Once set, spread the ice cream over the top of the pie. Cover and chill for 1 hour.

5. In a medium bowl, add the cream, powdered sugar, and vanilla and whip until it forms medium peaks. Spread over the top of the pie and freeze for 30 minutes before serving.

Dark-Chocolate Brownie Pie

This pie is layer upon layer of chocolate. If you want to cut back on the chocolate, feel free to use vanilla ice cream and a graham cracker crust.

INGREDIENTS | SERVES 8

Nonstick cooking spray

3 tablespoons unsalted butter

1 ounce bittersweet chocolate, chopped

3 tablespoons unsalted butter

1 cup sugar

1 egg

1 egg yolk

½ teaspoon vanilla

½ cup all-purpose flour

1 tablespoon Dutch-processed cocoa powder

½ teaspoon salt

½ cup chopped walnuts

1 quart chocolate ice cream

1 (9-inch) Chocolate Cookie Crust, baked and cooled (See Chapter 2)

¼ cup crisp rice cereal

½ cup chocolate fudge ice cream topping

¼ cup mini chocolate chips

1. Heat the oven to 350°F. Spray an 8" × 8" square baking pan with nonstick spray, line the pan with parchment paper, then spray the paper with nonstick spray.

2. In a small bowl, combine the butter and chopped chocolate. Melt in the microwave using 30-second bursts, stirring well in between, until smooth. Set aside to cool.

3. In a medium bowl, combine the second amount of butter, sugar, egg, egg yolk, and vanilla until smooth. Add the melted chocolate mixture and whisk to combine.

4. Sift in the flour, cocoa powder, and salt. Whisk until no large lumps of flour remain, then fold in the walnuts.

5. Spread it evenly in the prepared pan. Bake for 20 to 30 minutes, or until the brownies are set in the center. Remove from the oven and allow to cool completely in the pan. Once cool, cut into ¼-inch pieces.

6. In a large bowl, mix together the ice cream with 2 cups of the brownie pieces. Spread half of the ice cream mixture into the prepared crust.

7. Sprinkle half of the crisp rice cereal, half of the chocolate topping, and all the chocolate chips over the top. Cover both the pie and the remaining ice cream and freeze for 30 minutes.

8. Once cold, spread the remaining ice cream mixture over. Top with the reserved chocolate topping, crisp rice cereal, and brownie pieces. Cover and freeze for 2 hours. Let stand for 5 minutes before slicing.

Honey-Roasted Peanut and Caramel Pie

Honey-roasted peanuts are an easy way to add some flavor and crunch to your ice cream pies. In this pie, they are paired with salted caramel for a nutty treat.

INGREDIENTS | SERVES 8

1 quart vanilla ice cream

1 cup honey-roasted peanuts, divided

1 recipe Salted Caramel Sauce, divided (See Chapter 3)

1 (9-inch) Pretzel Crust, baked and cooled (See Chapter 2)

3 tablespoons honey

1. In a large bowl, combine the ice cream with ¾ cup of the peanuts. Drizzle in ¾ cup of the caramel sauce. Spread the ice cream into the prepared crust, then cover and freeze for 2 hours.

2. Once frozen, drizzle over the reserved caramel and honey, and garnish with the reserved peanuts. Let stand for 5 minutes before slicing.

Time Is of the Essence

When you are making an ice cream pie, it is best not to dawdle. You want the ice cream to be slightly soft, but if the ice cream gets too soft, it will lose some of its creaminess and become a little gritty when refrozen.

Mint Chocolate Cookie Pie

Sandwich cookies, peppermint patties, and mint chocolate chip ice cream are a super comfort-food combination.

INGREDIENTS | SERVES 8

1 quart mint chocolate chip ice cream

20 chocolate sandwich cookies, lightly crushed

4 regular, or 12 mini, peppermint patties, cut into ¼-inch pieces

1 (9-inch) Chocolate Cookie Crust, baked and cooled (See Chapter 2)

⅓ cup chocolate fudge ice cream topping

1. In a large bowl, combine together the ice cream, cookies, and peppermint patties until evenly distributed. Scoop into the prepared crust. Cover and freeze for 2 hours.

2. Once frozen, drizzle over the chocolate topping. Let stand for 5 minutes before slicing.

Triple-Berry Sorbet Pie

Strawberry and raspberry sorbet combine with fresh berries in this refreshing pie. A little whipped cream for garnish is a nice touch.

INGREDIENTS | SERVES 8

1 (9-inch) Traditional Graham Cracker Crust, baked and cooled (See Chapter 2)
1 pint strawberry sorbet
¼ cup fresh blueberries
¼ cup fresh raspberries
¼ cup fresh strawberries, diced
1 pint raspberry sorbet

1. On the bottom of the prepared crust, spread the strawberry sorbet in an even layer.

2. Arrange the berries over the sorbet, then spread the raspberry sorbet over the berries.

3. Cover and chill for 2 hours. Allow to stand for 5 minutes before serving.

Sorbet and Sherbet

Some people think sorbet and sherbet are the same, but they are not. Sorbet contains sweetened fruit juices, or fruit purée, that is frozen. Sherbet is very similar, except it also contains some milk or cream.

Peach Sorbet Pie

Fresh peaches are mixed with peach sorbet to create a light and refreshing pie. If you prefer it to be richer, use peach ice cream.

INGREDIENTS | SERVES 8

2 peaches, peeled, pitted, and cut into ¼-inch pieces
¼ teaspoon cinnamon
1 quart peach sorbet
1 (9-inch) Traditional Graham Cracker Crust, baked and cooled (Chapter 2)

1. In a large bowl, combine the peaches and the cinnamon. Toss so that the peaches are evenly coated. Add the sorbet and quickly mix to combine.

2. Spread the peach mixture into the prepared crust. Cover and freeze for 2 hours. Allow to stand for 5 minutes before serving.

Neapolitan Pie

Three layers of ice cream, fresh berries, and chocolate chips make this pie a cool summer favorite!

INGREDIENTS | SERVES 8

1 (9-inch) Traditional Graham Cracker Crust, baked and cooled (See Chapter 2)

1⅓ cups vanilla ice cream

⅔ cup diced fresh strawberries

1⅓ cups strawberry ice cream

⅔ cup mini chocolate chips

1⅓ cups chocolate ice cream

1 cup whipping cream

2 tablespoons powdered sugar

½ teaspoon vanilla

1. In a prepared crust, spread the vanilla ice cream evenly on the bottom. Arrange ½ cup of the strawberries over the top. Cover and freeze for 30 minutes.

2. Once chilled, spread the strawberry ice cream over the top. Arrange ½ cup of the chocolate chips on the top. Cover and chill for 30 minutes.

3. Once chilled, spread the chocolate ice cream over the top. Cover and chill for 2 hours.

4. In a medium bowl, add the cream, powdered sugar, and vanilla. Beat until the cream forms medium peaks.

5. Spread cream over the chilled pie. Garnish with the reserved strawberries and chocolate chips. Allow to stand 5 minutes before serving.

CHAPTER 16

Hand Pies

Blackberry Hand Pies

Feel free to use either fresh or frozen berries in this dessert. These pies are best served slightly warm or at room temperature.

2 cups blackberries

½ cup grated apple

½ cup sugar

2 tablespoons cornstarch

¼ teaspoon cinnamon

¼ teaspoon fresh grated nutmeg

2 recipes (9-inch) Flaky Pie Crust, not pressed into pie pans (See Chapter 2)

1 egg, beaten

A Spoonful of Sugar

If you want to sweeten things up and add a little decorative touch to your pies, try dusting the tops of egg-washed crusts with a little sugar. Table sugar will work fine, but if you want the sugar to stand out, try using sanding sugar. Sanding sugar is coarser and will not melt into the egg wash while baking.

1. In a medium saucepan over medium heat, combine the blackberries, apple, sugar, cornstarch, cinnamon, and nutmeg. Allow the mixture to come to a boil and thicken, about 5 minutes. Remove from the heat and cool to room temperature.

2. Heat the oven to 425°F and line a baking sheet with parchment paper.

3. Cut the pastry into 8-inch rounds or squares. Place about ⅓ cup filling onto the pastry slightly off center, brush the edges of the pastry with beaten egg, and fold the dough over the filling. Pinch or crimp with a fork to seal. Place the pies on the prepared baking sheet and brush with beaten egg. With scissors or a sharp paring knife, cut vents in pastry so that steam can escape.

4. Bake for 10 minutes, then reduce heat to 350°F and bake for an additional 25 to 30 minutes, or until the pastry is golden brown and juices are bubbling. Cool to room temperature before serving.

Peach Ginger Hand Pies

Sweet peaches and spicy ginger are a lovely combination. You may also make this pie with apricots when they are in season!

INGREDIENTS | SERVES 8

2 peaches, peeled, stoned, and finely diced

¼ cup packed light brown sugar

1 teaspoon fresh grated ginger

¼ teaspoon cinnamon

1 tablespoon cornstarch

2 recipes (9-inch) Flaky Pie Crust, not pressed into pie pans (See Chapter 2)

1 egg, beaten

1. In a medium saucepan over medium heat, combine the peaches, light brown sugar, ginger, cinnamon, and cornstarch. Cook until the mixture comes to a boil and thickens, about 5 minutes. Remove from the heat and cool to room temperature.

2. Heat the oven to 425°F and line a baking sheet with parchment paper.

3. Cut the pastry into 8-inch rounds or squares. Place about ¼ cup filling onto the pastry slightly off center, brush the edges of the pastry with beaten egg, and fold the dough over the filling. Pinch or crimp with a fork to seal. Place the pies on the prepared baking sheet and brush with beaten egg. With scissors or a sharp paring knife, cut vents in pastry so that steam can escape.

4. Bake for 15 minutes, then reduce heat to 350°F and bake for an additional 25 minutes, or until the pastry is golden brown and juices are bubbling. Cool to room temperature before serving.

Blueberry Lemon Cheese Hand Pies

This pie combines fresh blueberry filling with a thin layer of lemony cream cheese.

INGREDIENTS | SERVES 8

4 ounces cream cheese, softened

3 tablespoons sugar

1 egg

¼ teaspoon vanilla

1 tablespoon lemon zest

1½ cups fresh blueberries

¼ cup packed light brown sugar

1 tablespoon cornstarch

¼ teaspoon cinnamon

2 recipes (9-inch) Flaky Pie Crust, not pressed into pie pans (See Chapter 2)

1 egg, beaten

Testing for Doneness

How do you know if your hand pies are truly cooked all the way through? There are 3 ways to check. First, look at the bottom of the pie. It should be deeply golden brown. If it is pale, it needs more time. Second, the crust should feel firm to the touch. Gently press the center of the pie. It should not collapse or feel soggy. Finally, use a cooking thermometer to test the filling. Fillings with raw eggs are done when they reach 155°F.

1. In a large bowl, cream together the cream cheese and sugar until light and fluffy. Beat in the egg until well combined. Stir in the vanilla and lemon zest, then cover and chill for 1 hour.

2. In a medium saucepan over medium heat, combine the blueberries, light brown sugar, cornstarch, and cinnamon. Cook until the mixture comes to a boil and thickens. Remove from the heat and cool to room temperature.

3. Heat the oven to 425°F and line a baking sheet with parchment paper.

   Cut the pastry into 8-inch rounds or squares. Spread about 2 tablespoons of the cream cheese mixture into the center of the pastry. Place about ¼ cup filling onto the pastry slightly off center, brush the edges of the pastry with beaten egg, and fold the dough over the filling. Pinch or crimp with a fork to seal. Place the pies on the prepared baking sheet and brush with beaten egg. With scissors or a sharp paring knife, cut vents in pastry so that steam can escape.

4. Bake for 15 minutes, then reduce heat to 350°F and bake for an additional 20 to 30 minutes, or until the pastry is golden brown and juices are bubbling. Cool to room temperature before serving.

Pineapple Cream Cheese Hand Pies

Tart pineapple and tangy cream cheese make an unexpected and delicious filling for these pies.

INGREDIENTS | SERVES 8

8 ounces cream cheese, softened

⅓ cup sugar

1 tablespoon cornstarch

1 egg

1 egg yolk

¼ teaspoon vanilla

1 tablespoon orange zest

1 (8-ounce) can crushed pineapple, drained well

2 recipes (9-inch) Flaky Pie Crust, not pressed into pie pans (See Chapter 2)

1 egg, beaten

1. In a large bowl, cream together the cream cheese, sugar, and cornstarch until light and fluffy. Beat in the egg and egg yolk until well combined. Stir in the vanilla, orange zest, and pineapple until mixed well. Cover and chill for 1 hour.

2. Heat the oven to 425°F and line a baking sheet with parchment paper.

3. Cut the pastry into 8-inch rounds or squares. Evenly divide the cream cheese mixture among the pastries slightly off center, brush the edges of the pastry with beaten egg, and fold the dough over the filling. Pinch or crimp with a fork to seal. Place the pies on the prepared baking sheet and brush with beaten egg. With scissors or a sharp paring knife, cut vents in pastry so that steam can escape.

4. Bake for 15 minutes, then reduce heat to 350°F and bake for an additional 20 to 30 minutes, or until the pastry is golden brown and the filling is hot. Cool to room temperature before serving.

Country Apple Hand Pies

Bits of tart, fresh apple make a delicious filling for these portable pies.

Hand Pies into Fried Pies

Any hand pie made with a fruit filling can be made into a fried pie with a few simple modifications. First, do not cut a steam vent. The vent will allow oil to seep into the pie. Second, try to press out any air in the pastry before crimping. Fry the pies in oil heated to 350°F until puffed and golden.

1. In a medium bowl, combine the apple, cinnamon, sugar, and cornstarch until well mixed. Allow to stand 5 minutes.

2. Heat the oven to 425°F and line a baking sheet with parchment paper.

3. Cut the pastry into 8-inch rounds or squares. Place about ⅓ cup filling onto the pastry slightly off center, brush the edges of the pastry with beaten egg, and fold the dough over the filling. Pinch or crimp with a fork to seal. Place the pies on the prepared baking sheet and brush with beaten egg. With scissors or a sharp paring knife, cut vents in pastry so that steam can escape.

4. Bake for 15 minutes, then reduce heat to 350°F and bake for an additional 25 minutes, or until the pastry is golden brown and juices are bubbling. Cool to room temperature before serving.

Sweet Cheese Hand Pies

The filling for these pies can be flavored with citrus zest, or even cocoa powder, if you want to add some zip to your creation.

INGREDIENTS | SERVES 8

8 ounces cream cheese

4 ounces ricotta cheese

½ cup sugar

1 tablespoon cornstarch

1 egg

1 egg yolk

1 teaspoon vanilla

2 recipes (9-inch) Flaky Pie Crust, not pressed into pie pans (See Chapter 2)

1 egg, beaten

1. In a medium bowl, cream together the cream cheese and ricotta cheese until smooth. Add in the sugar and cornstarch until smooth, then beat in the egg, egg yolk, and vanilla until smooth. Cover and chill for 1 hour.

2. Heat the oven to 425°F and line a baking sheet with parchment paper.

3. Cut the pastry into 8-inch rounds or squares. Divide the filling evenly between the pastries, brush the edges with beaten egg, and fold the dough over the filling. Pinch or crimp with a fork to seal. Place the pies on the prepared baking sheet and brush with beaten egg. With scissors or a sharp paring knife, cut vents in pastry so that steam can escape.

4. Bake for 15 minutes, then reduce heat to 350°F and bake for an additional 25 minutes, or until the pastry is golden brown and juices are bubbling. Cool to room temperature before serving.

Spiced Pumpkin Hand Pies

Sometimes, after a big holiday meal, your guests are too full for dessert. Prepare these pies and send them home with your guests to be enjoyed later, when they are not so full.

INGREDIENTS | SERVES 8

⅓ cup sugar

½ teaspoon cinnamon

¼ teaspoon salt

⅛ teaspoon allspice

⅛ teaspoon ground cloves

1 egg

6 ounces pumpkin purée

2 ounces cream cheese, softened

2 recipes (9-inch) Flaky Pie Crust, not pressed into pie pans (See Chapter 2)

1 egg, beaten

1. In a medium bowl, combine together the sugar, cinnamon, salt, allspice, cloves, egg, pumpkin, and cream cheese until well combined. Cover and chill for 1 hour.

2. Heat the oven to 425°F and line a baking sheet with parchment paper.

3. Cut the pastry into 8-inch rounds or squares. Divide the filling evenly between the pastries, brush the edges with beaten egg, and fold the dough over the filling. Pinch or crimp with a fork to seal. Place the pies on the prepared baking sheet and brush with beaten egg. With scissors or a sharp paring knife, cut vents in pastry so that steam can escape.

4. Bake for 15 minutes, then reduce heat to 350°F and bake for an additional 30 to 35 minutes, or until the pastry is golden brown and the filling is hot. Cool to room temperature before serving.

Pumpkin Pie Spice

Many people prefer using commercially mixed pumpkin pie spice because they do not always have separate spices on hand. If you prefer a spice blend, you can easily substitute it for individual spices. Add up the amounts of the individual spices and substitute that total amount with pumpkin pie spice, for example ¼ teaspoon cinnamon plus ½ teaspoon allspice equals ¾ teaspoon pumpkin pie spice.

Creamy Chocolate Fried Pies

These pies are decadent, rich, and a hit with chocolate lovers. Some whipped cream and chocolate sauce are an easy way to doll them up for company.

INGREDIENTS | SERVES 8

1 cup milk or half-and-half

⅓ cup sugar

3 tablespoons Dutch-processed cocoa powder

2 tablespoons cornstarch

1 egg yolk

⅛ teaspoon salt

1 tablespoon butter

1 ounce semisweet chocolate, chopped

½ teaspoon vanilla

2 recipes (9-inch) Flaky Pie Crust, not pressed into pie pans (See Chapter 2)

1 egg, beaten

Oil, for frying

1. In a medium saucepan, combine the milk, sugar, cocoa powder, cornstarch, egg yolk, and salt. Whisk until smooth, then cook over medium heat, stirring constantly, until it begins to simmer and thicken.

2. Remove from the heat and add the butter, chopped chocolate, and vanilla. Stir until melted. Pour through a strainer into a separate bowl and place a layer of cling film directly on the custard. Chill for at least 4 hours or overnight.

3. Cut the pastry into 8-inch rounds or squares. Place about ⅓ cup filling onto the pastry slightly off center, brush the edges of the pastry with beaten egg, and fold the dough over the filling. Pinch or crimp with a fork to seal. Place the pies on the prepared baking sheet and chill for 1 hour.

4. Fill a deep pot at least 3 inches deep with oil, making sure the oil is at least 3 inches from the top of the pot. Heat the oil to 375°F.

5. Working in batches, fry the pies until golden brown on both sides, about 3 minutes for the first side and about 2 for the second side. Drain on a rack over a paper towel-lined baking sheet. Cool completely to room temperature before serving.

Fresh Peach Fried Pies

Serve these pies hot from the oil with a scoop of vanilla ice cream.

INGREDIENTS | SERVES 8

2 peaches, peeled, stoned, and finely diced

¼ cup packed light brown sugar

¼ teaspoon cinnamon

⅛ teaspoon nutmeg

1 tablespoon cornstarch

2 recipes (9-inch) Flaky Pie Crust, not pressed into pie pans (See Chapter 2)

1 egg, beaten

Oil, for frying

Make It in Advance

Fried pies and baked hand pies can be made in advance to help you save time. You can make them up the day before, cover with plastic, and chill before baking or frying. You may also make the pies up and freeze them on a baking sheet. Once the pies are frozen, transfer them to a zip-top freezer bag. When baking from frozen, allow an additional 10 minutes of cooking time. If frying, you need to defrost them in the refrigerator for best results.

1. In a medium bowl, combine the peaches, light brown sugar, cinnamon, nutmeg, and cornstarch until well combined.

2. Cut the pastry into 8-inch rounds or squares. Place about ⅓ cup filling into the pastry slightly off center, brush the edges of the pastry with beaten egg, and fold the dough over the filling. Pinch or crimp with a fork to seal. Place the pies on the prepared baking sheet and brush with beaten egg.

3. Fill a deep pot at least 3 inches deep with oil, making sure the oil is at least 3 inches from the top of the pot. Heat the oil to 375°F.

4. Working in batches, fry the pies until golden brown on both sides, about 3 minutes for the first side and about 2 for the second side. Drain on a rack over a paper towel-lined baking sheet.

Tart Lemon Fried Pies

The sharp citrus flavor of the filling makes these pies surprisingly refreshing!

INGREDIENTS | SERVES 8

2 egg yolks

3 tablespoons cornstarch

¾ cup water

½ cup sugar

⅛ teaspoon salt

1 tablespoon butter

¼ cup lemon juice

1 teaspoon lemon zest

2 recipes (9-inch) Flaky Pie Crust, not pressed into pie pans (See Chapter 2)

1 egg, beaten

Oil, for frying

1. In a medium saucepan, whisk together the egg yolks, cornstarch, water, sugar, and salt. Cook the mixture over medium heat, whisking constantly, until it comes to a boil. Boil for 1 minute, then remove from the heat and whisk in the butter and lemon juice.

2. Pour through a strainer into a separate bowl, stir in the lemon zest, then place a sheet of plastic wrap directly on the lemon filling and chill for at least 4 hours or overnight.

3. Cut the pastry into 8-inch rounds or squares. Place about ⅓ cup filling onto the pastry slightly off center, brush the edges of the pastry with beaten egg, and fold the dough over the filling. Pinch or crimp with a fork to seal. Place the pies on the prepared baking sheet and chill for 1 hour.

4. Fill a deep pot at least 3 inches deep with oil, making sure the oil is at least 3 inches from the top of the pot. Heat the oil to 375°F.

5. Working in batches, fry the pies until golden brown on both sides, about 3 minutes for the first side and about 2 for the second side. Drain on a rack over a paper towel-lined baking sheet.

Banana Cream Fried Pies

Nothing is more comforting than banana cream pie. This version takes it a step further and combines luscious custard and ripe bananas in a crisp fried crust.

INGREDIENTS | SERVES 8

¾ cup milk

¼ cup sugar

2 tablespoons cornstarch

1 egg yolk

⅛ teaspoon salt

1 tablespoon butter

½ teaspoon vanilla

2 recipes (9-inch) Flaky Pie Crust, not pressed into pie pans (See Chapter 2)

1 ripe banana, peeled and diced

1 egg, beaten

Oil, for frying

Frying Dos and Don'ts

When frying, here are a few things to keep in mind. *Do* make sure the oil is hot enough. Cold oil results in soggy pies. *Don't* overfill the oil in the pot. The oil could boil over and cause a fire. *Do* drain the fried food on something absorbent. It will help keep the food crisp. *Don't* let the oil get too hot. The oil will break down and taste burned, and the food will not cook evenly.

1. In a medium saucepan, combine the milk, sugar, cornstarch, egg yolk, and salt. Whisk until smooth, then cook over medium heat, stirring constantly, until it begins to simmer and thicken.

2. Remove from the heat and add the butter and vanilla. Stir until melted. Pour through a strainer into a separate bowl, then place a layer of cling film directly on the custard. Chill for 4 hours or overnight.

3. Cut the pastry into 8-inch rounds or squares. Place about ⅓ cup filling onto the pastry slightly off center, then add a few pieces of the diced banana. Brush the edges of the pastry with beaten egg and fold the dough over the filling. Pinch or crimp with a fork to seal. Place the pies on the prepared baking sheet and chill for 1 hour.

4. Fill a deep pot at least 3 inches deep with oil, making sure the oil is at least 3 inches from the top of the pot. Heat the oil to 375°F.

5. Working in batches, fry the pies until golden brown on both sides, about 3 minutes for the first side and about 2 for the second side. Drain on a rack over a paper towel-lined baking sheet. Cool completely to room temperature before serving.

Ham and Swiss Hand Pies

These little pies are perfect for a light lunch with a small salad or cup of soup.
If you prefer, feel free to substitute broccoli for the spinach.

INGREDIENTS | SERVES 8

4 ounces frozen, chopped spinach, thawed and drained well

8 ounces sliced ham, roughly chopped

1 cup shredded Swiss cheese

1 egg

¼ teaspoon ground red pepper

¼ teaspoon salt

⅛ teaspoon fresh grated nutmeg

2 recipes (9-inch) Flaky Pie Crust, not pressed into pie pans (See Chapter 2)

1 egg, beaten

Boosting Egg Wash's Browning Power

Want a shiny, deeply browned color for your pie crusts? In a small bowl, mix 2 egg yolks with 1 tablespoon of heavy cream until well combined. The egg yolks contain a lot of protein, which, when combined with the fat in both the egg yolks and cream, will result in a shiny brown crust.

1. In a medium bowl, combine the spinach, ham, cheese, egg, red pepper, salt, and nutmeg. Cover and chill for 1 hour.

2. Heat the oven to 425°F and line a baking sheet with parchment paper.

3. Cut the pastry into 8-inch rounds or squares. Place about ⅓ cup filling onto the pastry slightly off center, brush the edges of the pastry with beaten egg, and fold the dough over the filling. Pinch or crimp with a fork to seal. Place the pies on the prepared baking sheet and brush with beaten egg. With scissors or a sharp paring knife, cut vents in pastry so that steam can escape.

4. Bake for 15 minutes, then reduce heat to 350°F and bake for an additional 25 minutes, or until the pastry is golden brown and filling is hot. Cool for 20 minutes before serving.

Beef Picadillo Empanadas

Picadillo is a Latin American version of hash. This version has warm spices, fresh tomatoes, and sweet golden raisins.

INGREDIENTS | SERVES 8

2 teaspoons olive oil

½ medium onion, chopped (about ½ cup)

1 tablespoon tomato paste

½ pound ground beef

1 clove garlic, minced

1 tablespoon chili powder

¼ teaspoon cinnamon

¼ teaspoon allspice

½ cup diced tomatoes

¾ cup beef stock

⅓ cup golden raisins

½ teaspoon salt

½ teaspoon freshly cracked black pepper

2 recipes (9-inch) Flaky Pie Crust, not pressed into pie pans (See Chapter 2)

1 egg, beaten

Oil, for frying

1. In a large skillet over medium heat, add the oil. Once the oil shimmers, add the onion and tomato paste. Cook until the onions begin to soften and the tomato paste darkens in color, about 5 minutes.

2. Add the ground beef to the pan and cook, stirring constantly, until the meat is thoroughly browned. Add the garlic, chili powder, cinnamon, allspice, and tomatoes. Cook until the spices are fragrant and the tomatoes are softened, about 5 minutes.

3. Add the beef stock and raisins to the pan. Cook until the mixture simmers, then reduce the heat to low and allow the mixture to slowly reduce, about 10 minutes. Season with the salt and pepper. Remove the pan from the heat and cool to room temperature.

4. Cut the pastry into 8-inch rounds or squares. Place about ⅓ cup filling onto the pastry slightly off center, brush the edges of the pastry with beaten egg, and fold the dough over the filling. Pinch or crimp with a fork to seal. Place the pies on the prepared baking sheet and chill for 1 hour.

5. Fill a deep pot at least 3 inches deep with oil, making sure the oil is at least 3 inches from the top of the pot. Heat the oil to 375°F.

6. Working in batches, fry the pies until golden brown on both sides, about 3 minutes for the first side and about 2 for the second side. Drain on a rack over a paper towel-lined baking sheet. Enjoy warm.

Black Bean Empanadas

Using canned refried black beans makes this dish easy to assemble. If you cannot find refried black beans, feel free to use regular refried beans.

INGREDIENTS | SERVES 8

1 cup refried black beans

½ teaspoon cumin

2 tablespoons chopped cilantro

2 teaspoons lime juice

½ teaspoon salt

1 cup shredded pepper jack cheese

2 recipes (9-inch) Flaky Pie Crust, not pressed into pie pans (See Chapter 2)

1 egg, beaten

Oil, for frying

Refried Beans

Homemade refried beans are very easy and very tasty! Take 2 cans of pinto or black beans, drained and rinsed, and combine them in a medium pot with 1 cup of beef or chicken stock, ¼ cup fresh cilantro, 1 small chopped onion, 2 minced cloves of garlic, and 1 teaspoon cumin. Simmer, partially covered, for 1 hour, then roughly purée in a blender. Pour the mixture into a hot skillet with 2 tablespoons of lard or oil and cook until thickened.

1. In a medium bowl, combine the beans, cumin, cilantro, lime juice, salt, and cheese until well mixed. Cover and chill for 1 hour.

2. Cut the pastry into 8-inch rounds or squares. Place about ⅓ cup filling onto the pastry slightly off center, brush the edges of the pastry with beaten egg, and fold the dough over the filling. Pinch or crimp with a fork to seal. Place the pies on the prepared baking sheet and chill for 1 hour.

3. Fill a deep pot at least 3 inches deep with oil, making sure the oil is at least 3 inches from the top of the pot. Heat the oil to 375°F.

4. Working in batches, fry the pies until golden brown on both sides, about 3 minutes for the first side and about 2 for the second side. Drain on a rack over a paper towel-lined baking sheet. Enjoy warm.

Grilled Chicken and Pepper Jack Hand Pies

If you do not feel like grilling chicken, you can use roasted chicken breast in this recipe.
Just add ¼ teaspoon of smoked paprika to give the filling extra flavor.

INGREDIENTS | SERVES 8

1 chicken breast, pounded ½ inch thick

1 teaspoon vegetable oil

¼ teaspoon cumin

¼ teaspoon chili powder

¼ teaspoon salt

¼ onion, finely minced (about ¼ cup)

½ cup shredded pepper jack cheese

2 recipes (9-inch) Flaky Pie Crust, not pressed into pie pans (See Chapter 2)

1 egg, beaten

1. Place the chicken breast in a large zip-top plastic bag along with the vegetable oil, cumin, chili powder, and salt. Seal the bag and turn the bag to coat the chicken. Marinate for at least 1 hour in the refrigerator, then remove the bag from the refrigerator and let the chicken stand at room temperature for 30 minutes before grilling.

2. Heat the grill to medium heat. Grill the chicken breast until the flesh is opaque, the juices run clear, and the internal temperature is 160°F, about 6 minutes per side. Allow the chicken to rest for 20 minutes tented with foil, then dice into ¼-inch pieces.

3. Heat the oven to 425°F and line a baking sheet with parchment paper.

4. In a medium bowl, combine the chicken with the minced onion and shredded cheese.

5. Cut the pastry into 8-inch rounds or squares. Place about ⅓ cup filling onto the pastry slightly off center, brush the edges of the pastry with beaten egg, and fold the dough over the filling. Pinch or crimp with a fork to seal. Place the pies on the prepared baking sheet and brush with beaten egg. With scissors or a sharp paring knife, cut vents in pastry so that steam can escape.

6. Bake for 15 minutes, then reduce heat to 350°F and bake for an additional 20 to 25 minutes, or until the pastry is golden brown and juices are bubbling. Cool to room temperature before serving.

Chorizo Empanadas

Spicy Mexican chorizo is available in most markets in the meat section. Once cooked, the chorizo needs to be drained very well to keep the empanadas from being too greasy.

INGREDIENTS | SERVES 8

½ cup Mexican chorizo, removed from the casing

1 small onion, finely chopped

½ red bell pepper, finely chopped

1 small jalapeño, minced

1 clove garlic, minced

½ teaspoon cumin

8 ounces cream cheese, room temperature

1 cup shredded sharp Cheddar cheese

2 recipes (9-inch) Flaky Pie Crust, not pressed into pie pans (See Chapter 2)

1 egg, beaten

Oil, for frying

Chorizo

Chorizo is a pork sausage that comes in a variety of forms depending on the country of origin. In Spain and Portugal, chorizo is a cured sausage that has a deep smoky flavor and is popular in tapas bars. In Mexico and some Latin American countries, chorizo is sold uncooked and tends to be softer and spiced with chilies and paprika. It is popular cooked in stews and with eggs for breakfast.

1. In a medium skillet over medium heat, add the chorizo. Cook, stirring frequently, until the sausage is darker in color, about 5 minutes. Drain off the excess fat.

2. Return the skillet to the heat and add the onion, bell pepper, jalapeño, garlic, and cumin. Cook, stirring constantly, until the onions and peppers begin to soften, about 3 minutes. Remove the pot from the heat and allow the mixture to cool slightly.

3. In a medium bowl, beat the cream cheese until smooth. Stir in the chorizo mixture and Cheddar cheese. Mix until well blended, then cover and chill for 1 hour.

4. Cut the pastry into 8-inch rounds or squares. Place about ⅓ cup filling onto the pastry slightly off center, brush the edges of the pastry with beaten egg, and fold the dough over the filling. Pinch or crimp with a fork to seal. Place the pies on the prepared baking sheet and chill for 1 hour.

5. Fill a deep pot at least 3 inches deep with oil, making sure the oil is at least 3 inches from the top of the pot. Heat the oil to 375°F.

6. Working in batches, fry the pies until golden brown on both sides, about 3 minutes for the first side and about 2 for the second side. Drain on a rack over a paper towel-lined baking sheet. Enjoy warm.

Tomato, Basil, and Cheese Hand Pies

Fresh tomato and basil combine with ricotta and mozzarella cheese for a taste of Italy in a buttery crust.

INGREDIENTS | SERVES 8

4 ounces ricotta cheese

1 Roma tomato, seeded and finely chopped

1 cup shredded mozzarella cheese

1 egg

1 clove garlic, minced

1 tablespoon finely chopped basil

¼ teaspoon salt

⅛ teaspoon fresh grated nutmeg

2 recipes (9-inch) Flaky Pie Crust, not pressed into pie pans (See Chapter 2)

1 egg, beaten

1. In a medium bowl, combine the ricotta, tomato, shredded cheese, egg, garlic, basil, salt, and nutmeg. Cover and chill for 1 hour.

2. Heat the oven to 425°F and line a baking sheet with parchment paper.

3. Cut the pastry into 8-inch rounds or squares. Place about ⅓ cup filling onto the pastry slightly off center, brush the edges of the pastry with beaten egg, and fold the dough over the filling. Pinch or crimp with a fork to seal. Place the pies on the prepared baking sheet and brush with beaten egg. With scissors or a sharp paring knife, cut vents in pastry so that steam can escape.

4. Bake for 15 minutes, then reduce heat to 350°F and bake for an additional 25 to 30 minutes, or until the pastry is golden brown and filling is hot. Cool for 20 minutes before serving.

BBQ Pies

*Ready-cooked and shredded beef and pork BBQ are available
in most grocery stores in the meat department.*

INGREDIENTS | SERVES 8

2 cups shredded BBQ beef or pork

1 cup shredded Monterey jack cheese

1 medium onion, diced

2 recipes (9-inch) Flaky Pie Crust, not
pressed into pie pans (See Chapter 2)

1 egg, beaten

Slow Cooker BBQ

If you want to make your own BBQ filling,
just place a 1-pound beef chuck roast or
pork shoulder in your slow cooker along
with 1 cup of your favorite barbecue sauce,
1 sliced onion, 2 cloves minced garlic, and
1 tablespoon apple cider vinegar. Cook on
low for 8 hours, then remove from the pot
and shred.

1. In a medium bowl, combine the shredded meat, cheese, and diced onion.

2. Heat the oven to 425°F and line a baking sheet with parchment paper.

3. Cut the pastry into 8-inch rounds or squares. Place about ⅓ cup of the filling onto the pastry slightly off center. Brush the edges of the pastry with beaten egg and fold the dough over the filling. Pinch or crimp with a fork to seal. Place the pies on the prepared baking sheet and brush with beaten egg. With scissors or a sharp paring knife, cut vents in pastry so that steam can escape.

4. Bake for 15 minutes, then reduce heat to 350°F and bake for an additional 25 to 30 minutes, or until the pastry is golden brown and filling is hot. Cool for 20 minutes before serving.

Pepperoni Pizza Pie Pockets

This recipe makes a great snack or on-the-go meal that everyone will love. You can substitute cooked sausage or hamburger for the pepperoni if you prefer.

INGREDIENTS | SERVES 8

4 ounces ricotta cheese

2 tablespoons grated Parmesan cheese

1 cup shredded mozzarella cheese

1 egg

1 clove garlic, minced

1 tablespoon finely chopped basil

¼ teaspoon salt

1 cup tomato sauce

½ teaspoon dry oregano

¼ teaspoon ground fennel

¼ teaspoon crushed red pepper flakes

2 recipes (9-inch) Flaky Pie Crust, not pressed into pie pans (See Chapter 2)

32 pepperoni slices

1 egg, beaten

1. In a medium bowl, combine the ricotta, Parmesan, cheese, egg, garlic, basil, and salt. Cover and chill for 1 hour.

2. In a small saucepan, combine the tomato sauce, oregano, fennel, and red pepper flakes. Cook over medium heat until it comes to a simmer. Remove the pan from the heat and cool to room temperature.

3. Heat the oven to 425°F and line a baking sheet with parchment paper.

4. Cut the pastry into 8-inch rounds or squares. Place about ¼ cup of the cheese filling onto the pastry slightly off center. Top with 2 tablespoons of the tomato sauce and 4 pepperoni slices.

5. Brush the edges of the pastry with beaten egg and fold the dough over the filling. Pinch or crimp with a fork to seal. Place the pies on the prepared baking sheet and brush with beaten egg. With scissors or a sharp paring knife, cut vents in pastry so that steam can escape.

6. Bake for 15 minutes, then reduce heat to 350°F and bake for an additional 25 to 30 minutes, or until the pastry is golden brown and filling is hot. Cool for 20 minutes before serving.

CHAPTER 17

Special Occasion Pies

Tiramisu Pie

If you prefer, you can use mascarpone cheese instead of the cream cheese in this recipe.

INGREDIENTS | SERVES 8

6 ounces cream cheese, softened

1 cup powdered sugar

3 tablespoons cold strongly brewed coffee, divided

½ teaspoon powdered gelatin

1 cup heavy cream

½ teaspoon vanilla

1 (9-inch) Traditional Graham Cracker Crust, baked and cooled (See Chapter 2)

1 recipe Stabilized Whipped Cream (See Chapter 3)

Cocoa powder, for dusting

1. In a large bowl, cream together the cream cheese, powdered sugar, and 2 tablespoons of the coffee until thick and creamy.

2. In a small bowl, combine the remaining coffee with the gelatin. Allow to stand for 10 minutes to bloom. Once bloomed, heat in the microwave for 10 seconds to melt. Cool to room temperature.

3. In a medium bowl, beat the heavy cream with the vanilla until it begins to thicken. Slowly add in the gelatin mixture and beat until medium peaks form. Fold the whipped cream into the cream cheese mixture. Spread into the prepared pie crust, then cover and chill for 4 hours.

4. Once chilled, prepare the Stabilized Whipped Cream. Spread it over the pie. Chill for 1 hour. Dust the pie with cocoa powder before serving.

Pie Pops

These tiny pies are baked on lollipop sticks and are a fun project for kids. You can use any fruit filling you prefer, either store-bought or homemade.

INGREDIENTS | SERVES 12

2 recipes (9-inch) Flaky Pie Crust, not pressed into pie pans (See Chapter 2)
12 paper lollipop sticks
1 cup pie filling, homemade or prepared
1 egg, beaten
Sanding sugar

Colored Egg Wash

If you want to make your pies more festive, try using a colored egg wash. Mix an egg yolk with 5 to 10 drops of food coloring and ½ teaspoon of water. You can use this mixture to paint designs on everything from pies to cookies. The colors will darken while baking, and the finished designs will be very glossy.

1. Cut the pastry into 24 (2-inch) rounds with a sharp cookie or biscuit cutter. Gently press paper lollipop sticks into 12 of the pastry rounds, making sure the stick is no more than ¼ inch away from the top of the pastry circle.

2. Place about 1 tablespoon of filling into the center of the pastry, brush the edges of the pastry with beaten egg, and place a second 2-inch round over the filling, pressing out any trapped air. Crimp with a fork to seal. Place the pies on the prepared baking sheet and brush with beaten egg. With scissors or a sharp paring knife, cut small vents in pastry so that steam can escape. Dust the pies with sanding sugar.

3. Bake for 20 to 25 minutes, or until the pastry is golden brown and the filling is hot. Cool completely to room temperature before serving.

Triple Chocolate Brownie Pie

This is the best of both pie and brownies combined in one special dessert.

INGREDIENTS | SERVES 8

Nonstick cooking spray
2 eggs
1 cup sugar
½ cup butter, melted
½ cup all-purpose flour
⅓ cup Dutch-processed cocoa powder
¼ teaspoon salt
⅓ cup semisweet chocolate chips
¼ cup white chocolate chips
½ cup chopped walnuts, optional
1 teaspoon vanilla
1 pint vanilla ice cream

1. Heat the oven to 350°F and spray a 9-inch pie plate with nonstick cooking spray.

2. In a large bowl, whisk the eggs until they are well beaten. Add in the sugar and butter and whisk until well combined but not fluffy. Set aside.

3. In a medium bowl, sift together the flour, cocoa powder, and salt. Add the dry ingredients into the egg mixture and stir until just blended. The mixture will have some lumps.

4. Stir in the semisweet and white chocolate chips and the walnuts. Spread the batter into the prepared pan and bake for 30 to 35 minutes, or until the edges are set. The center will still be slightly gooey.

5. Cool to room temperature, then slice into wedges. Serve with vanilla ice cream.

Five-Spice Fruit Pie

Chinese five-spice adds a complex flavor to this very simple pie.

INGREDIENTS | SERVES 8

1 cup sugar

¼ cup cornstarch

½ teaspoon five-spice powder

½ teaspoon cinnamon

4 medium Granny Smith apples, peeled, cored, and sliced ¼-inch thick

4 medium Bosc pears, peeled, cored, and sliced ¼-inch thick

1 (9-inch) Mealy Pie Crust, unbaked (See Chapter 2)

1 (9-inch) Flaky Pie Crust, unbaked (See Chapter 2)

1 egg, beaten

What Is Five-Spice?

Chinese five-spice powder is an aromatic blend of spices that represent the five flavors: salty, sweet, sour, bitter, and savory. It is comprised of a mixture of anise, cinnamon, cloves, Szechuan pepper, and ground fennel and can be found in most grocery stores in the spice or Asian cooking section.

1. Heat the oven to 400°F.

2. In a large bowl, mix the sugar, cornstarch, five-spice, and cinnamon until well blended. Add the apples and pears and toss to coat. Allow to stand 10 minutes.

3. Fill the Mealy Pie Crust with the fruit mixture. Brush the edge of the bottom pie crust with the beaten egg so that the top crust will adhere. Top with the Flaky Pie Crust and trim the dough to 1 inch of the pan's edge. Tuck the edge of the top crust under the edge of the bottom crust. Crimp the dough using your fingers or a fork. Brush the entire top crust with the beaten egg and cut 4 or 5 slits in the top to vent steam.

4. Place the pie on a baking sheet and bake for 30 minutes, then reduce the heat to 350°F for an additional 30 to 40 minutes, or until the pie is bubbling and the juices are thick. Cool for 2 hours before slicing.

Chipotle Fudge Pie

Chipotle powder and cinnamon add spice and heat to this rich pie.
A drizzle of raspberry sauce is a nice addition to each slice.

INGREDIENTS | SERVES 8

2 ounces unsweetened chocolate, chopped

2 tablespoons butter

2 eggs

2 egg yolks

½ cup sugar

¾ cup corn syrup

½ teaspoon vanilla

1 tablespoon cocoa powder

½ teaspoon dry chipotle powder

½ teaspoon cinnamon

1 (9-inch) pastry crust, unbaked

1. Heat the oven to 375°F.

2. In a double boiler, melt the chocolate and butter until smooth. Remove from the heat.

3. In a large bowl, combine the eggs, egg yolks, sugar, and corn syrup. Add in the melted chocolate, vanilla, cocoa powder, chipotle powder, and cinnamon and whisk until well combined.

4. Pour the mixture into the pastry crust and place on a baking sheet. Bake for 30 to 35 minutes, or until the filling is just set. Serve slightly warm.

Chocolate Chip Cookie Pie

The flavor of gooey chocolate chip cookies makes this pie a family
favorite. It is excellent served with a scoop of ice cream.

INGREDIENTS | SERVES 8

2 eggs

1 egg yolk

¼ cup all-purpose flour

¼ cup sugar

¾ cup packed light brown sugar

¾ cup butter, softened

1½ cups semisweet chocolate chips

1 (9-inch) pastry crust, unbaked

1. Heat the oven to 325°F.

2. In a large bowl, whisk together the eggs and egg yolk until smooth. Add the flour, sugar, light brown sugar, and butter and whisk until well combined. Stir in the chocolate chips.

3. Pour the mixture into the pastry crust. Place the pie on a baking sheet and bake for 50 to 55 minutes, or until golden brown and the edges are set but the center is still slightly wobbly. Cool completely before serving.

Jam Tarts

These miniature tarts are the perfect sweet nibble for a tea party, shower, or any gathering where a dainty dessert is desired. You may use any seedless jam you prefer in this recipe.

INGREDIENTS | SERVES 10

Nonstick cooking spray
2 cups all-purpose flour
1 cup salted butter
¼ cup sugar
¼ cup milk
1 teaspoon vanilla
1 cup strawberry jam, seedless
Powdered sugar for dusting

Dough Tampers

A dough tamper is a tool that allows you to press dough into small muffin and tart pans evenly and quickly. The best tampers are made of sturdy wood and have a tamper on each side. To use the tamper, just dip it in flour and then press it evenly into the dough until it reaches the top edge of the pan.

1. Heat the oven to 350°F and spray a mini-muffin pan with nonstick cooking spray.

2. In the bowl of a food processor, combine the flour, butter, and sugar. Pulse 10 times, or until the butter is in pea-sized pieces. Add the milk and vanilla and process until the dough begins to clump around the blade.

3. Turn the dough onto a lightly floured work surface and lightly knead until the dough is smooth. Wrap the dough in plastic and chill for 20 minutes.

4. Once chilled, cut the dough into 3 even pieces. Cut each piece into 10 pieces and roll each piece into a ball.

5. Place the dough balls in the cups of a mini-muffin pan and, using a dough tamper or your fingers, press down until the dough reaches the top of the cup.

6. Fill each dough cup with 1 tablespoon of jam. Bake for 25 to 30 minutes, or until the tart crust is golden brown. Cool in the pan for 30 minutes, then transfer to a wire rack to cool completely. Dust with powdered sugar before serving.

Mango Chiffon Pie

Juicy mango gives this airy pie a refreshing flavor that is sure to please.

2 ripe mangos

¼ cup water

1 tablespoon powdered gelatin

5 eggs, separated

2 tablespoons lime juice

½ cup sugar, divided

1 teaspoon lime zest

¼ teaspoon salt

1 (9-inch) Traditional Graham Cracker Crust, baked and cooled (See Chapter 2)

1 recipe Stabilized Whipped Cream (See Chapter 3)

Selecting a Mango

It can be difficult to select a mango if you do not know what to look for. Mangos should be heavy for their size and very plump. A ripe mango should smell very sweet, and the flesh should just give under moderate pressure. Do not buy mangos that are oozing juice or have bruised or marred skins, or feel light for their size.

1. Peel and slice the mango into the work bowl of a blender. Purée until very smooth, about 3 minutes. You should yield 1½ cups of purée.

2. In a small bowl, combine the water and gelatin. Allow to stand for 10 minutes.

3. In a double boiler, combine the egg yolks, lime juice, ¼ cup sugar, lime zest, and mango purée. Cook the mixture, whisking constantly, until thickened. Remove from the heat and add the bloomed gelatin. Whisk until dissolved. Allow to cool until it thickens.

4. In a large, clean bowl, whip the egg whites with the salt until they are very frothy. Gradually add in the remaining sugar, beating constantly, until the whites form medium peaks.

5. Working in thirds, fold the egg whites into the mango mixture, making sure no large streaks of egg white remain. Pour the mixture into the prepared crust and chill until firm, about 4 hours.

6. Once chilled, prepare the Stabilized Whipped Cream. Top the pie and chill for 30 minutes before serving.

Chocolate Silk Pie

This rich, silky chocolate pie is the perfect ending to a dinner party or holiday gathering.

INGREDIENTS | SERVES 8

¾ cup butter, softened

1 cup sugar

3 ounces unsweetened chocolate, melted and cooled

1 teaspoon vanilla

¼ teaspoon almond extract

2 eggs

2 egg yolks

1 (9-inch) Chocolate Cookie Crust, baked and cooled (See Chapter 2)

1 recipe Stabilized Whipped Cream (See Chapter 3)

¼ cup mini chocolate chips

1. In a large bowl, cream together the butter and sugar until very smooth and fluffy, about 10 minutes. Beat in the chocolate, vanilla, and almond extract and mix for an additional 5 minutes.

2. Add eggs, one at a time, beating for 5 minutes after each. Add the egg yolks and beat for an additional 5 minutes. The filling should be thick and smooth.

3. Spoon the filling into the prepared crust. Cover with plastic and chill for at least 4 hours.

4. Once chilled, prepare the Stabilized Whipped Cream. Spread over the pie and garnish with the chocolate chips. Chill for 2 hours before serving.

Presidents' Day "Pie"

This recipe is a wonderful project for small children since there is no baking required. In fact, they get to prepare almost every part of the pie and eat it right away!

INGREDIENTS | SERVES 4

½ cup heavy cream

1 tablespoon powdered sugar

½ teaspoon vanilla

8 graham crackers

4 tablespoons butter

1½ cups prepared cherry pie filling

1. In a medium bowl, combine the cream, powdered sugar, and vanilla. Whisk until the mixture forms soft peaks. Chill until ready to use.

2. Place 2 graham crackers along with 1 tablespoon of butter in each zip-top plastic bag. Using your hands, mash the graham crackers with the butter until the mixture is well combined. Pour out onto a small plate and press into a firm disk.

3. Top with the cherry pie filling and whipped cream. Serve immediately.

Piña Colada Pie

Rum and coconut cream are delicious in the frosty cocktail, and they are even better in a pie! If you would like to avoid the alcohol, substitute ¼ teaspoon rum extract for the rum.

INGREDIENTS | SERVES 8

1 tablespoon unflavored powdered gelatin

¼ cup cold water

4 egg yolks

¼ cup sugar

1 tablespoon lime zest

2 tablespoons lime juice

1 tablespoon silver rum

⅓ cup sweetened cream of coconut

4 egg whites

¼ teaspoon salt

¼ cup sugar

1 (9-inch) pastry crust, baked and cooled

1 recipe Stabilized Whipped Cream (See Chapter 3)

¼ cup sweetened, shredded coconut, toasted

Cream of Coconut Versus Coconut Milk

Coconut milk and cream of coconut are not interchangeable. Coconut milk, or coconut cream, is the milk pressed from the flesh of a fresh coconut. Cream of coconut, on the other hand, is thick sugar-sweetened coconut syrup, similar to sweetened condensed milk. It can be found with drink mixers in most stores.

1. In a small bowl, combine the gelatin and the water. Allow to stand until completely bloomed, about 10 minutes.

2. In a double boiler, combine the egg yolks, sugar, lime zest, lime juice, rum, and cream of coconut. Cook the mixture, whisking constantly, until thickened and lighter in color. Remove from the heat and add the bloomed gelatin. Whisk until dissolved. Allow to cool until it starts to thicken.

3. In a large, clean bowl, whip the egg whites with the salt until they are very frothy. Gradually add in the sugar, beating constantly, until the whites form medium peaks.

4. Working in thirds, fold the egg whites into the coconut mixture, making sure no large streaks of egg white remain. Pour the mixture into the prepared crust and chill until firm, about 4 hours.

5. Once chilled, prepare the Stabilized Whipped Cream. Top the pie and garnish with the toasted coconut. Chill for 30 minutes before serving.

German Chocolate Pie

Filled with toasted pecans and coconut, this chocolate pie has all the best flavors of the popular cake.

INGREDIENTS | SERVES 8

1⅓ cups milk

2 tablespoons all-purpose flour

1 tablespoon Dutch-processed cocoa powder

1 cup sugar

6 tablespoons butter, softened

1 ounce unsweetened chocolate, melted and cooled

2 eggs

¼ teaspoon salt

1 teaspoon vanilla

¼ teaspoon coconut extract

½ cup sweetened shredded coconut, toasted

½ cup chopped pecans, toasted

1 (9-inch) pastry crust, unbaked

1. Heat the oven to 425°F.

2. In a medium saucepan, bring the milk to a simmer over medium heat. Remove from the heat and cool slightly.

3. In a large bowl, whisk together the flour, cocoa powder, sugar, butter, and melted chocolate until completely combined.

4. Add the eggs, salt, vanilla, and coconut extract and mix well. Slowly whisk in the warm milk until smooth. Fold in the coconut and pecans.

5. Pour the mixture into the prepared pastry crust and place on a baking sheet. Bake in the lower third of the oven for 10 minutes, then reduce the heat to 325°F and bake for an additional 30 to 40 minutes, or until the filling is set at the edges and just slightly wobbly in the center. Do not overbake or the custard will become watery. Cool completely before slicing.

Salted-Caramel Apple Pie

Salted caramel and tart apples bake together to make a buttery, delicious pie.

INGREDIENTS | SERVES 8

¾ cup sugar

¼ cup cornstarch

1 teaspoon cinnamon

½ teaspoon fresh grated nutmeg

8 medium Granny Smith apples, peeled, cored, and sliced ⅛-inch thick

1 recipe Salted Caramel Sauce (See Chapter 3)

1 (9-inch) Mealy Pie Crust, unbaked (See Chapter 2)

1 (9-inch) Flaky Pie Crust (See Chapter 2), cut into 10 1-inch strips

1 egg, beaten

1. Heat the oven to 400°F.

2. In a large bowl, mix the sugar, cornstarch, cinnamon, and nutmeg until well blended. Add the apples and toss to coat. Allow to stand 10 minutes.

3. Layer ⅓ of the apple mixture onto the bottom of the Mealy Pie Crust, then drizzle half the caramel sauce over it. Repeat, ending with a final layer of apples.

4. Lay out 5 strips of pie dough on top of the filling about ½ inch apart. Starting ½ inch from the edge of the pie, fold back every other strip and lay down 1 strip of pastry. Fold the pastry back down and fold back the other pieces. Lay down a second strip about ½ inch from the first strip. Repeat this process until all the strips are used. Trim the dough to 1 inch of the pan's edge. Tuck the edge of the top crust under the edge of the bottom crust. Crimp the dough using your fingers or a fork. Brush the lattice with beaten egg.

5. Bake for 15 minutes, then reduce the heat to 350°F and bake for an additional 30 to 40 minutes, or until the filling is bubbly in the center and the lattice is golden brown. Cool for 1 hour before serving.

Raspberry Chipotle Crumb Tart

Sweet raspberries pair surprisingly well with spicy chipotle pepper. If you like, you may add a drizzle of semisweet chocolate as a finishing touch.

INGREDIENTS | SERVES 8

1 (10-inch) Short Crust for Tarts, unbaked (See Chapter 2)

3 cups raspberries

¾ cup sugar

2 tablespoons cornstarch

2 tablespoons butter, melted

1 teaspoon lemon juice

½ teaspoon vanilla

½ chipotle pepper in adobo, finely chopped

¼ teaspoon cinnamon

¼ teaspoon salt

1 recipe Butter Crumble (See Chapter 3)

Chipotle in Adobo

In Spanish, *adobo* means "sauce," and in this case the sauce is a spicy marinade for smoked jalapeños. Chipotle peppers in adobo can be quite spicy, so if you are not a fan of heat, reduce the amount of chipotle in your recipes by half.

1. Heat the oven to 350°F.

2. Line the tart with parchment paper or a double layer of aluminum foil and add pie weights or dry beans. Bake for 12 minutes, then remove the paper and weights and bake for an additional 10 to 15 minutes, or until the crust is golden brown all over. Remove from the oven and set aside to cool. Leave the oven on.

3. In a large bowl, combine the raspberries, sugar, cornstarch, butter, lemon juice, vanilla, chipotle peppers, cinnamon, and salt until well combined. Spread into the prepared crust and top with the Butter Crumble.

4. Place the tart on a baking sheet and bake for 35 to 45 minutes, or until the filling is bubbling and the crumble is golden brown. Allow to cool completely before serving.

Shoofly Pie

Shoofly is a Southern tradition that has a moist, yet somewhat cakey, texture. If you like a robust molasses flavor, replace the corn syrup with molasses.

INGREDIENTS | SERVES 8

1¼ cups all-purpose flour

¾ cup packed light brown sugar

1 teaspoon cinnamon

¼ teaspoon salt

6 tablespoons butter, cut into ½-inch pieces and chilled

1 cup boiling water

¾ cup molasses

¼ cup light corn syrup

1 teaspoon baking soda

1 large egg, lightly beaten

1 (9-inch) pastry crust, unbaked

1. Heat the oven to 400°F.

2. In a large bowl, combine the flour, light brown sugar, cinnamon, and salt. Mix well.

3. Add in the butter and, with your fingers or a fork, rub it in until the mixture becomes crumbly. Cover and chill until ready to use.

4. In a medium bowl, whisk together the boiling water, molasses, and corn syrup until well blended. Whisk in the baking soda and egg until well mixed.

5. Pour the molasses mixture into the pastry crust and top with the crumb mixture. Place the pan on a baking sheet and bake for 10 minutes, then reduce the oven to 350°F and bake for an additional 35 to 45 minutes, or until the pie is golden brown and puffed. Cool completely before serving.

Strawberry Jalapeño Pie

Sweet, ripe strawberries are a surprisingly perfect match for fruity, spicy jalapeños.

INGREDIENTS | SERVES 8

1 quart fresh strawberries, hulled and quartered

¾ cup sugar

1 tablespoon butter

1 medium jalapeño, stemmed, seeded, and finely minced

3 tablespoons cornstarch

¼ teaspoon cinnamon

¾ cup cranberry juice

½ teaspoon vanilla

1 (9-inch) Traditional Graham Cracker Crust, baked and cooled (See Chapter 2)

1 recipe Stabilized Whipped Cream (See Chapter 3)

Reduce the Heat

Fresh jalapeños can be a little spicy, but you can reduce the heat by properly cleaning the flesh. Cut the stem off the jalapeño and slice the fruit in half. With a small spoon, scoop out the seeds, then scrape the inside of the flesh to remove the ribs. The ribs store the capsaicin, the compound that gives jalapeños their spice. Once fully scraped, just wash the jalapeño under cool water.

1. In a medium bowl, combine half of the strawberries with the sugar. With a potato masher or a fork, mash the berries until mostly smooth. Stir in the remaining berries and let stand for 10 minutes.

2. In a large saucepan, melt the butter until it foams. Add the minced jalapeño and cook, stirring constantly, for 1 minute.

3. In a bowl, combine the berry mixture, cornstarch, cinnamon, and cranberry juice. Add to the jalapeño and cook over medium heat until the mixture thickens and bubbles. Once thick, remove from the heat and stir in the vanilla.

4. Pour the mixture into the prepared crust and chill for 4 hours. Once chilled, prepare the Stabilized Whipped Cream and spread over the top. Chill for 30 minutes before serving.

Snickerdoodle Pie

This fluffy, cakelike pie tastes a lot like the popular cookie and is delicious with some whipped cream on top.

½ cup packed light brown sugar

½ cup butter, divided

3 tablespoons water

2 tablespoons corn syrup

¼ teaspoon cinnamon

2 teaspoons vanilla, divided

½ cup sugar

¼ cup powdered sugar

1 teaspoon baking powder

¼ teaspoon cream of tartar

½ teaspoon salt

1 egg

½ cup milk

1¼ cups all-purpose flour

1 tablespoon butter, melted

1 (9-inch) pastry crust, unbaked

1 tablespoon sugar

¼ teaspoon cinnamon

1. Heat the oven to 350°F.

2. In a medium saucepan, combine light brown sugar, ¼ cup butter, water, corn syrup, and cinnamon. Bring to a boil over medium heat, swirling the pan occasionally. Once boiling, let the mixture cook for 2 minutes. Remove from the heat and stir in 1 teaspoon vanilla. Set aside.

3. In a large bowl, cream together ¼ cup butter with the sugar and powdered sugar until creamy. Add in the baking powder, cream of tartar, salt, egg, milk, and flour and mix until smooth.

4. Brush the inside of the pastry crust with the melted butter. Combine the sugar with the cinnamon and dust the inside of the pastry evenly with the mixture. Spread the filling into the prepared pastry crust and then carefully pour the syrup over the top.

5. Place the pie on a baking sheet and bake for 45 to 50 minutes, or until the filling is browned and puffed. Cool for 30 minutes before serving.

CHAPTER 18

Quiches

Quiche Lorraine

This is a classic dish that is perfect for brunch, lunch, or even as dinner with a green salad.

INGREDIENTS | SERVES 8

1 (9-inch) pastry crust, unbaked

2 eggs

2 egg yolks

1 cup half-and-half

Pinch fresh grated nutmeg

½ teaspoon salt

½ teaspoon fresh cracked pepper

8 strips bacon, cooked crisp and chopped

1 cup grated Swiss or Gruyère cheese

1. Heat the oven to 375°F.

2. Line the pie crust with parchment paper or a double layer of aluminum foil and add pie weights or dry beans. Bake for 12 minutes, then remove the paper and weights and bake for an additional 10 minutes, or until the crust is golden brown all over. Remove from the oven and set aside to cool.

3. In a medium bowl, whisk together the eggs and egg yolks. Add the half-and-half, nutmeg, salt, and pepper and whisk until well combined.

4. Spread the bacon and cheese evenly on the bottom of the crust. Carefully pour over the egg mixture.

5. Bake for 30 to 40 minutes, or until the filling is set and starting to brown lightly on the top. Cool for 20 minutes at room temperature before serving.

Chorizo and Pepper Jack Quiche

Chorizo gives this quiche an exotic, spicy kick. Serve it with a cup of tortilla soup for a hearty meal.

INGREDIENTS | SERVES 8

1 (9-inch) pastry crust, unbaked
4 ounces chorizo sausage
½ cup diced onion
½ cup diced green bell pepper
½ cup diced red bell pepper
2 eggs
2 egg yolks
1 cup half-and-half
¼ teaspoon cumin
½ teaspoon salt
½ teaspoon fresh cracked pepper
⅔ cup grated pepper jack cheese

Substitutions for Chorizo

If chorizo is not available at your local market, feel free to substitute a spicy breakfast sausage, or ground beef or pork cooked with 2 teaspoons of taco seasoning.

1. Heat the oven to 375°F.

2. Line the pie crust with parchment paper or a double layer of aluminum foil and add pie weights or dry beans. Bake for 12 minutes, then remove the paper and weights and bake for an additional 10 minutes, or until the crust is golden brown all over. Remove from the oven and set aside to cool.

3. In a medium skillet over medium heat, add the chorizo. Cook, stirring frequently, for 5 minutes. Add the onion and peppers and cook until the vegetables are beginning to soften, about 3 minutes. Remove from the heat and set aside to cool slightly.

4. In a medium bowl, whisk together the eggs and egg yolks. Add the half-and-half, cumin, salt, and pepper and whisk until well combined.

5. Spread the chorizo mixture and cheese evenly on the bottom of the crust. Carefully pour over the egg mixture.

6. Bake for 30 to 40 minutes, or until the filling is set and starting to brown lightly on the top. Cool for 20 minutes at room temperature before serving.

Apple, Gruyère, and Caramelized Onion Quiche

Nutty Gruyère cheese pairs well with sweet caramelized onions and tart apples.

INGREDIENTS | SERVES 8

1 (9-inch) pastry crust, unbaked
2 eggs
2 egg yolks
1 cup half-and-half
Pinch fresh grated nutmeg
½ teaspoon salt
½ teaspoon fresh cracked pepper
1 medium apple, peeled, cored, and diced
1 cup grated Gruyère cheese
½ cup caramelized onions

Caramelized Onions

Thinly slice 2 large red onions and cook them in a heavy skillet over medium-low heat with 2 tablespoons olive oil and 1 tablespoon of sugar for 45 minutes to 1 hour. Stir often to prevent burning.

1. Heat the oven to 375°F.

2. Line the pie crust with parchment paper or a double layer of aluminum foil and add pie weights or dry beans. Bake for 12 minutes, then remove the paper and weights and bake for an additional 10 minutes, or until the crust is golden brown all over. Remove from the oven and set aside to cool.

3. In a medium bowl, whisk together the eggs and egg yolks. Add the half-and-half, nutmeg, salt, and pepper and whisk until well combined.

4. Spread the apples, cheese, and onions evenly on the bottom of the crust. Pour over the egg mixture.

5. Bake for 30 to 40 minutes, or until the filling is set and starting to brown lightly on the top. Cool for 20 minutes at room temperature before serving.

Apple Cheddar Quiche

Both sweet and savory, this quiche is perfect for a fall brunch served with a creamy soup.

INGREDIENTS | SERVES 8

1 (9-inch) pastry crust, unbaked
3 eggs
1 egg yolk
1 cup half-and-half
½ teaspoon salt
½ teaspoon fresh cracked pepper
2 medium apples, peeled, cored, and diced
1 cup grated sharp Cheddar cheese

1. Heat the oven to 375°F.

2. In a medium bowl, whisk together the eggs and egg yolk. Add the half-and-half, salt, and pepper and whisk until well combined.

3. Spread the apples and cheese evenly on the bottom of the crust. Carefully pour over the egg mixture.

4. Bake for 30 to 40 minutes, or until the filling is set and starting to brown lightly on the top. Cool for 20 minutes at room temperature before serving.

Spinach, Bacon, and Hash Brown Quiche

Hearty is the best way to describe this tasty quiche. Feel free to use fresh hash browns if you prefer; just drain them very well before cooking.

INGREDIENTS | SERVES 8

2 strips thick-cut bacon, chopped

1 cup frozen hash brown potatoes, thawed

4 ounces frozen chopped spinach, thawed and drained well

1 small onion, finely diced

1 clove garlic, minced

1 (9-inch) pastry crust, unbaked

3 eggs

1 egg yolk

½ cup half-and-half

½ cup sour cream

½ teaspoon salt

½ teaspoon fresh cracked pepper

1 cup shredded pepper jack cheese

1. In a medium skillet over medium heat, add the chopped bacon. Cook, stirring often, until the bacon is crisp. Remove the bacon from the pan to drain.

2. Add the hash browns to the pan and cook until browned and crisp, about 10 minutes. Remove from the pan to drain.

3. Add the spinach and onion and cook until the onions are soft, about 10 minutes. Add the garlic and cook until fragrant, about 1 minute. Set aside to cool. Drain off any excess water.

4. Heat the oven to 375°F.

5. Line the pie crust with parchment paper or a double layer of aluminum foil and add pie weights or dry beans. Bake for 12 minutes, then remove the paper and weights and bake for an additional 10 minutes, or until the crust is golden brown all over. Remove from the oven and set aside to cool.

6. In a medium bowl, whisk together the eggs and egg yolk. Add the half-and-half, sour cream, salt, and pepper and whisk until well combined.

7. Spread the spinach mixture, bacon, hash browns, and cheese evenly on the bottom of the crust. Carefully pour over the egg mixture.

8. Bake for 30 to 40 minutes, or until the filling is set and starting to brown lightly on the top. Cool for 20 minutes at room temperature before serving.

Asparagus and Pancetta Quiche

Fresh asparagus is available in the spring, but you can use frozen to make this dish year-round.

INGREDIENTS | SERVES 8

1 (9-inch) pastry crust, unbaked

½ pound fresh asparagus spears, trimmed and cut into ½-inch pieces

3 eggs

1 egg yolk

½ cup half-and-half

½ cup heavy cream

½ teaspoon salt

½ teaspoon fresh cracked pepper

4 ounces pancetta, cooked crisp and drained

½ cup grated mozzarella cheese

½ cup grated Parmesan cheese

Substitutes for Pancetta?

Pancetta is unsmoked, dry cured Italian bacon. Most markets carry it in the deli or meat section, or in an area with international or imported cheeses. If you cannot find it at the market, try using prosciutto or even a regular smoked bacon.

1. Heat the oven to 375°F.

2. Line the pie crust with parchment paper or a double layer of aluminum foil and add pie weights or dry beans. Bake for 12 minutes, then remove the paper and weights and bake for an additional 10 minutes, or until the crust is golden brown all over. Remove from the oven and set aside to cool.

3. Place asparagus in a steamer over 1 inch of boiling water and cover tightly with a lid. Cook until just tender, about 4 minutes. Drain and cool.

4. In a medium bowl, whisk together the eggs and egg yolk. Add the half-and-half, cream, salt, and pepper and whisk until well combined.

5. Spread the pancetta, asparagus, and cheeses evenly on the bottom of the crust. Carefully pour over the egg mixture.

6. Bake for 30 to 40 minutes, or until the filling is set and starting to brown lightly on the top. Cool for 20 minutes at room temperature before serving.

Bacon and Cheddar Quiche

Simple and tasty, this quiche is for bacon lovers!

INGREDIENTS | SERVES 8

½ pound thick-cut, hardwood smoked bacon, chopped

1 (9-inch) pastry crust, unbaked

3 eggs

2 egg yolks

1 cup half-and-half

½ teaspoon hot pepper sauce

½ teaspoon salt

½ teaspoon fresh cracked pepper

1 cup grated sharp Cheddar cheese

1. In a large skillet over medium heat, cook the bacon until brown and crisp. Remove from the pan and allow to cool to room temperature.

2. Heat the oven to 375°F.

3. Line the pie crust with parchment paper or a double layer of aluminum foil and add pie weights or dry beans. Bake for 12 minutes, then remove the paper and weights and bake for an additional 10 minutes, or until the crust is golden brown all over. Remove from the oven and set aside to cool.

4. In a medium bowl, whisk together the eggs and egg yolks. Add the half-and-half, hot pepper sauce, salt, and pepper and whisk until well combined.

5. Spread the bacon and cheese evenly on the bottom of the crust. Carefully pour over the egg mixture.

6. Bake for 30 to 40 minutes, or until the filling is set and starting to brown lightly on the top. Cool for 20 minutes at room temperature before serving.

Pork Sausage, Onion, and Hash Brown Quiche

This quiche was inspired by a hearty country breakfast. If you want to bump up the color and flavor, add ⅓ cup finely diced green pepper with the onions.

INGREDIENTS | SERVES 8

3 tablespoons butter, divided
1 cup shredded potato, drained well
1 small onion, finely chopped
8 ounces bulk pork breakfast sausage
1 (9-inch) pastry crust, unbaked
2 eggs
2 egg yolks
1 cup half-and-half
½ teaspoon hot pepper sauce
½ teaspoon salt
½ teaspoon fresh cracked pepper
¾ cup grated Colby-Jack cheese

1. In a medium skillet over medium heat, melt 2 tablespoons of the butter until it foams. Add the shredded potato and cook until it begins to brown and become crisp, about 12 minutes. Remove the potatoes from the pan and cool.

2. In the same pan, heat the remaining butter until it foams. Add the onion and cook until just translucent. Add the pork sausage and cook, stirring constantly, until the sausage is cooked through and browned, about 10 minutes. Remove the pan from the heat and cool.

3. Heat the oven to 375°F.

4. Line the pie crust with parchment paper or a double layer of aluminum foil and add pie weights or dry beans. Bake for 12 minutes, then remove the paper and weights and bake for an additional 10 minutes, or until the crust is golden brown all over. Remove from the oven and set aside to cool.

5. In a medium bowl, whisk together the eggs and egg yolks. Add the half-and-half, hot pepper sauce, salt, and pepper and whisk until well combined.

6. Spread the hash browns, sausage mixture, and cheese evenly on the bottom of the crust. Carefully pour over the egg mixture.

7. Bake for 30 to 40 minutes, or until the filling is set and starting to brown lightly on the top. Cool for 20 minutes at room temperature before serving.

Broccoli and Mushroom Quiche

This quiche has a lot of earthy flavors, and it is perfect as a main course for lunch or dinner.

INGREDIENTS | SERVES 8

1 (9-inch) pastry crust, unbaked

2 tablespoons unsalted butter

10 ounces frozen chopped broccoli, thawed

8 ounces button mushrooms, sliced

3 eggs

2 egg yolks

1 cup half-and-half

½ teaspoon salt

½ teaspoon fresh cracked pepper

1 cup grated Swiss cheese

Broccoli

Broccoli is a member of the cabbage family and is rich in vitamins and minerals. The best way to cook broccoli to preserve its health benefits is steaming. Broccoli is shown to contain a number of cancer-fighting compounds, as well as being high in vitamin C and dietary fiber.

1. Heat the oven to 375°F.

2. Line the pie crust with parchment paper or a double layer of aluminum foil and add pie weights or dry beans. Bake for 12 minutes, then remove the paper and weights and bake for an additional 10 minutes, or until the crust is golden brown all over. Remove from the oven and set aside to cool.

3. In a medium skillet over medium heat, melt the butter until it foams. Add the broccoli and mushrooms and cook until they are soft, about 8 minutes. Drain off any liquid and allow to cool to room temperature.

4. In a medium bowl, whisk together the eggs and egg yolks. Add the half-and-half, salt, and pepper and whisk until well combined.

5. Spread the broccoli mixture and cheese evenly on the bottom of the crust. Carefully pour over the egg mixture.

6. Bake for 30 to 40 minutes, or until the filling is set and starting to brown lightly on the top. Cool for 20 minutes at room temperature before serving.

Jalapeño and Roast Chicken Quiche

*Fresh jalapeños add the best flavor to this pie. You can substitute
cooked turkey to this quiche, or even chopped ham.*

INGREDIENTS | SERVES 8

1 (9-inch) pastry crust, unbaked
1 tablespoon butter
½ medium onion, finely chopped
1 large jalapeño, seeded and minced
2 cloves garlic, minced
½ teaspoon salt
½ teaspoon chili powder
¼ teaspoon smoked paprika
½ teaspoon fresh cracked pepper
2 eggs
2 egg yolks
1 cup half-and-half
1 cooked chicken breast, shredded
1 cup grated Monterey jack cheese

1. Heat the oven to 375°F.

2. Line the pie crust with parchment paper or a double layer of aluminum foil and add pie weights or dry beans. Bake for 12 minutes, then remove the paper and weights and bake for an additional 10 minutes, or until the crust is golden brown all over. Remove from the oven and set aside to cool.

3. In a medium skillet over medium heat, melt the butter until it foams. Add the onion and jalapeño. Cook, stirring occasionally, until they begin to soften, about 5 minutes.

4. Add the garlic, salt, chili powder, paprika, and pepper and cook until fragrant, about 1 minute. Remove from the heat and allow to cool slightly.

5. In a medium bowl, whisk together the eggs and egg yolks. Add the half-and-half and whisk until well combined.

6. Spread the chicken, jalapeño mixture, and cheese evenly on the bottom of the crust. Carefully pour over the egg mixture.

7. Bake for 30 to 40 minutes, or until the filling is set and starting to brown lightly on the top. Cool for 20 minutes at room temperature before serving.

Chicken and Potato Quiche

Frozen hash browns make this quiche a snap to make, but you can use fresh grated potato if you prefer.

INGREDIENTS | SERVES 8

1 (9-inch) pastry crust, unbaked
1 chicken breast
¾ teaspoon salt, divided
¼ teaspoon poultry seasoning
¼ teaspoon smoked paprika
1 tablespoon butter
1½ cups frozen hash brown potatoes, thawed
2 eggs
2 egg yolks
1 cup half-and-half
½ teaspoon fresh cracked pepper
1 cup grated Swiss cheese

Rotisserie Chicken

Most grocery stores offer fresh roasted chickens in their deli sections. These chickens are seasoned and ready to use, which can be a great time-saver. Just remove the chicken you need for the recipe. The rest can be used for chicken salad or chicken soup, or eaten as it is.

1. Heat the oven to 375°F.

2. Line the pie crust with parchment paper or a double layer of aluminum foil and add pie weights or dry beans. Bake for 12 minutes, then remove the paper and weights and bake for an additional 10 minutes, or until the crust is golden brown all over. Remove from the oven and set aside to cool.

3. Season the chicken breast with ¼ teaspoon of the salt, poultry seasoning, and smoked paprika. Bake for 25 to 30 minutes, or until the internal temperature reaches 160°F and the meat is no longer pink. Rest for 10 minutes, then dice into ½-inch cubes. Set aside.

4. In a medium skillet over medium heat, melt the butter until it foams. Add the hash browns and cook, stirring occasionally, until brown and crisp. Remove from the heat and allow to cool slightly.

5. In a medium bowl, whisk together the eggs and egg yolks. Add the half-and-half, the remaining salt, and pepper. Whisk until well combined.

6. Spread the chicken, hash browns, and cheese evenly on the bottom of the crust. Carefully pour over the egg mixture.

7. Bake for 30 to 40 minutes, or until the filling is set and starting to brown lightly on the top. Cool for 20 minutes at room temperature before serving.

Roasted Red Pepper and Mozzarella Quiche

Roasted red peppers add a lot of delicious flavor to this quiche. If you like, you can use an Italian cheese blend in place of the shredded mozzarella.

INGREDIENTS | SERVES 8

1 (9-inch) pastry crust, unbaked
3 eggs
1 egg yolk
½ cup half-and-half
½ cup heavy cream
½ teaspoon salt
½ teaspoon fresh cracked pepper
2 roasted red peppers, chopped
1 cup fresh mozzarella cheese, cut into ¼-inch pieces
¼ cup grated Parmesan cheese

1. Heat the oven to 375°F.

2. Line the pie crust with parchment paper or a double layer of aluminum foil and add pie weights or dry beans. Bake for 12 minutes, then remove the paper and weights and bake for an additional 10 minutes, or until the crust is golden brown all over. Remove from the oven and set aside to cool.

3. In a medium bowl, whisk together the eggs and egg yolk. Add the half-and-half, cream, salt, and pepper and whisk until well combined.

4. Spread the roasted red pepper, mozzarella, and Parmesan cheese evenly on the bottom of the crust. Carefully pour over the egg mixture.

5. Bake for 30 to 40 minutes, or until the filling is set and starting to brown lightly on the top. Cool for 20 minutes at room temperature before serving.

Crab Cake Quiche

This quiche has all the best flavors of crab cakes and is perfect with a cup of creamy chowder.

INGREDIENTS | SERVES 8

1 (9-inch) pastry crust, unbaked
1 tablespoon unsalted butter
½ cup diced green bell pepper
½ cup diced onion
1 clove garlic, minced
2 eggs
2 egg yolks
1 cup half-and-half
1 teaspoon Old Bay seasoning
½ teaspoon salt
½ teaspoon fresh cracked pepper
4 ounces fresh lump crabmeat, picked through and drained
½ cup grated Parmesan cheese
½ cup grated Swiss cheese

Crab or Krab?

If real crab is not available or too expensive, you have another option. Imitation crabmeat, or krab, is made of processed white fish paste called surimi. While similar in taste and texture to real crab, it is lower in cholesterol, more affordable, and readily available in most seafood markets.

1. Heat the oven to 375°F.

2. Line the pie crust with parchment paper or a double layer of aluminum foil and add pie weights or dry beans. Bake for 12 minutes, then remove the paper and weights and bake for an additional 10 minutes, or until the crust is golden brown all over. Remove from the oven and set aside to cool.

3. In a medium skillet over medium heat, melt the butter until it foams. Add the diced peppers and onions and cook until tender, about 5 minutes. Add the garlic and cook until fragrant, about 30 seconds. Remove from the heat and set aside to cool.

4. In a medium bowl, whisk together the eggs and egg yolks. Add the half-and-half, Old Bay, salt, and pepper and whisk until well combined.

5. Spread the peppers and onions, crabmeat, and cheeses evenly on the bottom of the crust. Carefully pour over the egg mixture.

6. Bake for 35 to 45 minutes, or until the filling is set and starting to brown lightly on the top. Cool for 20 minutes at room temperature before serving.

Smoked Salmon Quiche

*Smoked salmon makes this quiche rich and flavorful. If fresh herbs are
not available, feel free to use half as much of the dried kind.*

INGREDIENTS | SERVES 8

1 (9-inch) pastry crust, unbaked
3 eggs
1 egg yolk
½ cup half-and-half
½ cup sour cream
2 tablespoons fresh chopped dill
2 tablespoons fresh chopped chives
½ teaspoon salt
½ teaspoon fresh cracked pepper
4 ounces cold smoked salmon, chopped
1 cup shredded Swiss cheese

1. Heat the oven to 375°F.

2. Line the pie crust with parchment paper or a double layer of aluminum foil and add pie weights or dry beans. Bake for 12 minutes, then remove the paper and weights and bake for an additional 10 minutes, or until the crust is golden brown all over. Remove from the oven and set aside to cool.

3. In a medium bowl, whisk together the eggs and egg yolk. Add the half-and-half, sour cream, dill, chives, salt, and pepper and whisk until well combined.

4. Spread the smoked salmon and Swiss cheese evenly on the bottom of the crust. Carefully pour over the egg mixture.

5. Bake for 30 to 40 minutes, or until the filling is set and starting to brown lightly on the top. Cool for 20 minutes at room temperature before serving.

Ham, Leek, and Gruyère Quiche

This quiche has a mild, sophisticated flavor. For a special touch, use Serrano or Parma ham.

INGREDIENTS | SERVES 8

2 tablespoons butter

2 leeks, white part only, cleaned and chopped

1 (9-inch) pastry crust, unbaked

2 eggs

2 egg yolks

1 cup half-and-half

Pinch fresh grated nutmeg

½ teaspoon salt

½ teaspoon fresh cracked pepper

4 ounces thinly sliced smoked ham, chopped

1 cup grated Gruyère cheese

Cleaning Leeks

The easiest and most effective way to clean the grit out of leeks is to slice them into rings and soak them in cold water. As they soak, the grit will fall to the bottom of the bowl. Once soaked, give them a good rinse in cold water before using to wash away any lingering dirt.

1. In a medium skillet over medium heat, melt the butter until it foams. Add the leeks and sauté until softened, about 5 minutes. Remove from the heat and allow to cool.

2. Heat the oven to 375°F.

3. Line the pie crust with parchment paper or a double layer of aluminum foil and add pie weights or dry beans. Bake for 12 minutes, then remove the paper and weights and bake for an additional 10 minutes, or until the crust is golden brown all over. Remove from the oven and set aside to cool.

4. In a medium bowl, whisk together the eggs and egg yolks. Add the half-and-half, nutmeg, salt, and pepper and whisk until well combined.

5. Spread the leeks, ham, and cheese evenly on the bottom of the crust. Carefully pour over the egg mixture.

6. Bake for 30 to 40 minutes, or until the filling is set and starting to brown lightly on the top. Cool for 20 minutes at room temperature before serving.

Spinach, Mushroom, and Swiss Quiche

Don't throw away your mushrooms stems. Use them to make some mushroom soup to go with this quiche!

INGREDIENTS | SERVES 8

2 tablespoons butter

1 pint shitaki or crimini mushrooms, stemmed and cut in half

4 ounces frozen chopped spinach, thawed and drained well

1 small onion, finely diced

1 clove garlic, minced

1 (9-inch) pastry crust, unbaked

3 eggs

1 egg yolk

½ cup half-and-half

½ cup sour cream

2 tablespoons fresh chopped dill

2 tablespoons fresh chopped chives

½ teaspoon salt

½ teaspoon fresh cracked pepper

1 cup shredded Swiss cheese

1. In a medium skillet over medium heat, melt the butter until it foams. Add the mushrooms and cook, stirring occasionally, until they are browned and softened, about 5 minutes.

2. Add the spinach and onion and cook until the onions are soft, about 10 minutes. Add the garlic and cook until fragrant, about 1 minute. Set aside to cool. Drain off any excess water.

3. Heat the oven to 375°F.

4. Line the pie crust with parchment paper or a double layer of aluminum foil and add pie weights or dry beans. Bake for 12 minutes, then remove the paper and weights and bake for an additional 10 minutes, or until the crust is golden brown all over. Remove from the oven and set aside to cool.

5. In a medium bowl, whisk together the eggs and egg yolk. Add the half-and-half, sour cream, dill, chives, salt, and pepper and whisk until well combined.

6. Spread the spinach mixture and cheese evenly on the bottom of the crust. Carefully pour over the egg mixture.

7. Bake for 30 to 40 minutes, or until the filling is set and starting to brown lightly on the top. Cool for 20 minutes at room temperature before serving.

Shrimp and Spinach Quiche

You could replace the Monterey jack cheese with Swiss or Gruyère in this dish.

INGREDIENTS | SERVES 8

1 (9-inch) pastry crust, unbaked
1 tablespoon unsalted butter
1 medium onion, chopped
4 ounces frozen chopped spinach, thawed and drained well
1 clove garlic, minced
2 eggs
2 egg yolks
1 cup half-and-half
½ teaspoon smoked paprika
1 teaspoon hot sauce
½ teaspoon salt
½ teaspoon fresh cracked pepper
4 ounces cooked shrimp, chopped
½ cup grated Parmesan cheese
½ cup grated Monterey jack cheese

Cooking Shrimp

Never buy frozen cooked shrimp. They have a mealy, mushy texture. Instead buy the freshest shrimp available and cook them yourself. The easiest way is to boil them in salted water for 3 to 4 minutes or sauté them in butter and garlic until they just become opaque and begin to curl.

1. Heat the oven to 375°F.

2. Line the pie crust with parchment paper or a double layer of aluminum foil and add pie weights or dry beans. Bake for 12 minutes, then remove the paper and weights and bake for an additional 10 minutes, or until the crust is golden brown all over. Remove from the oven and set aside to cool.

3. In a medium skillet over medium heat, melt the butter until it foams. Add the onions and cook until tender, about 5 minutes. Add the spinach and garlic and cook until fragrant, about 1 minute. Remove from the heat and set aside to cool.

4. In a medium bowl, whisk together the eggs and egg yolks. Add the half-and-half, paprika, hot sauce, salt, and pepper and whisk until well combined.

5. Spread the onions, shrimp, and cheeses evenly on the bottom of the crust. Carefully pour over the egg mixture.

6. Bake for 35 to 45 minutes, or until the filling is set and starting to brown lightly on the top. Cool for 20 minutes at room temperature before serving.

Roasted Butternut Squash Quiche

Roasted butternut squash gives this quiche a deep, slightly sweet flavor.

INGREDIENTS | SERVES 8

1 tablespoon vegetable oil

2 cups butternut squash, cut into ¼-inch pieces

1 tablespoon butter

1 small onion, diced

2 cloves garlic, minced

1 (9-inch) pastry crust, unbaked

2 eggs

2 egg yolks

1 cup half-and-half

½ teaspoon fresh chopped rosemary

¼ teaspoon cinnamon

¼ teaspoon mace

½ teaspoon salt

½ teaspoon fresh cracked pepper

4 strips bacon, cooked crisp and chopped

1 cup grated Cheddar cheese

1. Heat the oven to 425°F and line a baking sheet with parchment paper.

2. In a medium bowl, combine the vegetable oil and butternut squash. Toss until evenly coated. Spread the squash out on the baking sheet and roast for 40 to 50 minutes, or until fork-tender. Cool completely.

3. In a medium skillet over medium heat, melt the butter until it foams. Add the onion and cook until tender, about 3 minutes. Add the garlic and cook until fragrant. Set aside to cool.

4. Heat the oven to 375°F.

5. Line the pie crust with parchment paper or a double layer of aluminum foil and add pie weights or dry beans. Bake for 12 minutes, then remove the paper and weights and bake for an additional 10 minutes, or until the crust is golden brown all over. Remove from the oven and set aside to cool.

6. In a medium bowl, whisk together the eggs and egg yolks. Add the half-and-half, rosemary, cinnamon, mace, salt, and pepper and whisk until well combined.

7. Spread the squash, onions, bacon, and cheese evenly on the bottom of the crust. Carefully pour over the egg mixture.

8. Bake for 30 to 40 minutes, or until the filling is set and starting to brown lightly on the top. Cool for 20 minutes at room temperature before serving.

CHAPTER 19

Pies for Special Diets

Reduced-Fat Pastry Crust

This flavorful crust is tender yet crisp, and it has 62 percent less butter than a traditional pastry crust.

INGREDIENTS | YIELDS 1 (9-INCH) CRUST

1¼ cups all-purpose flour

1 tablespoon sugar, or granular sucralose

½ teaspoon salt

3 tablespoons unsalted butter, cubed and chilled

3 tablespoons skim milk

3–4 tablespoons ice water

Watch the Clock

Baked goods made with sugar substitutes tend to bake more quickly than those made with sugar. When substituting granular sucralose for sugar in a recipe, you will want to check early for doneness. Start checking 10 minutes early to avoid burning.

1. In a large bowl, sift together the flour, sugar or sucralose, and salt.

2. Add the butter and, using your fingers, rub it into the flour until the mixture looks like coarse sand.

3. Add the milk along with 2 tablespoons of water and mix until the dough forms a rough ball. Add more water, 1 tablespoon at a time, if needed.

4. Turn the dough out onto a lightly floured surface and form a disk. Wrap in plastic and chill for at least 30 minutes or up to 3 days.

5. Remove the dough from the refrigerator for 10 minutes before rolling out. Roll out on a lightly floured surface to a ⅛-inch-thick, 12-inch circle, turning the dough often to make sure it does not stick. Dust the surface with additional flour if needed.

6. If molding into a pie pan, fold the dough in half and place it into a 9-inch pie plate. Unfold and carefully press the dough into the pan. Use kitchen scissors or a paring knife to trim the dough to 1 inch of the pan's edge.

7. Cover with plastic and chill until ready to bake.

Reduced-Fat Graham Cracker Pie Crust

A little butter goes a long way in this crisp graham cracker crust.
The secret ingredient is something very simple . . . water!

INGREDIENTS | SERVES 8

1⅓ cups graham cracker crumbs
3 tablespoons sugar
2 tablespoons unsalted butter, melted
¼ cup water

Light Butter?

Light butter is a mixture of butter, water, fillers, and emulsifiers that give the finished product a texture similar to butter. Those fillers and emulsifiers do not melt or bake like real butter and can change the texture and flavor of the finished product. It is better to add just a little of the real thing.

1. Heat the oven to 350°F.

2. Combine the graham cracker crumbs, sugar, butter, and water in a medium bowl until well combined. Press the mixture evenly into a 9-inch pie pan.

3. Bake for 10 to 12 minutes, or until the crust is golden brown and the center is firm when pressed lightly. Cool completely before filling.

Reduced-Sugar Butter Crumble

A little sugar is needed for browning this crumble, but you can replace it with sucralose
if desired. It may not brown as well if you do, but it will still taste delicious.

INGREDIENTS | YIELDS ENOUGH CRUMBLE FOR 1 (9-INCH) PIE

¼ cup all-purpose flour
3 tablespoons granular sucralose
1 tablespoon light brown sugar
Pinch of salt
3 tablespoons unsalted butter, cubed and chilled

1. In a bowl, blend the flour, sucralose, light brown sugar, and salt.

2. Using your fingers, rub in the butter until the mixture resembles coarse sand.

3. Chill the crumble for 30 minutes before use.

Gluten-Free Pastry Crust

Most health and natural food stores carry white rice flour and potato starch.
If you can't find them locally, you can easily find them on the Internet.

INGREDIENTS | YIELDS 1 (9-INCH) CRUST

¾ cup white rice flour

¼ cup potato starch

¼ cup tapioca flour

2 tablespoons almond flour

1 tablespoon sugar

¼ teaspoon salt

8 tablespoons cold butter, cut into small pieces

1 large egg, beaten

4 tablespoons ice water

1. In a large bowl, sift together the white rice flour, potato starch, tapioca flour, almond flour, sugar, and salt.

2. Add the butter and, using your fingers, rub it into the flour until the mixture looks like coarse sand.

3. Add the egg, along with 2 tablespoons of water, and mix until the dough forms a rough ball. Add more water, 1 tablespoon at a time, if needed.

4. Turn the dough out onto a surface dusted with white rice flour and form a disk. Wrap in plastic and chill for at least 30 minutes or up to 3 days.

5. Remove the dough from the refrigerator for 10 minutes before rolling out. Roll out on a lightly floured surface to a ⅛-inch-thick, 12-inch circle, turning the dough often to make sure it does not stick. Dust the surface with additional flour if needed.

6. If molding into a pie pan, fold the dough in half and place it into a 9-inch pie plate. Unfold and carefully press the dough into the pan. Use kitchen scissors or a paring knife to trim the dough to 1 inch of the pan's edge.

7. Cover with plastic and chill until ready to bake.

Reduced-Sugar Pecan Streusel

A little dark brown sugar adds a little caramel flavor to this topping that complements the pecans.

INGREDIENTS | YIELDS ENOUGH CRUMBLE FOR 1 (9-INCH) PIE

¼ cup granular sucralose

1 tablespoon dark brown sugar

½ cup all-purpose flour

¼ cup unsalted butter, cubed and chilled

⅓ cup chopped pecans

1. In a bowl, blend the sucralose, dark brown sugar, and flour.

2. Using your fingers, rub in the butter until the mixture resembles coarse sand. Add the pecans and mix well.

3. Chill for 30 minutes before use.

Topping Additions

When making a streusel topping, you can use any nuts you prefer. Ground almonds and walnuts are always nice. You can also add quick-cooking oats to your streusel. Just put the oats in the blender and pulse.

No-Sugar-Added Peanut Butter Pie

Make this pie with a chocolate graham cracker crust for an extra-special touch.

INGREDIENTS | SERVES 8

¾ cup creamy peanut butter

4 ounces cream cheese, softened

1¼ cups granular sucralose, divided

1 cup heavy cream

1 teaspoon vanilla

1 (9-inch) Reduced-Fat Graham Cracker Pie Crust, baked and cooled (See Chapter 19)

1. In a large bowl, cream together the peanut butter, cream cheese, and 1 cup of the sucralose. Set aside.

2. In a separate bowl, whip the heavy cream with the remaining sucralose and vanilla until it forms medium peaks.

3. Beat half of the whipped cream into the peanut butter mixture until almost combined, then add the remaining whipped cream and beat until no streaks of cream remain.

4. Pour into the prepared crust and chill overnight. Serve cold.

No-Sugar-Added Chocolate Pie

This filling packs in the chocolate flavor while cutting the fat and sugar.

2 cups 2% milk

⅔ cup granular sucralose

⅓ cup Dutch-processed cocoa powder

¼ cup cornstarch

1 egg

¼ teaspoon salt

1 tablespoon butter

2 ounces semisweet chocolate, chopped

1 teaspoon vanilla

1 (9-inch) reduced-fat Graham Cracker Crust, baked and cooled (See Chapter 19)

½ cup heavy cream

1 tablespoon granular sucralose

¼ teaspoon vanilla

1. In a medium saucepan, combine the milk, sucralose, cocoa powder, cornstarch, egg, and salt. Whisk until smooth, then cook over medium-low heat, stirring constantly, until it begins to simmer and thicken. If the mixture becomes lumpy, pour it into a blender and purée until smooth.

2. Remove from the heat and add the butter, chopped chocolate, and vanilla. Stir until melted. Pour through a strainer into a separate bowl, then pour directly into the prepared crust.

3. Place a layer of cling film directly on the custard and chill for at least 6 hours or overnight.

4. Once the pie has chilled, prepare the whipped cream. In a medium bowl, combine the cream, sucralose, and vanilla. Beat until the mixture forms medium peaks. Pipe or spread on the pie. Serve immediately.

No-Sugar-Added Pumpkin Chiffon Pie

Making a no-sugar-added pumpkin chiffon pie ensures the filling will stay silky, moist, and flavorful.

INGREDIENTS | SERVES 8

1 envelope unflavored powdered gelatin

¼ cup cold water

1 cup granular sucralose

2 eggs

1 egg yolk

2 tablespoons cornstarch

¼ teaspoon salt

½ teaspoon cinnamon

¼ teaspoon allspice

¼ teaspoon ground cloves

⅛ teaspoon fresh grated nutmeg

1½ cups pumpkin purée

1 teaspoon vanilla

4 egg whites

¼ teaspoon salt

1 (9-inch) Reduced-Fat Graham Cracker Pie Crust, baked and cooled (See Chapter 19)

1. In a small bowl, combine the gelatin and the water. Allow to stand until completely bloomed, about 10 minutes.

2. In a medium saucepan, combine the sucralose, eggs, egg yolk, cornstarch, salt, cinnamon, allspice, cloves, nutmeg, and pumpkin. Cook over a double boiler, whisking constantly, until thickened.

3. Remove from the heat and add the gelatin and vanilla. Mix until well blended, then allow to cool until slightly warm.

4. In a large, clean bowl, whip the egg whites with the salt until the whites form medium peaks.

5. Working in thirds, fold the egg whites into the pumpkin mixture, making sure no large streaks of egg white remain. Pour the mixture into the prepared crust and chill until firm, about 4 hours, before serving.

Whole Wheat Pastry Flour

Looking to add a little more fiber and whole grains to your diet? Try using whole wheat pastry flour in your baking. Whole wheat pastry flour is finely milled, so it will not weigh down your pastries and cakes. You can substitute half of the white flour in most recipes with whole wheat pastry flour with no loss of texture.

No-Sugar-Added Vanilla Cream Pie

Use the best-quality vanilla you have available for this pie. A dash of almond extract is also nice in this pie to round out the flavor.

INGREDIENTS | SERVES 8

1 (9-inch) Reduced-Fat Pastry Crust, unbaked (See Chapter 19)

2 cups 2% milk

⅔ cup granular sucralose

¼ cup cornstarch

2 eggs

¼ teaspoon salt

2 tablespoons butter

1 teaspoon vanilla

½ cup heavy cream

1 tablespoon granular sucralose

¼ teaspoon vanilla

1. Heat the oven to 350°F.

2. Line the pie crust with parchment paper or a double layer of aluminum foil and add pie weights or dry beans. Bake for 12 minutes, then remove the paper and weights and bake for an additional 10 to 15 minutes, or until the crust is golden brown all over. Remove from the oven and set aside to cool.

3. In a medium saucepan, combine the milk, sucralose, cornstarch, eggs, and salt. Whisk until smooth, then cook over medium-low heat, stirring constantly, until it begins to simmer and thicken. If the mixture becomes lumpy, pour it into a blender and purée until smooth.

4. Remove from the heat and add the butter and vanilla. Stir until melted. Pour through a strainer into the prepared crust. Place a layer of cling film directly on the custard and chill for at least 6 hours or overnight.

5. Once the pie has chilled, prepare the whipped cream. In a medium bowl, combine the cream, sucralose, and vanilla. Beat until the mixture forms medium peaks. Pipe or spread on the pie. Serve immediately.

No-Sugar-Added Apple Pie

Use very fresh, not too tart apples in this pie for the best flavor.

INGREDIENTS | SERVES 8

1 cup granular sucralose

¼ cup cornstarch

1 teaspoon cinnamon

½ teaspoon allspice

¼ teaspoon fresh grated nutmeg

8 medium Gala apples, peeled, cored, and sliced ¼ inch thick

2 Reduced-Fat Pastry Crusts, unbaked, 1 molded into a pie pan (See Chapter 19)

2 tablespoons butter

1 egg, beaten

Browning

Sugar helps pastry crusts brown. When you reduce or remove the sugar, you may notice your pastry does not achieve a golden brown color, even when it is fully baked. For double-crust pies or pies topped with a lattice that use sucralose, you will want to brush on an egg wash to help the crust get some color.

1. Heat the oven to 400°F.

2. In a large bowl, mix the sucralose, cornstarch, cinnamon, allspice, and nutmeg until well blended. Add the apples and toss to coat.

3. Fill the bottom crust with the apple mixture and dot the top with the butter. Brush the edge of the bottom pie crust with the beaten egg so that the top crust will adhere. Top with the second crust and trim the dough to 1 inch of the pan's edge. Tuck the edge of the top crust under the edge of the bottom crust. Crimp the dough using your fingers or a fork. Brush the entire top crust with the beaten egg and cut 4 or 5 slits in the top to vent steam.

4. Place the pie on a baking sheet and bake for 30 minutes, then reduce the heat to 350°F for an additional 30 to 40 minutes, or until the pie is bubbling and the juices are thick. Cool for 2 hours before slicing.

Reduced-Fat Banana Cream Pie

Watching your weight does not mean you have to sacrifice dessert. This pie uses lots of ripe bananas and silky custard so good you will not miss any of the fat!

INGREDIENTS | SERVES 8

1 (9-inch) Reduced-Fat Pastry Crust, unbaked (See Chapter 19)

4 ripe bananas, cut into ¼-inch-thick slices

1½ cups 2% milk

⅓ cup sugar

3 tablespoons cornstarch

1 egg

¼ teaspoon salt

1 tablespoon butter

1 teaspoon vanilla

½ cup heavy cream

1 tablespoon powdered sugar

¼ teaspoon vanilla

1. Heat the oven to 350°F.

2. Line the pie crust with parchment paper or a double layer of aluminum foil and add pie weights or dry beans. Bake for 12 minutes, then remove the paper and weights and bake for an additional 10 to 15 minutes, or until the crust is golden brown all over. Remove from the oven and cool completely. Once cooled, layer the sliced bananas into the crust. Set aside.

3. In a medium saucepan, combine the milk, sugar, cornstarch, egg, and salt. Whisk until smooth, then cook over medium-low heat, stirring constantly, until it begins to simmer and thicken.

4. Remove from the heat and add the butter and vanilla. Stir until melted. Pour through a strainer into the prepared crust. Place a layer of cling film directly on the custard and chill for at least 6 hours or overnight.

5. Once the pie has chilled, prepare the whipped cream. In a medium bowl, combine the cream, powdered sugar, and vanilla. Beat until the mixture forms medium peaks. Pipe or spread on the pie. Serve immediately.

No-Sugar-Added Cherry Pie

A little extra butter keeps the filling of this pie silky. A little lemon zest would also give this pie a little extra zip.

INGREDIENTS | SERVES 8

20 ounces frozen pitted cherries

1 cup granular sucralose

½ cup cornstarch

2 tablespoons butter

¼ teaspoon salt

1 teaspoon lemon juice

¼ teaspoon cinnamon

¼ teaspoon almond extract

1 (9-inch) Reduced-Fat Pie Crust, unbaked (See Chapter 19)

1 recipe Reduced-Sugar Butter Crumble (See Chapter 19)

Frozen Fruit

Frozen fruit is an excellent resource for those who are watching their sugar intake. Because the fruit is frozen at its peak of freshness, you will be sure to get fruit with a naturally sweet, robust flavor. Use frozen fruit in smoothies or pies, or topped with a little whipped cream.

1. Heat the oven to 375°F.

2. Thaw the cherries and drain the juices into a measuring cup. Add enough water to the juice to equal ½ cup.

3. Combine the juice, sucralose and cornstarch until smooth in a small saucepan. Cook over medium-low heat until the mixture begins to thicken. If the mixture becomes lumpy, remove from the heat and whisk until smooth.

4. Add the butter, salt, lemon juice, cinnamon, and almond extract. Mix well and then fold in the cherries. Cool to room temperature.

5. Pour into the pie shell and top with the crumble. Bake for 40 to 45 minutes, or until the filling is bubbly in the center and the crumble is golden brown. Cool for 30 minutes before serving.

Reduced-Sugar Pecan Pie

Agave nectar replaces the corn syrup in this pie, reducing the sugar without reducing the flavor!

1. Heat the oven to 350°F.

2. Whisk together the flour and sucralose. Add the eggs, agave syrup, salt, butter, and vanilla. Whisk until smooth.

3. Spread the pecans into the crust in an even layer. Pour the filling over the pecans and tap the pie gently on the counter to release any air bubbles.

4. Place the pie on a baking sheet and bake for 45 to 55 minutes, or until the filling is puffed all over and set. Cool to room temperature before serving.

Glycemic Index

The glycemic index measures the effects of carbohydrates on blood sugar. As carbohydrates break down, they convert into sugar and can cause spikes in blood sugar and weight gain. Foods that are low on the glycemic index do not cause those blood sugar spikes. These include most fruits, vegetables, legumes, nuts, and foods low in carbohydrates.

Reduced-Fat Lemon Pudding Pie

Sweet, tart, and creamy, this lemon pie is a wonderful treat during swimsuit season.

INGREDIENTS | SERVES 8

1 (9-inch) Reduced-Fat Graham Cracker Pie Crust, baked and cooled (See Chapter 19)

2 cups 2% milk

⅔ cup granular sucralose

¼ cup cornstarch

2 egg yolks

2 teaspoons lemon zest

¼ teaspoon salt

2 tablespoons butter

½ teaspoon vanilla

3 tablespoons lemon juice

½ cup heavy cream

1 tablespoon granular sucralose

¼ teaspoon vanilla

1. In a medium saucepan, combine the milk, sucralose, cornstarch, egg yolks, lemon zest, and salt. Whisk until smooth, then cook over medium-low heat, stirring constantly, until it begins to simmer and thicken. If the mixture becomes lumpy, pour it into a blender and purée until smooth.

2. Remove from the heat and add the butter, vanilla, and lemon juice. Stir until melted. Pour through a strainer into the prepared crust. Place a layer of cling film directly on the custard and chill for at least 6 hours or overnight.

3. Once the pie has chilled, prepare the whipped cream. In a medium bowl, combine the cream, sucralose, and vanilla. Beat until the mixture forms medium peaks. Pipe or spread on the pie. Serve immediately.

Reduced-Sugar Chocolate, Vanilla, and Fresh Strawberry Ice Cream Pie

Who does not love berries and ice cream? If you want, you can use raspberries in place of the strawberries.

INGREDIENTS | SERVES 8

1 Reduced-Fat Graham Cracker Pie Crust, baked and cooled (See Chapter 19)

1⅓ cups sugar-free/reduced-sugar vanilla ice cream

1 cup diced fresh strawberries, divided

1⅓ cups sugar-free/reduced-sugar chocolate ice cream

1 cup whipped cream

¼ cup sugar-free chocolate sauce

¼ cup mini chocolate chips

1. In a prepared crust, spread the vanilla ice cream evenly on the bottom. Arrange ¾ cup of the strawberries over the top. Cover and freeze for 30 minutes.

2. Once chilled, spread the chocolate ice cream over the top. Cover and freeze for 2 hours.

3. Garnish with the reserved strawberries, chocolate sauce, and chocolate chips. Allow to stand for 5 minutes before serving.

Reduced-Sugar Mocha Almond Ice Cream Pie

If you are unable to find a reduced-sugar or sugar-free mocha ice cream, add 2 tablespoons of very strong coffee for each pint of ice cream, then mix and freeze for 30 minutes before making this pie.

INGREDIENTS | SERVES 8

1 cup toasted flake almonds

⅓ cup mini chocolate chips

1 quart reduced-sugar/no-sugar-added mocha ice cream, softened slightly

1 Reduced-Fat Graham Cracker Pie Crust, baked and cooled (See Chapter 19)

¼ cup sugar-free chocolate syrup

1. In a large bowl, combine the almonds, chocolate chips, and ice cream and mix until evenly combined.

2. Spread into the prepared crust and freeze for 2 hours to set.

3. Garnish with chocolate syrup. Allow to stand for 5 minutes before serving.

Reduced-Fat Blueberry Ricotta Tart

The combination of blueberries, ricotta cheese, and pecan topping makes this a dessert you will be proud to serve, and no one will know it is missing anything!

INGREDIENTS | SERVES 8

¾ cup reduced-fat ricotta cheese

1 teaspoon cornstarch

2 teaspoons lemon zest

1 teaspoon vanilla

2 tablespoons agave syrup

2 tablespoons granular sucralose

1 egg white

¼ teaspoon salt

1 (12-inch) round Reduced-Fat Pastry Crust, chilled

1 cup fresh blueberries

1 recipe Reduced-Sugar Pecan Streusel (See Chapter 19)

1. In a large bowl, whisk together the ricotta, cornstarch, lemon zest, vanilla, agave, sucralose, egg white, and salt. Cover and chill for 30 minutes.

2. Heat the oven to 350°F and line a baking sheet with parchment paper.

3. Place the chilled pastry on the prepared baking sheet. Spread the ricotta mixture onto the pastry, leaving a ½-inch border. Arrange the berries over the ricotta mixture, then fold the pastry just over the edge of the filling. Top with the Reduced-Sugar Pecan Streusel.

4. Bake for 40 to 50 minutes, or until the fruit is bubbling, and both the crumble and pastry are golden brown. Cool to room temperature before serving.

Reduced-Fat Chicken Potpie

*Cutting the fat does not mean sacrificing flavor. This pie is
creamy, rich, and satisfying with much less guilt.*

INGREDIENTS | SERVES 8

1 tablespoon olive oil

1 large onion, diced

2 stalks celery, diced

3 carrots, peeled and diced

1 bay leaf

1 teaspoon fresh thyme

½ teaspoon salt

½ teaspoon fresh cracked black pepper

3 cups fat-free chicken broth, divided

½ cup all-purpose flour

¼ cup 2% evaporated milk

1 cooked skinless chicken breast, shredded

1 Reduced-Fat Pastry Crust, cut into 12 (1-inch) strips (See Chapter 19)

1 egg, beaten

Getting the Most Impact

I'm sure you have heard the saying that first you eat with your eyes, and it is true! When cutting the fat, it is important to use higher-fat components, like crust and whipped cream, to get the most visual impact. In potpies use a single crust for a decorative top. The first thing you see is crust, and that is very satisfying!

1. Heat the oven to 400°F.

2. In a medium saucepan over medium heat, heat the olive oil until it shimmers. Add onion, celery, and carrots and cook until they begin to soften, about 5 minutes.

3. Add the bay leaf, thyme, salt, and pepper and cook for 3 minutes more, or until the herbs are fragrant.

4. Add 1 cup of the chicken broth and bring to a simmer. Cook, covered, for 10 minutes.

5. In a medium bowl, whisk together the remaining chicken broth, flour, and evaporated milk until smooth. Slowly pour it into the simmering vegetables, whisking constantly, and cook until it begins to simmer and thicken. Turn off the heat and add the shredded chicken. Allow to cool to room temperature.

6. Transfer the chicken mixture into a 2½-quart baking dish. Lay out 6 strips of pie dough on top of the filling about 1 inch apart. Starting 1 inch from the edge of the pie, fold back every other strip and lay down 1 strip of pastry. Fold the pastry back down and fold back the other pieces. Lay down a second strip about ½ inch from the first strip. Repeat this process until all the strips are used. Trim the dough to 1 inch of the pan's edge. Tuck the edge of the top crust into the edges of the pan. Brush the lattice with beaten egg.

7. Place the dish on a baking sheet and bake for 20 minutes, then reduce the heat to 350°F for an additional 35 to 45 minutes, or until the pie is bubbling and the crust is golden brown. Cool for 30 minutes before serving.

Reduced-Fat Turkey Sausage and Cheddar Quiche

Most grocery stores carry a variety of fully cooked turkey and chicken sausage in gourmet flavors.

INGREDIENTS | SERVES 8

1 (9-inch) Reduced-Fat Pastry Crust, unbaked (See Chapter 19)

2 eggs

2 egg whites

1 teaspoon cornstarch

Pinch fresh grated nutmeg

½ teaspoon salt

½ teaspoon fresh cracked pepper

1 cup 2% milk

4 ounces turkey sausage, chopped

1 cup grated 2% milk Cheddar cheese

Ground Turkey

Not all ground turkey is the same. Some ground turkey includes a significant amount of fat from the skin and dark meat of the bird. If you are looking to save fat, you need to find ground turkey breast. You can use the ground turkey to make your own turkey sausage by adding your favorite spices and ground vegetables and forming it into patties.

1. Heat the oven to 350°F.

2. Line the pie crust with parchment paper or a double layer of aluminum foil and add pie weights or dry beans. Bake for 12 minutes, then remove the paper and weights and bake for an additional 10 to 15 minutes, or until the crust is golden brown all over. Remove from the oven and set aside to cool.

3. In a medium bowl, whisk together the eggs and egg whites. Add the cornstarch, nutmeg, salt, and pepper and whisk until well combined. Slowly whisk in the milk.

4. Spread the sausage and cheese evenly on the bottom of the crust. Carefully pour over the egg mixture.

5. Bake for 30 to 40 minutes, or until the filling is set and starting to brown lightly on the top. Cool for 20 minutes at room temperature before serving.

Reduced-Fat Ham and Spinach Quiche

Canadian bacon offers a lot of smoky flavor, but if you cannot find it, use any smoked ham you prefer.

INGREDIENTS | SERVES 8

1 (9-inch) Reduced-Fat Pastry Crust, unbaked (See Chapter 19)

1 teaspoon olive oil

½ medium onion, finely chopped

½ stalk celery, finely chopped

1 clove garlic, minced

1 roasted red pepper, drained and finely chopped

2 eggs

2 egg whites

1 teaspoon cornstarch

½ teaspoon salt

½ teaspoon fresh cracked pepper

1 cup 2% milk

2 ounces Canadian bacon, chopped

½ cup grated 2% milk Swiss cheese

1. Heat the oven to 350°F.

2. Line the pie crust with parchment paper or a double layer of aluminum foil and add pie weights or dry beans. Bake for 12 minutes, then remove the paper and weights and bake for an additional 10 to 15 minutes, or until the crust is golden brown all over. Remove from the oven and set aside to cool.

3. In a medium skillet over medium heat, add the olive oil. Once it shimmers, add the onions and celery and cook until just softened, about 3 minutes. Add the garlic and red pepper and cook for 1 minute more. Remove from the heat and cool.

4. In a medium bowl, whisk together the eggs and egg whites. Add the cornstarch, salt, and pepper and whisk until well combined. Slowly whisk in the milk.

5. Spread the vegetables, Canadian bacon, and cheese evenly on the bottom of the crust. Carefully pour over the egg mixture.

6. Bake for 30 to 40 minutes, or until the filling is set and starting to brown lightly on the top. Cool for 20 minutes at room temperature before serving.

Glossary

Baking sheet: A flat metal pan used for baking.

Beat: To vigorously mix a batter using a whisk or spoon until smooth.

Blind baking: The process of baking a pastry crust without a filling. Used primarily for pies where the filling is not baked.

Bloom: To soften gelatin in cool water.

Brown sugar: Granular sugar that contains certain impurities that give it a distinctive flavor.

Creaming: A mixing method where fat is blended with another ingredient, usually sugar, to form a uniform, lightened mixture.

Crimp: To seal together by pinching or pressing.

Custard: A mixture that thickens due to the coagulation of egg protein during cooking.

Docking: The process of piercing small holes in a pastry crust before baking to prevent bubbling and excess rising.

Double boiler: A combination of a pot with a heatproof bowl on top. Used for slow, gentle cooking of food in the bowl by the action of simmering water in the pot below.

Dust: To lightly coat a surface or baked item with flour or sugar.

Dutch-processed cocoa: Cocoa that is processed with alkali to reduce acidity.

Fold: To blend a lighter mixture into a heavier mixture.

Frothing: The process of incorporating air by whipping egg whites or other ingredients.

Lattice crust: A decorative pastry crust made up of strips of woven pastry dough.

Leavening: The production of, or incorporation of ingredients that produce, gasses that cause mixtures to increase in volume.

Meringue: A mixture of beaten egg whites, sugar, and sometimes an acid.

Parchment paper: Baking paper impregnated with silicone. Used in baking to prevent sticking without using additional oil or fat.

Pasteurization: A process where food items, typically milk and egg products, are heat-treated to kill harmful bacteria.

Wash: A liquid, frequently beaten egg or milk, that is applied to a pastry item prior to baking.

Sources for Pie-Making Supplies

Bob's Red Mill

An excellent source for all-natural ingredients.
www.bobsredmill.com

Cooking.com

From serving ware and electric mixers to knives and pans, this store has it all.
www.cooking.com

Gluten-Free Supermarket

Wide variety of gluten-free ingredients including mixes, specialty flours, and recipes.
www.glutenfree-supermarket.com

Honeyville Food Products

The producers of very refined almond flour, as well as other specialty nut and grain flours.
www.honeyvillegrain.com

King Arthur Flour

Wide variety of flours and other ingredients, as well as baking tips and recipes.
www.kingarthurflour.com

Kitchen Krafts

If you are looking for things to give your baking an extra bit of oomph in the decorating department, this is the shop for you.
www.kitchenkrafts.com

My Spice Sage

Wide variety of spices, chilies, and exotic flavors.
www.myspicesage.com

Penzeys Spices

Excellent resource for spices, spice blends, and dry herbs. They also sell vanilla beans and various extracts.
www.penzeys.com

Sur la Table

Specialty gourmet store with a wide variety of tools and appliances.
www.surlatable.com

Williams-Sonoma

Kitchen gadgets, pans, and other equipment. They are a great resource for specialty items and gourmet ingredients.
www.williams-sonoma.com

Standard U.S./Metric Measurement Conversions

VOLUME CONVERSIONS	
U.S. Volume Measure	Metric Equivalent
⅛ teaspoon	0.5 milliliters
¼ teaspoon	1 milliliters
½ teaspoon	2 milliliters
1 teaspoon	5 milliliters
½ tablespoon	7 milliliters
1 tablespoon (3 teaspoons)	15 milliliters
2 tablespoons (1 fluid ounce)	30 milliliters
¼ cup (4 tablespoons)	60 milliliters
⅓ cup	90 milliliters
½ cup (4 fluid ounces)	125 milliliters
⅔ cup	160 milliliters
¾ cup (6 fluid ounces)	180 milliliters
1 cup (16 tablespoons)	250 milliliters
1 pint (2 cups)	500 milliliters
1 quart (4 cups)	1 liter (about)

WEIGHT CONVERSIONS	
U.S. Weight Measure	Metric Equivalent
½ ounce	15 grams
1 ounce	30 grams
2 ounces	60 grams
3 ounces	85 grams
¼ pound (4 ounces)	115 grams
½ pound (8 ounces)	225 grams
¾ pound (12 ounces)	340 grams
1 pound (16 ounces)	454 grams

OVEN TEMPERATURE CONVERSIONS	
Degrees Fahrenheit	Degrees Celsius
200 degrees F	100 degrees C
250 degrees F	120 degrees C
275 degrees F	140 degrees C
300 degrees F	150 degrees C
325 degrees F	160 degrees C
350 degrees F	180 degrees C
375 degrees F	190 degrees C
400 degrees F	200 degrees C
425 degrees F	220 degrees C
450 degrees F	230 degrees C

BAKING PAN SIZES	
American	Metric
8 x 1½ inch round baking pan	20 x 4 cm cake tin
9 x 1½ inch round baking pan	23 x 3.5 cm cake tin
11 x 7 x 1½ inch baking pan	28 x 18 x 4 cm baking tin
13 x 9 x 2 inch baking pan	30 x 20 x 5 cm baking tin
2 quart rectangular baking dish	30 x 20 x 3 cm baking tin
15 x 10 x 2 inch baking pan	30 x 25 x 2 cm baking tin (Swiss roll tin)
9 inch pie plate	22 x 4 or 23 x 4 cm pie plate
7 or 8 inch springform pan	18 or 20 cm springform or loose bottom cake tin
9 x 5 x 3 inch loaf pan	23 x 13 x 7 cm or 2 lb narrow loaf or pate tin
1½ quart casserole	1.5 litre casserole
2 quart casserole	2 litre casserole

Index

We Have

EVERYTHING

on Anything!

With more than 19 million copies sold, the Everything® series has become one of America's favorite resources for solving problems, learning new skills, and organizing lives. Our brand is not only recognizable—it's also welcomed.

The series is a hand-in-hand partner for people who are ready to tackle new subjects—like you!

For more information on the Everything® series, please visit *www.adamsmedia.com*

The Everything® list spans a wide range of subjects, with more than 500 titles covering 25 different categories:

Business	History	Reference
Careers	Home Improvement	Religion
Children's Storybooks	Everything Kids	Self-Help
Computers	Languages	Sports & Fitness
Cooking	Music	Travel
Crafts and Hobbies	New Age	Wedding
Education/Schools	Parenting	Writing
Games and Puzzles	Personal Finance	
Health	Pets	